# To Nepal With Love

A Travel Guide for the Connoisseur

To Nepal With Love
Edited by Kim Fay and Cristi Hegranes
Photography by Kraig Lieb



Credits and copyright notices for the individual essays in this collection are given starting on 197.



To Asia With Love series created by Kim Fay
Cover and book design by Janet McKelpin/Dayspring Technologies, Inc.
Copy-editing by Elizabeth Mathews
Book production by Paul Tomanpos, Jr.

Please be advised that restaurants, shops, businesses, and other establishments in this book have been written about over a period of time. The editor and publisher have made every effort to ensure the accuracy of the information included in this book at the time of publication, but prices and conditions may have changed, and the editor, publisher, and authors cannot assume and hereby disclaim liability for loss, damage, or inconvenience caused by errors, omissions, or changes in regard to information included in this book.

For information regarding permissions, write to:
ThingsAsian Press, San Francisco, California USA
www.thingsasian.com
Printed in Hong Kong

ISBN-13: 978-1-934159-09-5
ISBN-10: 1-934159-09-3

# Table of Contents

# Introduction

Imagine that on the eve of your upcoming trip to Nepal, you are invited to a party. At this party are dozens of guests, all of whom live in or have traveled extensively through the country. Among this eclectic and well-versed group of connoisseurs are contributors to acclaimed travel guides, popular newspaper writers, veteran gourmets, and pioneering adventurers. As the evening passes, they tell you tales from their lives in these exotic places. They whisper the names of their favorite shops and restaurants; they divulge the secret hideaways where they sneak off to for an afternoon or a weekend to unwind. Some make you laugh out loud, and others seduce you with their poetry. Some are intent on educating, while others just want to entertain. Their recommendations are as unique as their personalities, but they are united in one thing ... their love of Nepal. If you can envision being welcomed at such a party, then you can envision the experience that *To Nepal With Love* aspires to give you.

Kim Fay
Series Editor, To Asia With Love

When I arrived in Nepal, I was twenty-three. Not only was it my first time in Asia, it was my first time anywhere, really. I was there to finish my master's thesis and to work as a stringer for a few news organizations. I will never forget that late night disembarkation. The smell of wood smoke, diesel, and incense converged to produce a perfume that seemed to envelope the whole country. As my taxi careened toward its destination, I did my best to speak the words of Nepali I had learned from my dear friend Anil in New York during the months leading up to my trip. After I got to my room and unpacked my few belongings, I walked up one flight of stairs to find a tiny roof garden atop my hotel, just outside Thamel, the main tourist area of Kathmandu.

As I looked around and took another deep breath of that rich air, I felt like a giddy teenager in love for the first time. I remember gazing out across Kathmandu and thinking, almost wishing, *I never want to leave.*

Those first months in Nepal inspired and changed me to a degree I hadn't thought possible. As I trekked and trudged my way through the country—recording stories, writing news articles, and meeting people—I had what would be a career-changing, a life-changing epiphany: I was the wrong person to be reporting the news.

I spoke decent Nepali, and I had rounded up a strong base of local sources as I reported on everything from maternal health to the rural realities of the civil war. But there was something I lacked—there was something all foreign correspondents lacked.

Context. Social, historical, political context. I realized that my "dream job" of becoming a foreign correspondent was not all it was cracked up to be. It was the lack of context, I found, that filled news pages only with stories of war, disaster, and disease from developing countries. There were so many other stories I wanted to tell. But I didn't have access. And I couldn't find an editor interested in anything else.

When I met Pratima, a woman living in a tiny, remote village in Eastern Nepal, I realized there was another way. Pratima was the community matriarch with access to fascinating stories about the region. She was savvy, inspired, and passionate about her community. And she was a natural storyteller. What if women like Pratima were given the opportunity to be trained as journalists and were given a credible global platform to share their reporting? I could not stop thinking about the world-changing news coverage they could produce. But no such training opportunity or publication existed.

I decided that I would create one.

Just eighteen months after I took my first step off the plane in Nepal, I founded an international nonprofit organization called Global Press Institute (GPI). GPI uses journalism as a development tool to educate, employ, and empower women, who produce high-quality local news coverage that elevates global awareness and catalyzes social change. Today, GPI operates independent news desks in twenty-four countries. But it was the women of the Nepal news desk who demonstrated that the idea worked and that it is powerful.

In many ways the wish I made on that first night in Nepal—to never leave—has come true, as my new career allows me to visit often. Each time I get off the plane I am reminded of that first trip to Nepal that changed my life, my career, and my dreams.

That is why I wanted to be a part of this book. In Nepal there is magic everywhere. In the bustle of the streets, in the majesty of the mountains, in the kindness of the people, and in the perfume of the night sky. In this book you will find an array of authentic experiences that encompass the full reality of Nepal. From trekking the famous Himalayas and riding through

Chitwan National Park atop an elephant to delving into the treats and treasures of restaurants and shops in Kathmandu, the contributors in this book have painted a true picture of the beauty, passion, and potential of Nepal. Each writer shares a love for and a gratitude to the country, as I do. As you turn each page you will see how their dreams came true and their lives were changed as they traveled through this magnificent place.

Cristi Hegranes
Coeditor, *To Nepal With Love*

## How This Book Works

*A good traveler has no fixed plans, and is not intent on arriving.*
~Lao Tzu

*To Nepal With Love* is a unique guidebook with chapters organized by theme as opposed to destination. This is because it focuses foremost on the sharing of personal experiences, allowing each place to serve as the colorful canvas on which our writers overlay vivid, individual impressions. Within each themed chapter you will find the recommendations grouped by region, and then by towns or areas within each region.

Chapters begin in the capital city of Kathmandu and flow out to the Kathmandu Valley and such popular destinations as Patan/ Lalitpur and Boudha. From here the essays travel across the country from west to east, beginning in Western Nepal before moving on to Central Nepal and Annapurna, which includes the Annapurna Circuit trekking region, as well as Lumbini (birthplace of Buddha). Finally, each chapter ends in Eastern Nepal and Everest. For attractions or experiences by destination, a complete index of cities can be found at the end of this book.

Each recommendation consists of two parts: a personal essay and a fact file. Together, they are intended to inspire and inform. The essay tells a story while the fact file gives addresses and other serviceable information. Because each contribution can stand alone, the book does not need to be read in order. As with an old-fashioned miscellany, you may open to any page and start reading. Thus every encounter with the book is turned into its own distinctive armchair journey.

Keep in mind that *To Nepal With Love* is selective and does not include all of the practical information you will need for daily travel. Instead, reading it is like having a conversation with a friend who just returned from a trip. You should supplement that friend's stories with a comprehensive guidebook, such as Lonely Planet or Rough Guide.

Confucius said, "A journey of a thousand miles begins with a single step." We hope that this guide helps you put your best foot forward.

## Key Terms and Important Information

Religious terms: Throughout the book you will find various Hindu and Tibetan Buddhist terms, which are not always defined, so as not to interrupt the flow of the story. Because of the prevalence of such terms in Nepal, it is helpful to brush up on the basics before you go. Numerous glossaries of Tibetan Buddhist and Hindu terms can be found online.

Civil War: From 1996 to 2006, Nepal experienced a violent civil war that resulted in fifteen thousand deaths, the internal displacement of more than a hundred thousand people, and the overthrow of the centuries-old monarchy. The country is now officially known as the Federal Democratic Republic of Nepal, and although peace has been declared, the conflict still impacts the day-to-day lives of many Nepalese. For a better understanding of the country's civil war and how it affects Nepal today, check out the recommendations in the resources chapter of this book.

METRIC SYSTEM: Although we are an American publisher, we have used the metric system for all measurements. For easy conversion, go to WWW.METRIC-CONVERSIONS.ORG.

THE NEWAR: This indigenous group makes up about half the population of the Kathmandu Valley. Travelers' explorations in this area often include experiences with Newari food, architecture, and traditions that date back centuries.

TREKKING: Naturally, this book is filled with stories of trekking, and while each contains basic information, none provides everything needed to prepare for your trip. Supplies and safety are touched on, but you will need expert advice if you plan to explore the mountains of Nepal. Use the stories in this book as inspiration, and then spend time with comprehensive guides such as the Lonely Planet guide to trekking Nepal or *Trekking in the Everest Region* (see page 181).

*New year chariot, Kathmandu*

# Moveable Feasts

*A tasting menu of exotic flavors*

Some countries are known as foodie destinations (i.e., France and Japan), while others gain their reputations from different types of attractions. Nepal is definitely one of the "others." When this small former kingdom is mentioned in conversation, Sir Edmund Hillary—rather than a Nepalese Julia Child—springs to mind. People think of the soaring Himalayas and brave mountaineers tackling the peaks. This is not a place to come for grand gastronomic pleasures. But if you're determined, you can find some very good meals, as well as memorable culinary adventures.

Sustenance is crucial when trekking, and most travelers joke about the ubiquitous lentil dish of *dal bhat* that is found in most corners of Nepal, and especially along the trekking routes. If you're craving a bit more variety, take inspiration from Ellen Shapiro. With three essays in a row in this chapter, she sips and nibbles her way around the Annapurna Circuit, discovering a traditional local brew and the satisfaction of apple pie and Snickers bars (creatively prepared!) at altitude. Simplicity, in fact, seems to be the key to culinary fulfillment after a long day spent on the trail. Whether it's the potatoes Clint Rogers encounters in Samdo village or the doughnuts savored by Linzi Barber in Tengboche, even the most basic foods are all the more fulfilling when eaten among the highest mountain peaks in the world.

Lower down in Kathmandu, international and local flavors mingle. For a taste of Nepal, follow Brian Smith's suggestions for the city's best Newari cuisine and Emily Eagle's advice on hunting down a superior *momo*. And if you're hankering for something more international, join Charis Boke at a sushi restaurant that surprises with freshness in a landlocked country. Additional recommendations are enhanced by David Markus's insight on how to separate the wheat from the chaff among the restaurants of the Thamel tourist district.

From descriptions of eating buffalo milk curd to drinking rhododendron wine to learning to cook vegetarian *chukauni*, the writers in this chapter make it clear that while Nepal may not be vast in its cuisine, it is at least varied, offering a culinary experience that is as intimate and unique as the country itself.

*Nepalese women sorting grain in the Annapurna region*

# Kathmandu

## *Brian Smith recommends more than dal bhat in Kathmandu*

My Nepalese friend Pradip always jokes that in Nepal all people eat is "*dal bhat, dal bhat.*" Upon first moving here that's about all I ate for three weeks, too—a simple meal of steamed white rice served with lentil soup and *takari*, boiled vegetables flavored with curry. Most Nepalese eat this twice a day, every day, but my Western taste buds, spoiled by years of constant variety, needed something else. While Kathmandu has plenty of international foods done with varying degrees of success, I knew there had to be more to Nepali food than the ubiquitous *dal bhat*. Thankfully the Newar, an indigenous group prevalent in the Kathmandu Valley, have a rich tradition of a much more diverse cuisine.

The food served at Newari restaurants is usually reserved for festivals, holidays, and special occasions by the Newar. In keeping with this tradition, at the Krishnarpan restaurant at Dwarika's Hotel, it's presented in courses, from six to a gut-busting twenty-two, though à la carte items are offered. You can also ask for a vegetarian menu, but you'll miss out on the better part of the experience, as the meats are what make Newari cuisine special and unique to the region. Among my top picks is *choyla*, a grilled meat, normally buff (water buffalo), that is marinated in fresh herbs and mustard seed oil. *Momos*, a Nepali staple, are another very popular Newari dish (though some claim it is Tibetan) that can be bought on nearly any street corner. Fried or steamed, these dumplings are filled with seasoned meats or curried vegetables and potatoes.

Like good French cuisine, Newari food makes excellent use of organ meats. At my favorite Newari restaurant, Wunjala Moskva in Naxal, I enjoy dishes like *ma mena* (boiled tongue) and *swan puka* (pan-seared lung stuffed with herbs and spices). I had actually eaten these a few times before a Nepalese friend of mine informed me of what I was eating. With a shrug I just kept on chewing. As far as I'm concerned, it's better to follow your taste buds than your prejudices when dining.

The main course at a Newari meal is usually brought out on a large plate with a variety of items on it. Its base is essentially *dal bhat*, with the addition of dishes like *suku la achaar* (dried buff chutney), *phasikwa* (sweet pumpkin-based curry), *henya la* (duck meat cooked in a large quantity of ginger), *saag* (spinach) boiled or pan-seared with cumin seeds, more grilled meats, and other meats stewed in curry sauces. Occasionally it will also include fried freshwater fish.

Rounding out this meal, dessert often consists of *chai*, a very sweet tea that can be ordered with or without milk, and a yogurt dish or curd served either plain, with sugar, or with honey and fruit. Naturally, all of this leaves me quite full, and my need for variety is suitably quenched. It also proves that despite what Pradip says, there is more to Nepali cuisine than "*dal bhat, dal bhat.*"

### Newari cuisine in Kathmandu

*Krishnarpan*
Dwarika's Hotel
Battisputali District
Kathmandu

www.dwarikas.com

*Thamel House*
Thamel Tole District
Kathmandu

thamelhouse@gmail.com

*Wunjala Moskva*
Naxal Petrol Pump
Opposite police headquarters' main gate
Naxal District
Kathmandu

www.nepalicuisine.com

## *David Markus redeems Kathmandu's tourist cuisine*

Cross-cultural confusion is par for the course in Kathmandu these days. Screwdrivers served with Newari cuisine. Chicken fajitas eaten to the sound of Hindu chanting. Even at the finest Nepali and Indian restaurants one is liable to find a ham sandwich listed under the Continental section of the menu. Utility overrides all aspirations to good taste, especially in the tourist district of Thamel, where restaurant owners have as much experience catering to families with fussy children as they do serving American tourists with childish palates.

The long-popular Northfield Café, located in the center of Thamel and known for its "Mexican" dishes, epitomizes this sort of unapologetic cross-cultural mélange. With a cabana-style bar overlooking a spacious dining court covered by a corrugated tin roof reminiscent of a Louisiana smoke house, it boasts Italian-restaurant-style tablecloths, Chinese lanterns, and a menu spanning several continents, making the word *eclectic* a gross understatement.

You would think a person possessing any culinary sophistication would vow never to eat Mexican cuisine in Kathmandu. But when you've experienced day after day of more than your fair share of *dal bhat*, sometimes there is no direction to go but west—southwest, in my case. Sitting in Northfield Café, sipping from a tall mug of Everest beer and waiting for my fajitas to arrive, I contemplated whether or not I should take it as an insult that the manager of my hotel thought this was a place I would enjoy.

How liberating it is to confront one's hidden prejudices!

As I lounged under the corrugated roof, surveying the mix of British families, Indonesian couples, and Israeli postarmy types, all unabashedly gorging on the transcontinental cuisine, I suddenly realized how much cultural pretense is built into the consideration of something as simple as where to dine tonight. Whether we take globalization as a good thing or not, a few days in Thamel make it perfectly clear: the Asian-bound traveler who arrives at an international destination like Kathmandu with the attitude "I didn't come here for lasagna *al forno*" harbors views of cultural "otherness" that are so twentieth century.

Cultural cross-pollination is a fact of life in Kathmandu. Case in point: while some local women wear traditional dress on a daily basis, others reserve this custom for religious holidays and are happy going about in a leather jacket and jeans—far more practical for navigating the winding streets of this frenetic city atop a moped. And when you are dining in a modern Nepali home in an urban community, your hosts will gladly show off their favorite national dishes, but they will also hold no reservations about the fact that nontraditional foods make up a large part of their diet. Besides, as anyone who has spent a significant amount of time outside Nepal's more touristy destinations will tell you, lentils and rice every day is nothing to write home about.

As for the fajitas at Northfield Café, let's just say they are no worse than those served up at the kind of family restaurants you see in strip malls across America. And for Nep-Mex, well, that's not half bad.

*Northfield Café*
Thamel Northwest
Near Pilgrim's Feed 'n Read
Thamel District
Kathmandu

## *Charis Boke fishes around for wasabi in Kathmandu*

"I know a sushi place in Kathmandu," my friend said.

I paused. I thought about raw fish, the one allowance I give myself as a vegetarian, and about how long it had been since I tasted decent wasabi. In my own private lexicon, *sushi* is synonymous with *vehicle for wasabi*. That night I dreamed about sushi and took it as a sign—must have raw fish!

I've always enjoyed going to dinner by myself, so a day after my conversation with my friend, I went to Kotetsu in Lazimpat, an area of Kathmandu just north of the Royal Palace Museum. Lazimpat is home to several embassies, including the U.S. and Japanese, and is a less intrusive version of the tourist district, with some very nice gift shops along the main road.

I walked a couple of kilometers from my house up through the Ranibari woods onto Lazimpat Road. Five hundred meters up from the Japanese embassy, I saw the Bajaj motorcycle dealership that my friend had mentioned as a landmark. A small side door led upstairs, with a sign that read *Kotetsu*.

The doors to Kotetsu proper were the half-length black-patterned curtains that I've come to associate with sushi over the years. Brushing them aside, I stepped in to behold a proper sushi bar, chefs chopping and dicing, and five or six waitresses and hosts calling "*namaste*" to me.

Inexplicably, I've always been a bit intimidated by the sushi bar. Also, in order to properly read the academic text that I'd brought with me, I needed to spread out—so I sat in the small side room with two tables. I looked at the menu—ahhh. Sashimi, nigiri, sushi, tempura. It all seemed promising, but since I'm familiar with the state of rivers in much of Nepal and South Asia, I was suspicious about the freshness of the fish. I asked about it.

"Oh yes," came the reply, "the fish comes from Japan."

"From Japan?" My jaw dropped.

"Yes, twice a week the owner flies in fish from Japan."

"Oh," I replied, stunned, and immediately decided to treat myself to 1,000 rupees (about $16) worth of yummy raw fish and a pot of green tea.

The tea came in a beautiful stoneware pot, made and fired in Nepal by traditional Newari potter families. The drink itself was smooth, without the dry bitter aftertaste I associated with green tea—presentation plus taste made it the best I'd had in my life. And the sashimi came delicately arranged on a simple plate, with plenty of pickled ginger and extra wasabi when I requested it.

Even though I had an entire pot of green tea, after I finished the eight pieces of sashimi, I felt relaxed, drowsy even. Apparently, because the fish is raw, all the hormones stay in it, rather than being decomposed by cooking, and they can actually make you feel intoxicated—or as I like to call it, *the sushi high*.

Since that first visit to Kotetsu I've been back many times. Each time I am greeted like an old friend, and each time the wasabi is fresh and the tea is good. I always try to tell myself I should really order something besides the sashimi. The menu is full of other delicious options. But inevitably, it's the eight-piece sashimi for me, with lots of wasabi, of course—a surprising treat in the heart of Nepal.

*Kotetsu*
Near the Japanese embassy
Lazimpat Road
Lazimpat District
Kathmandu

## *Brian Smith nibbles his way around Kathmandu*

**1905 Restaurant**
www.1905restaurant.com

Almost every Saturday morning I make my way down to 1905 on central Kantipath for its excellent farmers' market (cheese, organic vegetables, etc.) and brunch with friends. The restaurant was once an exclusive club that entertained the city's elite next to the famous Royal Hotel. It's located in central Kathmandu, but it feels like a country villa, tucked away on the valley rim, surrounded by fountains, gardens, and man-made ponds. The menu consists of some of the best Continental food in Kathmandu, beginning with Eggs Florentine and crepes for breakfast. Later in the day, good wines accompany cheese plates and dishes as diverse as sizzling garlic prawns, *aloo sadheko* soufflé, and leg of lamb with beluga lentils and sautéed artichoke.

**Brian's Grill House**
Located on the ninth floor of the Sunrise Business Park building on Charakahl, just around the corner from City Center Mall, my own restaurant has awesome views of the Himalayas on clear days and of the whole valley any time of year. Brian's was born out of a want for authentic, well-made, Western pub-style food, which I was always craving after a trek. The menu includes more than fourteen types of burgers and real Tex-Mex dishes, as well as American-style BBQ and plenty of vegetarian options. To make sure the textures and flavors are authentic, many of the cheeses (such as Colby and Swiss) and spices (such as chipotle peppers and vanilla beans) are shipped in special. The bar has one of the widest cocktail selections in town, produces its own infused vodkas, and slings some mean frozen drinks.

**Hotel New Gajur**
A little-known Chinese hotel and restaurant in eastern Thamel on Jyatha Road, Hotel New Gajur offers authentic Chinese hot pot cuisine. This is a great place to take a group of friends, as the hot pot sits in the center of the table and is perfect for communal dining. The pot comes with a spicy or vegetable broth—if you can't decide, order the split pot. The ingredients available for dunking in the broths range from the tame, such as tofu, vegetables, dumplings, and thinly sliced pork, to more exotic options: brains, chicken feet, seaweed, and other Chinese delicacies.

**Nargila**
A first-floor hole-in-the-wall across from Northfield Café and below Tom &

Jerry's Pub, this is my favorite cheap lunch place in Thamel. Nargila does not offer as extensive a selection of Middle Eastern food as OR2K, but the dishes it does have are excellent. At the top of my list: the *shawarma lafa*, a large wrapped sandwich containing tahini, hummus, fresh cucumber and tomato, French fries, and grilled lamb. There is also a vegetarian version that replaces the lamb with falafel, and the falafel is quite good. The hummus plates and baba ghanoush plates are also worth ordering and reasonably priced. Finally, the restaurant offers some really good teas made with cinnamon bark, fresh ginger, or honey, depending on the type you order. I recommend ordering the pots, as they are excellent value.

**Shogun**
After passing by the horribly polluted Bagmati River, the last thought on the mind of any visitor to Kathmandu is sushi, but amazingly, you can get quality sushi in small, landlocked Nepal. Located at Babar Mahal Revisited, a collection of upscale shops and restaurants set in a renovated Rana palace stable, Shogun enjoys a spectacular setting that is quiet and has tons of atmosphere. The food is excellent and safe, as the fish is flown in regularly, and if sushi isn't your thing, you can order other dishes, such as teriyaki chicken and seaweed or avocado salad. Make sure to try the green tea, and afterward, if you have any appetite left, stop by the excellent Chez Caroline for some of the best desserts in town.

## Kathmandu & Kathmandu Valley

### *Emily Eagle exclaims over the momos of Kathmandu*

The dumpling you'll dream about long after you've returned home, *momos* are the prize street food of Nepal. Although some claim the *momo* was a tasty gift from the country's indigenous Newar, and others say that it came from Tibetan exiles, there is no other country on earth where this delicious dish is so plentiful!

*Momos* are deceptively simple: just ground chicken, buffalo meat, or veggies wrapped in pastry dough and steamed. But thanks to the fresh ingredients and the spicy sauces (most often a tomato-based "*achar*," much like a cooked salsa and every bit as delicious), the *momo* comes to life on your tongue. It's sure to be a part of your lasting culinary memories of your time spent in the Himalayas.

Many tourists instinctively turn to the familiarity of the chicken *momo*. The brave try out the buff *momo*, made from water buffalo meat. But my favorite are the vegetarian *momos*, which boast complexities not found in their meaty cousins, as they are filled with multiple combinations of cauliflower, carrots, potatoes, peas, cabbage, cilantro, and other veggies I have yet to identify.

*Momos* make a quick, filling lunch during a day of sightseeing, or a welcome snack after hours of high-altitude trekking. You're sure to notice their popularity on the streets of Kathmandu, as dozens of people will gather around a stall with a large round cauldron where *momos* are being freshly steamed. As for any worries about getting sick if you eat *momos* from street vendors—if the dumplings are served fresh and hot, they're safe. That they are one of the cheapest meals you will find in Nepal makes them all the more enjoyable.

### Momos around Kathmandu

#### *Dolma Momo Center*

Although just a hole-in-the-wall (located down the street from Hotel Utse), the Momo Center serves some of the tastiest and cheapest *momos* in town.

Jyatha Road
Thamel District
Kathmandu

#### *The Green Café*

A great choice for *momos*, this place serves excellent Newari food.

Pulchowk Road
Patan (Lalitpur)

#### *Royal Alina's Bakery Café*

Many Lalitpur locals agree that this Royal Alina's outlet is the best place to get *momos* in Kathmandu.

Jawalakhel Road
Patan (Lalitpur)

#### *Rex Turgano weighs in*

Oh, how I miss the *momos* at Belle Momo (on Durba Marg in Royal Saino), as it was the only place I knew of that made eight different varieties of *momos*. (Now the shop sells even more!) It is also in a central location, where volunteers from around the city can meet to catch up and talk about the highs and lows of volunteer work ... not to mention everything else but work. The *momos*, soup, fries, and drink special is a steal for the price. We always sat outside on the patio, and the same smiling, friendly guard always greeted us at the gate.

## Boudha

## *Jacquelin Sonderling dines with a view in Boudha*

The climb to the rooftop terrace of the Stupa View Restaurant is worth every step of the steep three flights of stairs. Once there, you'll find one of my favorite views, direct and spectacular over the great stupa, Boudhanath.

Truthfully, I can't tell you much about the interior of the restaurant because I always make my way up to the roof. I do know that it's crowded, though—this is a popular place—and the restroom facilities are very good (something you come to appreciate quickly in Nepal). As I do on every visit to Boudhanath, I seek out the terrace and settle in at one of the green metal-and-wood folding chairs at a matching picniclike table.

A vegetarian restaurant run by European expats, Stupa View has a good-sized menu with a surprisingly wide selection of local dishes, including *momos*. These dumplings are a staple all over Nepal, but they're especially tasty in the neighborhood around the stupa, known as "Little Tibet." The Stupa View serves very good *momos* filled with cheese and spinachlike greens in a tomato sauce.

Another recommendation is the traditional Nepali *dal bhat* (lentils and rice with a veggie curry). I also love the *thukpa*, a soupy mixture of vermicelli noodles and veggies. But if you're feeling in the mood for something familiar, this restaurant, like the many other touristy places in the area, also has a Continental section on its menu featuring pizzas, veggie patties, pastas, and even a Greek salad.

I particularly enjoy my evening visits to the stupa. I take my usual rooftop seat at Stupa View and order a large pot of *masala* tea. Relaxed, I watch the prayer flags on the stupa dance in the wind as the sun sets on another amazing day in Kathmandu.

### *Getting to Boudha*

Boudha is approximately five kilometers from Kathmandu's Thamel neighborhood. The easiest way to get back and forth is in a taxi or tuk-tuk, especially if you're planning on returning with your arms full. Another alternative is to take a taxi to the Pashupatinath temple, and then walk to Boudha in time for sunset before taking a taxi back to Thamel.

### *Stupa View Restaurant*

This restaurant is located right at the Boudhanath Stupa. The stupa can be reached by taxi or by bus from the City Bus Park (Ratna Park).

## Bhaktapur

*Laura Gyre craves the king of curds in Bhaktapur*

I had only a few days left in Nepal, and there was one last thing I had to try—the yogurt in Bhaktapur.

Now Nepal is not known for its dairy products, and Bhaktapur is famed for ancient Newari culture, crafts, and architecture. The town is classified as a UNESCO world heritage site, and its monuments are certainly a must-see, but I was focused on a lesser-known local gem—*ju ju dhau*, or "king of curds."

Bhaktapur felt to me like an open-air museum, with its ornate wooden buildings and dusty craft-filled streets. Wandering among the temples, homes, and shops, I felt as if I had traveled into Nepal of the past, when Westerners, taxis, and tour guides didn't exist. Potting is a major industry in Bhaktapur, and around every corner we found merchants selling a variety of clay wares, spread out on blankets in the warm afternoon sun. Naturally, I couldn't help but buy a few pieces as souvenirs as we wandered around, but this was all just a prelude to the main event: yogurt.

We had no specific destination in mind, but luckily for us, the yogurt vendors were almost as plentiful as potters. The yogurt shops were actually just tiny wooden stalls, with no signs or noticeable markings. Still, it was easy to find what we were looking for, since most shops were bare except for a few large earthen pots filled with fresh plain yogurt. We bought a small pot to share, figuring that we'd come back for another.

We ate ours with a bit of chopped fruit and raw sugar, and it really did surpass our expectations. It was thick, rich, tart, and creamy, made with buffalo milk instead of cow's and served in clay pots, following a centuries-old tradition. The particular curd used in Bhaktapur yogurt is native to the area, and it commands a premium price on the dairy market owing to its consistently good taste, which I can certainly attest to.

After we finished our *ju ju dhau*, the shopkeeper told us to leave the pot behind. He proceeded to smash it into small pieces. We must have looked shocked, because he quickly explained that the clay was unfinished. Merchants do not reuse the pots but rather return the clay to the soil. We liked this—not only is the yogurt of Bhaktapur delicious, it's a wonderful example of recycling and sustainability within a local, traditional community.

### *Getting to Bhaktapur*

Bhaktapur is located just east of Kathmandu. You can take a taxi for 300-500 rupees or a minibus for much less. Buses leave nearly hourly from Kathmandu's Bagh Bazar (not the main bus park; ask for directions). If taking a taxi, be sure to bargain for the fare. The hour-plus trip one way should be 500 Nepali rupees at the very most. The last bus leaves around 9 p.m., and after that, taxi prices can be expected to go up.

### *Touring Bhaktapur*

Because the town is a UNESCO World Heritage Site, there is a $10 entry fee for Westerners. For your pass, bring two passport-size photos and a photocopy of your passport including your Nepal visa. The town is small enough to see pretty thoroughly in one day, but if you think you'll come more than once, let the official know when you get your pass so that it will cover more than one visit.

www.btdc.com.np

### *Where to find yogurt*

We heartily recommend trying *ju ju dhau* outdoors rather than in a restaurant. Hole-in-the-wall yogurt vendors are easy to find, scattered throughout the winding streets.

## Tansen

*Joe Bindloss reveals Tansen's sophisticated culinary secret*

The remote town of Tansen may once have been a royal capital, but it still surprised me when I found a place as sophisticated as Nanglo West tucked away among the winding cobbled lanes and metal-casting workshops. Facing the public square where the Ranas of Palpa used to parade on the backs of armored elephants, this stylish restaurant specializes in traditional Newari cuisine—an intriguing blend of Tibetan, Indian, Chinese, and Central Asian cooking styles.

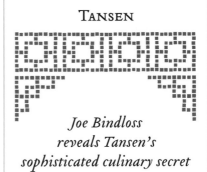

Hidden behind a tall Newari facade with carved window frames, this is one of my favorite Nepali eateries, swimming in the atmosphere of Rana-era Nepal. Reached through a stone courtyard, the dining room is decked out with old family treasures—hand-carved furniture, stained wooden butter pots, and ceremonial Hindu and Buddhist effigies. Shoes must be left at the threshold, waiters wear waistcoats and topis (traditional caps), and meals are served at low tables, laid with handwoven napkins and tablecloths.

The menu includes some familiar Nepali dishes, including a respectable plate of buff *momos* (that's buffalo meat for the uninitiated) and imaginatively spiced *dal bhat*, but the main reason to go is for the Newari cuisine. During harsh Nepali winters, Newari traders would carry *choyla* on the trails. At Nanglo West, this roasted and dried duck or buffalo meat, spiced with ground chili and fresh ginger, is served with *chura* (rice pounded into oatlike flakes) and potatoes in spiced curd, all washed down with pegs of Khukri rum.

During the conflict in Nepal, Nanglo West faced a lean time, but since 2008, gourmet travelers have started coming back to Tansen. Even so, the town, like the restaurant, is a well-kept secret. Shops in the cobbled bazaar sell brassware and woven *dhaka* fabric not to backpackers but to village traders, while volunteers at the tiny tourist office suggest day trips to temples, tribal villages, and Himalayan viewpoints in the surrounding hills ... all of which are ideal activities for working up an appetite for a leisurely meal at Nanglo West.

### *Getting to Tansen*

Located in Palpa District, Tansen is a four-hour bus ride from Pokhara or a two-hour bus ride uphill from Butwal on the road between Kathmandu and Sunauli at the Indian border.

### *Nanglo West*

Nanglo West is located on the north side of Sitalpati, the public square in front of the palace.

### *Newari landmarks*

While in Tansen, check out the Newari temples dotted around the cobbled streets. The most impressive is the pagoda-style Amar Narayan Mandir at the bottom of the steep road running east from Sitalpati. Built in 1807, it features some surprisingly risqué erotic carvings on the roof struts and a series of skulls and animal heads on the lintels above the doors.

### *Local walks*

Just west of Sitalpati and open every day except Saturday, GETUP (Group for Environment and Tourism Upgrading Palpa) is a mine of local information, including maps for local walks at the cost of just a few rupees. For Himalayan views and peaceful rural scenes, try the three-hour walk to the village of Ghansal or the one-hour stroll to the Buddha statue at the east end of Srinagar Danda, the huge hill rising behind Tansen. The best longer walk is the strenuous day-hike to Ranighat Durbar, a crumbling, river-view, Nepali-baroque palace built to house an exiled Rana in 1896.

## *Elizabeth Sharpe makes Palpa's signature chukauni*

Shanta handed me a stainless steel cup of hot steaming tea with a faint citrusy smell. The black tea wasn't diluted with creamy fresh buffalo milk because, she explained with apology, the buffalo had given birth a few weeks earlier.

"Oh, I don't mind." I took a sip, holding the rim of the cup gingerly. The tea was sweet, very sweet, so she had added *kagati* (lemon). "It's delicious," I assured her.

I had stopped to visit my friend Shanta in Chirtungdhara, a small village an hour outside of Tansen in the Palpa District. Inside her one-room home, I sat on a woven mat covering a wooden bed frame. Another similar set of mats had been laid side by side on the floor, and a comforter was rolled up so the frame could be used as a bench by day and bed at night.

The small shuttered windows were wide open, but the room was still dark and cool, compared to the hot day outside. I could barely make out the small posters hanging on the red, foot-thick walls that had been mortared with the plentiful dirt that stained the terraced hills outside. One poster was of Lakshmi, goddess of fortune and beauty, and the other of Vishnu, the supreme god in the Hindu faith.

Under the watchful gaze of these deities, Shanta asked her younger sister to run next door for some *dahi*, a yogurt that was made in the village from buffalo milk. Then she took a few potatoes from a pot and began to peel the skin, dicing them thickly in her hand with a knife. Next she lit the kerosene stove, and spices began to pop and sizzle, the fragrance of the air growing pungent from frying peppers. Her sister soon came running back, balancing a small covered bowl. Shanta added the contents to the potatoes before she mixed in the other ingredients.

"Have you ever tried *chukauni*?" she asked, offering me a plate containing something that looked a bit like potato salad and a few pieces of *sel roti*, a circular fried bread that is readily available at Nepali tea shops and made for nearly every festival and celebration.

As I tasted it, she told me that *chukauni* was a specialty of Palpa. The blend of spices and yogurt gave the potatoes a distinctive flavor, a sourness that was set off with a mild heat from the chili. It was delicious. I insisted that she teach me how to make it.

I didn't mean that day, and certainly not right then and there, but Shanta turned to her sister and asked her to go out for more *dahi*. This time I watched closely as she chopped and fried the ingredients, noting everything carefully so that I could re-create not only the dish, but this moment with my dear friend, once I got back home.

### *Cooking Nepali cuisine*

If you're interested in cooking Nepali dishes, check out Jyoti Pathak's *Taste of Nepal* cookbook (www.tasteofnepalcookbook.com). To get started, you can try Elizabeth's simple recipe for Palpali *chukauni* (serves 6).

**Ingredients:**

- 1 lb potatoes (*aloo*)
- 2 cups plain yogurt (*dahi*)
- 2-3 hot red chilies (*khursani*)
- 1 Tbsp mustard oil (*tori ko tel*)
- 1 tsp fenugreek seeds (*methi*)
- 1 tsp turmeric (*besar*)
- Pinch of salt (*nun*)
- 1 small diced onion, optional (*pyaj*)

**Directions:**

1. Wash potatoes well. Keep skins on, and cover potatoes with water. Boil potatoes 20 to 25 minutes, or until a fork can easily slide into a potato. Strain water from potatoes and rinse them with cold water. Let cool.
2. Using a mortar and pestle, grind whole red peppers with a pinch of salt. Add a sprinkle of water to help make a paste. The number of peppers used depends on preferred spiciness.
3. Peel skins of potatoes when cool. The skin should slide off easily. Then cut potatoes into bite-sized cubes. In a bowl, mix potatoes with yogurt.
4. In a small frying pan, heat mustard oil. When oil is hot, add fenugreek seeds. When seeds begin to turn dark brown, add turmeric and chili paste. Stir several times, then take the pan off the heat.
5. Mix ingredients from the frying pan with potatoes.

Serve *chukauni* chilled with diced onions on top.

### *Getting to Chirtungdhara*

Chirtungdhara is about an hour out of Tansen, on the highway that leads to Pokhara in the north and Butwal in the south.

## Chomrong

### *Ellen Shapiro admires creative deep frying in Chomrong*

I love food. I'm married to a food writer. My son, who is not quite four years old, talks about naan and Thai rice and coconut soup. And no, we don't have any Asian relatives.

Within the general category of food, I gravitate toward a subcategory: sweets. I'm a fanatic. So you can imagine my delight, shock, astonishment, and wonder when I came across a menu in Nepal that listed an item called "Snickers rool." What could a Snickers rool possibly be, my friend and I wondered, giggling a bit since we knew that the menu should have read "Snickers roll"—though for us it would forever be a rool.

We were in the Annapurna Sanctuary, and my friend was a first-time visitor to Nepal. I was delighted to be showing her around, and we were both excited to try something new together. I don't know where we first saw mention of Snickers rool, but it was appearing with great frequency on teahouse menus along the trail. Rather than race to try it, we savored anticipation of the day we would sample what we could only assume to be a local delicacy.

But as we climbed stone steps higher and higher, the Snickers rool never quite happened. In one spot we were too exhausted. In another, too out of breath. Then, one day, to our horror, we noticed that the Snickers rool had all but disappeared off the local menus. We walked from teahouse to teahouse picking up speed as each menu taunted us with the absence of Snickers rool. I chided myself. How could I have let this happen? By the time we made it to Annapurna Base Camp, it was official—Snickers rool had disappeared.

But wait! We realized that on our return trip we would retrace our steps for a couple of days. Maybe there was still hope. We talked with great anticipation about where we should try our very first Snickers rool, and we settled on Chomrong. We even knew the place. We would taste it on the patio of the Chomrong Guest House.

Days later, our arrival in Chomrong was a joyous one. Not only had we just climbed up hundreds of stone steps from the Chomrong River, but we were about to try our long-anticipated treat. We dropped our gear and headed for the guesthouse. We looked at a menu, but this was only a courtesy. Of course we knew exactly what we were going to order: a Snickers rool, to share.

When it arrived, we were giddy. It looked like a giant *momo*. The outside was fried golden brown, and when we cut into it ... milk chocolate oozed out. My friend took a bite. A thin stream of chocolate dribbled down her chin as she gestured wildly, pointing happily with her utensils toward the dessert. I took the next bite, and a quiet groan inadvertently escaped my lips. We polished off the first Snickers rool in no time flat and ordered a second. Clearly, half a Snickers rool apiece wasn't going to cut it.

As we waited, we discussed the merits of our newfound delicacy. Who knew a Snickers candy bar could be deep fried like a *momo* and become an instant trekking delicacy? It was a creative blending of cultures, and I loved everything about it!

### *Snickers rool*

Ellen has seen Snickers rool only at teahouses along the Annapurna Sanctuary Trail. She cannot say that the Snickers rool at the Chomrong Guest House is best as it is the only one that she has tried, but she can tell you this—it's delicious!

*Chomrong Guest House*

This guesthouse is located in the lower part of the upper section of Chomrong. The name is painted in huge white letters on the roof and is therefore impossible to miss en route to Annapurna Base Camp.

## Tukuche

*Ellen Shapiro sips her way through Annapurna*

I'm not really a drinker. It's not that I'm opposed on principle to drinking, or that I don't occasionally enjoy a drink, but weeks can go by before I might think to myself, "Gee, wouldn't it be nice to have a cocktail." Yet somehow, when I'm trekking around Annapurna, it's something that's *always* in the back of my mind.

The reason being, I love a good brandy. When I was a girl, I had the misfortune of contracting a searing toothache. The pain was intense, and it awakened me from a dead sleep in the night. A couple of tablets of acetaminophen were not going to do the trick. My father went down to our basement, cracked open a gallon jug of Prohibition-era, homemade moonshine, soaked a wad of cotton in it, and said, "Put this on your tooth and suck on it. It'll numb that tooth in no time."

Ever since, I've had a soft spot for fruit brandies (the glass jug had been stuffed full of apricots, with the moonshine poured over it and then the jar resealed for aging). So I considered it my good fortune to stumble upon the signs for the Tukuche Distillery as I trekked around Annapurna for the first time in 1992, far from home and my ailing father. I took the detour (as I have done many times since) and walked down a long narrow lane between two high walls. I had already come over Thorong La Pass and trekked beyond Kagbeni, and I was now in apple country. Above me, branches laden with red apples were visible from the orchards on the other side of the walls, which were built from stones pulled out of the ground around the trees.

I continued along, turning around periodically to see if I had taken a wrong turn or gotten lost somehow, until I saw a second small marker pointing me to the right along another narrow lane. When I reached the distillery, there was a big yellow sign out front announcing: "Tukuche Distillery, Tukuche, Mustang," with a listing below of the varieties of brandy made there: apple, apricot, orange, and carrot.

I walked through the archway to enter the building and found myself in a lovely courtyard ... with no one in sight. This was not only a distillery, but clearly also someone's home. I didn't know which of the three doors to enter—left, right, or center—so I stood dumbly, trying not to look too out of place, and waited for someone to discover me there.

Eventually, I heard clanging, and when I looked toward where I thought the noise was coming from, I saw large barrels by the doorway to the right. I tentatively made my way over to the door and tried to push it open. The person who was clanging looked up, opened the door, and invited me in.

Inside there were large, covered, waist-high barrels of what I could only assume was brandy. I surveyed the wall of bottles and saw a selection of sizes ranging from fifths to one-liter beer bottles (recycled) to one-and-a-half-liter bottles. A bespectacled woman, clearly the matron of the establishment, offered me a sample. Of course, I couldn't refuse.

The apple brandy was a sure hit, as was the apricot. I wasn't as thrilled with the orange, and the carrot, well, it wasn't for me. Now: decisions, decisions. How much should I get?

Ordinarily, this would not be a concern—back home I just buy what I want, and if I run out, I hop back around to the corner store and restock. Here, that was not an option. Whatever I bought, I would have to carry in my backpack for the next ten days, before toting in on a bus to Kathmandu, and hopefully (if it lasted that long), onto an airplane and back to the United States. I settled on three one-liter bottles, weighing, I figured, approximately nine pounds.

This load lightened as I moved on. I enjoyed that brandy along the trail, and later when I met up with friends to trek into the Annapurna Sanctuary from Annapurna Base Camp, we used it to toast a pink-hued Machhapuchhare at sunset.

I return to Nepal often, and while I have trekked many routes and enjoyed them all immensely, I always feel a twinge of regret when I miss the opportunity to get to Tukuche and pick up another bottle or two.

### *Tukuche*

The village of Tukuche is on the Annapurna Circuit south of Kagbeni and Jomsom. When you are coming down from Thorong La Pass, continue through the village almost until the very end. There is a sign posted along one of the whitewashed stone walls, but it's almost as hard to find as the distillery. So as you pass through the village, make sure to look on the walls at every left turn, and you will eventually see an arrow pointing you in the right direction—to the left. If all else fails, ask a local. You might make a couple wrong turns before arriving, but Ellen promises you, it's worth the effort. Cheers!

# MANANG/ANNAPURNA

## *Ellen Shapiro longs for apple pie in Manang*

There is nothing—and I mean nothing—as welcoming as the smell of a bakery when you've just trekked to more than three thousand meters.

As I rush into the Manang Valley on the high route from Pisang, I have only one thing on my mind. It's not a hot shower or where I'll rest my weary bones for the night. All I can think about is my favorite bakery. The last hours of our trek pass excruciatingly slowly as my thoughts are consumed with the taste of fresh-baked apple pie or strudel. I cross my fingers in hopes that the local bakery will be open late.

Once in town, I walk purposefully, watching every passerby to make sure she is not eating *my* piece—possibly the last piece—of apple pie.

I arrive at the bakery and have to restrain myself from pushing my face up against window. I search quickly but see no apple pie. I fling the door open, trying not to seem desperate. Maybe, I tell myself, there's an apple strudel in the display case inside. My eyes dart from side to side, and I calm down a bit when I see a pile of cinnamon rolls. At least there's that. For an immediate fix, I order one and then casually inquire about the pie. No? How about the strudel?

I must look crestfallen, because guy behind the counter offers me the last piece of apple crumble. But as kind as his offer is, that just won't do. All day only one thing pushed me forward: apple strudel or apple pie. He assures me that there will be fresh batches first thing in the morning. "Come back then," he says.

Oh, I'll be there. You can bet your trekking boots on that!

### *Manang Bakery*

If you've made it as far as Manang, you'll have no trouble finding this bakery, as there's only one street in town. As you enter the *kani* (archway) to town en route from Pisang, the bakery comes up quickly on your right. If you get to the turnoff for the Himalayan Rescue Association (HRA), you've gone too far. If all else fails, follow your nose.

### *Pie with a view*

It's hard to go wrong with any of the goods offered at the Manang Bakery, but the apple strudel, apple pie, and cinnamon rolls top Ellen's list, and she certainly wouldn't turn down the chocolate bread. There's a nice garden area, perfect for enjoying the mountain views, but wait until the sun climbs high enough over the mountains and warms the patio—unless you're planning on wearing your down coat and doing jumping jacks between bites.

## Samdo Village

*Clint Rogers finds heaven on earth in Samdo village*

Samdo is a village in the northern Gorkha District in Nepal. I selected it as the field site for my research on cross-border trade between Nepal and Tibet because it sits on a major caravan route just a few hours' walk from the border. When the patriarch of Samdo—a single-toothed grandpa with a quick smile—invited me to stay in his house, I was thrilled.

Here I was in a serene, remote setting, located within spitting distance of Mt. Manaslu (the world's eighth-tallest peak), where four high-mountain passes connect the village with adjacent regions in Tibet and Nepal. I knew it would be perfect for my research. What I didn't know was that Samdo would turn out to be the home of the most amazing potatoes I'd ever eaten.

Admittedly, my first few weeks in Samdo were rough. I quickly became accustomed to the local bathing habits—once a year—and was soon visited by my first case of lice. Not long after the lice, I was bedridden with a bout of giardiasis, popularly known as backpacker's diarrhea. Fortunately, I had brought my own medicine and so was able to avoid the local remedy of fresh chicken's blood.

After a few days' recovery, I was pleased to finally partake in some local delicacies. The daily staple in Samdo is *tsampa*, a concoction of barley flour mixed in a cup of salt-butter tea, but for me the true treat of the village is the typically unassuming *pomme de terre*.

I am completely convinced that the villagers of Samdo grow the world's best potatoes. Local residents prepare their delectable *aloo* (Nepali for potato) by boiling the small lumps to perfection in a broth of melted yak butter, Tibetan rock salt, and a spice called *jimbu*, which is picked wild in Tibet. If that isn't enough to take you to potato nirvana, the buttery tubers are then dipped in fresh yak milk curd. Life in Samdo was difficult in many ways, but because of the potato, I was certain I'd found heaven on earth.

### *Getting to Samdo*

The best way to reach Samdo village is by contacting one of the two trekking companies in Kathmandu listed below, both of which Clint knows and trusts. Explain that you want to trek "around Manaslu."

The duration of this trek is about three weeks. You will begin in

Gorkha (reached by bus from Kathmandu or Pokhara) and finish in Besisahar (with buses back to Kathmandu or Pokhara). Unlike the more established trekking destinations in the Everest and Annapurna regions, there are very few guesthouses along the way, so be prepared to camp. The best season for the Manaslu trek is autumn, particularly mid-October to mid-November.

**Project Himalaya**
www.project-himalaya.com

**Everest Parivar Expeditions**
http://mountclimbing.com

### *Trek highlights*

Clint's top picks include: viewing Manaslu peak close-up from its east, north, and west sides; eating boiled potatoes and salt-butter tea with traditional caravan traders in Samdo village; and taking a day trip from Sama village to the lake-studded meadows of Pungyen Gompa at the base of Manaslu's sheer southeast face.

### *Picture perfect*

If you plan to use a digital camera, bring extra batteries. In this remote area you will not be able to recharge or purchase batteries.

### *Author, author!*

To read more about Samdo village, purchase a copy of Clint's book, *Where Rivers Meet: A Tibetan Refugee Community's Struggle to Survive in the High Mountains of Nepal.* It is published by Mandala Book Point and available from the publisher or Amazon.com.

www.mandalabookpoint.com

## Tengboche

### *Linzi Barber cherishes chocolate doughnuts in Tengboche*

Reaching Tengboche—on day 4 of our trek from Lukla to Everest Base Camp—gave us a reason to celebrate. We had successfully reached thirty-eight hundred meters.

Soon after arriving, we headed for the huge open space in front of the Tengboche Monastery, where trekkers and ponies alike were enjoying the late afternoon sunshine. After six days without communication with my best friend, I assumed the highlight of Tengboche was going to be the only Internet café above three thousand meters en route to base camp. I was soon to be proved wrong.

As I finished sending my email, I noticed a coffee shop across the street. Although we were officially avoiding caffeine because of the altitude, I figured we could at least sit and have a nice cup of herbal tea. As I pushed open the heavy door to the café, the smell of homemade baked goods hit me. We were greeted by the welcome sight of cakes and pastries so beautiful that we felt as if we had walked into an upscale urban patisserie.

My mouth watered, and I struggled to make my choice. Finally, my eyes fell on the chocolate doughnuts. Just when I thought it couldn't get any better, the smiling proprietor of one of the world's highest bakeries offered to warm one up for me. At this point I decided: to hell with the no caffeine rule!

Wrapped in fleeces outside Café Tengboche, we enjoyed the luxury of hot coffee and freshly baked doughnuts on top of the world. We sat for a long time, just watching life pass by. Ponies licked sugar off the recently vacated tables, then knocked them over in their hurry to escape the proprietors, who frequently opened the windows to shout and wave their arms. When the sun began to set, we walked down to the monastery to listen to evening prayer. Maybe it was the chocolate, but the world had become a better place.

Base Camp was undoubtedly the highlight of our trip, but along with my memory of reaching the summit of Kala Patthar, Café Tengboche is still high on my list of favorite experiences. Needless to say, Tengboche was a scheduled stop on the way back down the mountain.

## *Kathmandu to Everest Base Camp*

Linzi adds: Although some people still walk to Lukla on the historical route from Jiri (this takes about a week), we flew from Kathmandu to Lukla. I recommend allowing extra time in your schedule for this, since the weather often delays the flights, especially in the early mornings. Then we went from Lukla (2,804 meters) down to Phakding (2,610 meters), since sleeping lower than you started on your first day is important for acclimatization. After an overnight in Phakding, we trekked up to Namche Bazaar (3,440 meters), which is considered the last "civilized" place on this route, with its shops and Internet cafés. We stayed here for two nights to acclimatize and found plenty to do, including visiting a great Sherpa museum.

From Namche we made our way to Tengboche (3,860 meters), and from there to Dingboche (4,410 meters). By this stage in the trek the days were feeling much longer, because walking was slower as we adjusted to the thinning air. After two nights at Dingboche, which included another acclimatization day, we headed to Lobuje (4,910 meters) and then on to our highest sleeping point, Gorak Shep (5,153 meters). This was not only the point from which we made our attempt at base camp, but also the point from where we climbed Kala Patthar for excellent views of Mt. Everest. Our trek to base camp from Gorak Shep took around eight hours round-trip, and there were no facilities at all on the way. It was essential to carry enough water and snacks for the entire journey.

### *Kathmandu to Lukla*

Flights between Kathmandu and Lukla are operated by Gorkha Airlines.

www.gorkhaairlines.com

### *The basics*

Linzi stayed in basic teahouse lodging, with either private or dorm rooms, all of which require providing your own sleeping bag. It's best to use local Sherpa guides, readily available from the airport at Lukla. They will be able to help arrange accommodation—most travelers do not book in advance. Water can be purchased along most of the trails, but it's better to use running water from teahouses and restaurants and purify it yourself, since you will need to carry your plastic bottles with you until you get back to Lukla, where you can dispose of them.

### *Café Tengboche*

You can get your chocolate doughnut fix on the main road, just across from the only Internet café in town.

### *Sherpa museum*

The Sherwi Khangba center in Namche Bazaar offers travelers a deeper understanding of the traditional way of life of the Sherpa people, who are hired to work as porters for treks in the Himalayas. The museum also emphasizes the important role Sherpas have played in hiking Mt. Everest.

www.sherpa-culture.com.np

### *Altitude sickness*

Altitude sickness may occur above three thousand meters, and it's important to ascend slowly. With an itinerary like Linzi's, plenty of days are figured in for acclimatization. If you feel any symptoms at all of altitude sickness, you should descend immediately. Sometimes, simply descending fifty meters can help. On your way back down, make time to visit the clinic near Lukla, which appeals to travelers to donate any unused first aid equipment on their return from base camp.

## Singalila Ridge

### *Karen Coates drinks in the flowers on the Indian border*

Were it not for the sweet pink elixir of rhododendron wine, I might very well have frozen my petunias off during our first night in Nepal. There was almost no firewood to be found on the Nepal side of the trail that borders India's Singalila National Park. That was because the Indian government prohibited villagers from cutting wood a few months earlier, and the Nepal side had been stripped long ago.

The result: icy-cold nights and cookstoves fueled by gas. While I'm all for saving the trees, I wholeheartedly empathized with the villagers bundled in hats and blankets, shivering through months of winter.

So there we were in Gairibas, barely a village on the edge of a military outpost, where the wind howled against the flimsy walls of an airy lodge. But our host, Diki Sherpa, rescued us when she hauled out a jug of rhododendron wine.

In springtime, these flowers cover the Himalayas. So why not make use of all those pretty blossoms? I learned that the flowers are crushed with yeast and millet or rice, and then cooked in a big pot. The juice slowly drips into a container, creating something of a makeshift distillery.

The wine tasted light and flowery upfront, with a hint of the kicky aftertaste you get in a serious rice wine. This was a good thing. I needed something warm that winter night in the high mountains of Nepal.

*Singalila Ridge*
To read more about this area of Nepal, go to page 128.

## General Nepal

### *Charis Boke perks up for real espresso around Nepal*

I'm not your typical coffee snob. In the face of no other option, I will drink pretty much anything that is handed to me. My java snobbery developed only after a year of working at a high-end coffeehouse in Berkeley, so it's not deep-seated. Still, it' exists, which is why, when I got to Kathmandu, I decided I should track down a few good coffee shops—not only for the caffeine, but also because I do my best work in these kinds of cafés.

### Imago Dei Café and Gallery

A few years ago, I knew of only one or two places in Kathmandu that served "real" coffee—not just the Nescafé that is oh so common here. All of these real-coffee coffee shops were in the tourist district of Thamel, so when I heard about Imago Dei from a friend, I was surprised. What's a Latin name meaning "in the image of god" doing attached to a Nepali café? I walked to the east side of the former royal palace one day to find out, and boy, was I pleasantly surprised!

Set back in a courtyard, in which there are two art galleries and a duty-free shop, Imago Dei Café and Gallery has the atmosphere of any upscale urban beverage-consuming venue. The walls are all glass—that means great light, which is hard to come by indoors in Nepal—and a new set of paintings is displayed every month ... also hard to come by here. Though a little spendy, the food is pretty good, the lattes are beautiful, and the espresso is strong and flavorful.

### Lazimpat Gallery Café

My second little coffee sanctuary was discovered by chance. Walking up Lazimpat Road, thinking vaguely about stopping somewhere for a glass of water, I saw a sign reading "Lazimpat Gallery Café." The words alone didn't get me—it was the stylish lettering, the modern touch of the sign's coloring that pulled me in. We may say that it's wrong to judge a book by its cover, but at least in this case it wasn't such a bad thing. I sat down to check out the menu and was shocked (yes, shocked) to see espresso on it. *What*? I looked up at the counter, and there it was, the Holy Grail: an espresso machine. Happily, I ordered a cup, and since that lucky day I've gotten some really good work done here, synthesizing research, writing presentations, and taking care of all the other jazz that comes with living and working in Nepal.

### Cafe Society

My good friend and his Nepalese business partner decided to launch their own coffee bean roastery right here in Kathmandu. I was thrilled. Fresh-roasted coffee always tastes better than the packaged stuff. As for this particular coffee ... though I love the other shops I've written about here, their brews pale in comparison. The *crema* on the fresh espresso ... the scent of newly roasted beans ... the calm that comes with tasting a truly fine coffee. Not something you find every day in Nepal.

### High Plains Inn

As for a random and remote place for good coffee, I recommend the High Plains Inn in Tukuche in the Annapurna region in the Himalayas. I had been to about five villages north of Tukuche when I first heard of this place from another traveler in Kagbeni. Noting my bag of ground coffee and my struggle to make coffee through a tea filter, she said, "You should really check out the High Plains Inn. They have great coffee, and they're the best place for lunch on the whole trek." She wasn't kidding, as I later discovered. On a day hike from Marpha to see some temples and monasteries in Tukuche and Larjung, I noticed a sign reading "Dutch filter coffee and espresso." I convinced my friends that we should eat lunch early. It was only after about half an hour that I realized we must be in the place my Kagbeni acquaintance had mentioned—no way were there two restaurants with coffee that good in the same tiny town! I was so impressed that I made sure to stop in for a snack on the way back through.

### Coffee in Kathmandu

*Cafe Society*

This coffee shop is next door to the European Bakery and across the street from the Grihini Departmental Store.

Baluwatar District
Kathmandu

*Imago Dei Café and Gallery*

East Gate of Royal Palace Museum
Nag Pokhari District
Kathmandu

imago.dei.gallery@gmail.com

*Lazimpat Gallery Café*

This café is located south of the Shangri-La Hotel & Resort. For more information, you can find the café on Facebook.

Lazimpat District
Kathmandu

lazimpatgallerycafe@hotmail.com

*Getting online*

All three of the Kathmandu-based coffee shops are equipped with good Wi-Fi, which guests can use for free.

### Coffee high in the Himalayas

*High Plains Inn*

Tukuche Village
Mustang District

www.highplainsinn.com

# Seeing the Sights

*Fresh perspectives on must-see attractions*

Although Nepal has its share of conventional sights worth seeing, its museums and monuments pale in comparison to its greatest attraction: the views. There is perhaps no more impressive sight in the world than the Himalayan Mountain Range.

This is why a full third of the essays in this chapter focus on views. Using Pokhara as their base, Joe Bindloss, David Markus, and Joshua Esler hike and bike the surrounding area, searching for the best angles from which to marvel at the grandeur of Machhapuchhare, Nepal's famous "Fish Tail" peak. They study it at all hours of the day, though it is most enticing at sunrise, as are the Himalayas' many other mountainscapes. As Devon Wells discovers on his hike to Poon Hill, no matter how difficult the journey, the dawn-hour vista is worth the effort.

But views aren't the only reason to explore the trekking routes. Other types of sights illuminate the uniqueness of mountain culture, from horse races to rope bridges to remote monasteries. Because spirituality is such an essential part of life in Nepal, we have included holy destinations off the slopes, as well, beginning with Lumbini. The birthplace of Buddha, this is one of the most sacred sites in the world, and that is why we offer essays from two perspectives, to show how the pilgrimage site means different things to different people.

As for Kathmandu, this chapter takes you from the great stupa of Boudha to the palace of the Living Goddess to family-friendly spots along the outlying valley. As with every other destination written about here—located high or low—each will give you an appreciation of the blend of natural beauty and spiritual tradition that makes sightseeing in Nepal such a transcendental experience.

*Boudhanath Stupa in Kathmandu*

# KATHMANDU

*Scott Berry befriends a former Living Goddess in Kathmandu*

In the mid-1980s my wife and I, along with our two daughters, ages eight and ten, spent a year living in one room near the old Hanuman Dhoka Palace and Kumari Ghar, the house of the "Living Goddess." Our girls, Maya and Laxmi, became fascinated with this child, just a bit younger than they were, who lived such a different life from their own, or indeed from that of most Nepalese children.

In Nepal, the Kumari goddess is a little girl of high caste. She is said to be the incarnation of the fierce goddess Taleju, and from the ages of four to twelve, she lives in her own temple dressed all in red. My daughters and I made daily visits to the young Kumari's courtyard hoping to get a glimpse of her. One day, after appearing at her window for a group of tourists, she called down to the girls in Nepali, "I have a ball. Do you want to play?"

It was the beginning of an unusual friendship. Kumari was not allowed outside, except during festival times, when she was dressed up and carried around, and our girls, not being Hindus, were not allowed in her temple. Her guardians suggested a compromise. Maya and Laxmi could stand at the bottom of the steps, Kumari at the top. They could throw toys and sweets back and forth and chat. During festivals they could get close enough to have their photos taken together as long as they did not talk or distract her from her duties.

In the monsoon month of August, 2001, my wife and I made our first return visit to Nepal in about fifteen years. What, we wondered, had happened to the child goddess of long ago? Once the goddesses hit puberty, we had been told, they are kicked out of the palace and a replacement is chosen. We wondered about the little girl that our own little girls had gotten to know—had adjusting to normal life been difficult?

One day my wife was having a piece of jewelry repaired. The goldsmith was a member of the Shakya community, the caste from which all Kumaris are chosen. Thinking he might know what had become of her, we showed him an old photo. "Oh yes, Rashmila," he said immediately. His brother phoned the family, arranged a meeting, and gave us directions to the house.

Having heard tales of spoiled and unapproachable ex-goddesses, we had no idea if she would remember our girls, or what kind of a person she might be. It turned out we needn't have worried. She was waiting in a courtyard in the heart of the oldest part of Kathmandu. The intervening years had eroded our Nepali language skills to almost nothing, so we were pleasantly surprised when she spoke to us in excellent English. She had no idea who we were until we showed her the pictures of our daughters. Her face lit up, and she exclaimed, "Maya and Laxmi!"

After that we were often guests of Rashmila and her family. A self-assured young woman in her early twenties, she was just about to begin university (having completed her degree in IT, she now works full-time as a software designer while also pursuing her MA). Gradually, from Rashmila and her sisters, we heard stories of how she transformed from pampered goddess to well-adjusted mortal. Though she had been spoiled rotten during her reign as Kumari, and had almost no schooling, she eventually caught up and was proud to have made a happy adjustment to normal life.

### *Kumari Ghar*

Also known as Kumari Chowk or Kumari Che, the home of the Living Goddess is located in Kathmandu's Durbar Square, and the ornate courtyard is usually open during the daylight hours, except from noon to four, when the goddess is having private tuition—an improvement since Rashmila's time. The incumbent Kumari is usually willing to appear at the upstairs window. A small donation is appreciated.

### *The life of a goddess*

There are many wild tales about the selection process and a Kumari's life. Some guidebooks and guides will tell you that as part of the process she is required, at the age of four, to prove her courage by walking through a room of freshly severed buffalo heads while priests make frightening noises. You might also be told that she never gets to see her family and has no playmates. Rashmila has stressed again and again that these stories have no basis in fact. She was chosen on the basis of her horoscope, saw her family regularly (they sometimes spent the night), and had a houseful of playmates.

### *Viewing Kumari*

The best time to get a good look at Kumari is during one of the festivals, when she comes outside. It is possible to give only approximate dates, since they change every year. Her most spectacular festival, Indra Jatra, is held in September. She is carried out briefly to the Taleju temple the evening before, then on three occasions is pulled through the town on a huge chariot and worshipped by adoring crowds. The best time to get a really close look at her is the evening after Gai Jatra, which usually falls in August, when she is taken to visit a number of temples to view their treasures.

### *The story continues*

To read more about Rashmila's life, track down a copy of *From Goddess to Mortal*, coauthored by Scott and the former child goddess.

## *Jacquelin Sonderling worships in her own way in Boudha*

No matter how often I go to Kathmandu, I'm drawn to the great stupa of Boudhanath. It thrills me every time, as though it were my first visit. Boudhanath consistently stays near the top of my "to do" list, right after Pilgrim's Feed 'n Read bookstore and the spice stalls in the Thamel District. My heartbeat always speeds up as I get close enough to recognize the entrance of this extraordinary landmark—the religious center for much of Nepal's Tibetan population and a primary pilgrimage destination for Buddhists of the Himalayas.

While no one knows exactly how old Boudhanath is, experts generally agree that the origins of this UNESCO World Heritage Site date from sometime around the seventh century AD. The sense of history here is so strong that it's palpable. Stepping through the gates and into the forecourt, I feel as if I'm walking back into a time that's long since passed. I close my eyes, and the honking horns of taxis and speeding motorbikes disappear. Instead, I can hear the yak caravans passing by, the bells around the necks of the big beasts ringing gently as they lumber along, slowly pulling carts piled high with goods bound for market.

The stupa sits on an ancient trade route that ties Nepal with Tibet. For centuries, Tibetan merchants would stop to rest and offer prayers. When the Chinese communists invaded Tibet in the 1950s, many refugees fled to Nepal, settling around Boudhanath. The area became known as "Little Tibet," and it's a great place to get a feel for Tibetan lifestyle.

The base of the stupa is also a fascinating place to people watch. Visions of the Tibetans and Nepalese I have seen around Boudhanath sit atop my memories of Nepal. I once spotted a monk in his crimson robes and running shoes, a Nike backpack over his shoulders, spinning the prayer wheels as he circumambulated the stupa. I watched a group of men sitting on small stools playing a game of cards, and later that same day, at least half a dozen women presided over tables full of the butter candles that are lit to honor Buddha. The dozens of burning candles add to the spiritual atmosphere, whose pull I feel whenever I visit.

My first time there, I was captivated by the massive whitewashed monument and the dancing prayer flags, which are known as Wind Horses. Hundreds, maybe even thousands, snap in the breeze, straining at their strings—bright red, blue, green, yellow, and white—fluttering against the blue sky. They're magical, the way they wave and tumble in a nonstop ballet around the stupa's magnificent combination of art and architecture. The base is shaped like a mandala, which signifies the earth. On top of this tiered foundation sits the famously recognizable white dome, symbolizing water. The spire shoots up into the sky, like the column of flame it represents. Perched on top of that is the umbrella (air) and, finally, the pinnacle (ether).

From the square base of the spire that tops the white dome, the eyes of Buddha gaze out in four directions, keeping careful watch over the ever-present faithful performing *kora*, the ritual circling of the stupa: pilgrims, monks, old women, and even the occasional Westerner. They pray as they walk, fingering their *mala* beads, chanting, reaching out to spin the prayer wheels in the brick wall that surrounds the stupa. The murmured words of the immortal mantra, *om mani padme hum*, provide a soft background music as I begin each visit by firing off at least a dozen photos—in my ongoing attempt to capture the perfect image—and then begin my own ritual of circumambulation.

*Getting to Boudha*

Go to page 21.

*Legendary details*

Robert Tompkins adds: According to legend, the builders of Boudhanath collected dew to mix with mortar since the stupa was constructed during a period of severe drought. Another apocryphal story regarding its origins claims that a widow petitioned the king for land the size of which could be covered by a buffalo hide. When the land was granted, she cut the buffalo skin into strips, roped them together, and claimed the substantially larger area on which the stupa was built.

## Kurintar & Gorkha

*Joe Bindloss braves a family day trip out of Kathmandu*

You know how it is. When you make a place home, you rarely visit the sights. Despite living in Kathmandu for years, several of my expat friends had never roamed beyond the Kathmandu Valley, put off by the stresses of traveling on Nepal's crowded roads with a young family. Determined to put this right, a few of us planned a Saturday out with the children—aged two, four, and nine—along the highway between Kathmandu and Pokhara.

Setting off early by jeep, we left the Kathmandu Valley at Thankot and plunged down into the valley of the Trisuli River. Distances in Nepal look short on the map, but the tortured topography adds miles to every journey. To help the time pass, we sang along to Rolf Harris songs on the tape player. A few sights along the route attracted the children's attention—vendors with racks of pongy smoked fish in Malekhu, inflatable rafts on the rapids near Benighat, gangs of rhesus monkeys begging for food along the roadside—but tempers were starting to fray by the time we reached our first stop.

The Riverside Springs Resort was founded by one of Nepal's most successful entrepreneurs as a luxury retreat for families fleeing the noise and crowds in the capital. With its shingled cottages, shady gardens, and huge outdoor swimming pool, it provided a real haven after the hectic traffic on the Prithvi Highway. The children had a field day, splashing around in the morning sunshine, while the grownups enjoyed a well-earned *chota peg* (a "small drink" of alcohol).

A quick lunch of fried chicken and vegetable soup—mildly spiced for young taste buds—and we set off for the next stage of the journey, the cable car ride to the Manakamana temple. Built by Swiss engineers in 1998, the cableway travels 2.8 kilometers and swoops 1,000 meters up the valley wall to the temple of the "wish-fulfilling goddess," replacing an arduous five-hour trek from the village of Mugling. From our gently rocking carriage, the view stretched along the gorge, with the river glinting like a silver ribbon almost a kilometer below.

The wooden pagoda at Manakamana was built in the seventeenth century by devotees of the Hindu goddess Bhagwati. Nepali Hindus aim to make the pilgrimage here at least once before they die, bringing goats, chickens, and pigeons as animal sacrifices. The cable car even has a dedicated carriage for the goats. We were a little concerned as to how the children would react to the fate of the baby goats milling around in the courtyard, but we needn't have worried. If anything, they seemed more comfortable with the concept of life and death than the adults, cheerfully waving goodbye to the goats as they were led into the sacrificial compound.

The journey home was the hardest part of the day. We faced a constant struggle to keep the children from falling asleep before bedtime. Fortunately, fizzy drinks kept most of the party alert, helped by endless choruses of "Nellie the Elephant" and "Jake the Peg." Nevertheless, when we finally pulled into Kathmandu, three sleeping children had to be carried inside, exhausted from a big day out.

### *Manakamana temple*

The temple is on the main Prithvi Highway between Kathmandu and Pokhara. Any bus between the two towns can drop you at the bottom cable car station at Cheres. The cable car runs from 9 a.m. to 5 p.m. with an hour-and-a-half break starting at noon. Tickets cost $12 return, and there's a small rupee fee for bulky items of luggage. Note that there is often a long queue for the cable car early in the morning and late in the afternoon.

If you want to stay at Manakamana, there are several decent pilgrims' hotels on the path from the top cable car station to the temple. The simple but friendly Sunrise Home (064-460055) offers the best value for money, with big clean rooms and a restaurant serving both vegetarian and nonvegetarian dishes.

*Riverside Springs Resort*

Also on the highway, on the way to the temple from Kathmandu, the resort offers rooms in wooden cabins or a bright, airy central lodge. If you stop by for lunch, children can use the pool for free.

www.rsr.com.np

## Khokana & Bungamati

*Devon Wells meets "regular people" outside Kathmandu*

"You've come all this way—don't you want to understand what you're seeing?" My driver peered at me over his mirrored shades as I sat in his rickshaw outside Durbar Square.

"You know, that makes sense. Sure, I'll hire you."

I grabbed his arm as he helped me down from the seat. He was dressed in a leather jacket, and with his slicked-back hair, he reminded me of John Stamos—a little rounder, a little more tanned, but Stamos nonetheless.

"Call me Milan," he said.

But despite having a guide, and despite the historical and cultural significance, Durbar Square was a bust. It was the Saraswati Puja festival the day I visited, and the Hanuman Dhoka palace complex was closed. And, as usual, I was underwhelmed with the string of temples and shrines. Regular people going about their regular lives always hold my attention better.

Soon, Milan and I stopped to get some tea at a rooftop café and chat awhile. "So, we've seen everything here?" I asked.

"Everything *here*, yes," said Milan. "But I think you maybe want to see where real people live, to understand the culture."

*How convenient*, I thought. "That's *exactly* what I want to see."

We paid up, found a taxi, and headed somewhere south. Milan said we were going past Patan, but I was too focused on keeping my head from cracking on the roof of the car with every bump to pay attention. Along highways and rocky paths, through small hills and valleys, we traveled for about half an hour, until the driver pulled over on the side of a dirt road.

Milan got out. "We have to walk from here," he said. The sun was beaming down over tiers of grain gardens as we descended into the valley, dodging mud and stones from construction along the way.

We were in Khokana, a traditional Newari village known mostly for its production of mustard oil. That might sound as interesting as drywall, until you realize that life here has barely changed in the past few hundred years. The same Newari townhouses still stand sandwiched together on the hillsides, while descendents of descendents of descendents still card wool by hand in the public squares and wield hammers to crush turmeric plucked fresh from the earth.

Milan led me along dirt and cobblestone paths until an old man with sun-tempered skin approached us, clad in a traditional Newari vest, jodhpurs, and topi hat. We stood outside a large clay building without windows as the elder started talking.

"He's saying this is where they press the mustard," explained Milan. "Or they used to. Now they ship it to an electric press. I think that's what he's saying. He's speaking Newari, and I only understand a little."

Even tiny villages in the mountains usually had people who spoke English, but here, the eldest residents couldn't even speak Nepali, preserving the complex Newari language hardly used outside the Kathmandu Valley.

With a pleasant "*namaste*," we continued down past more houses tucked on hillsides, across a river, past fields of mustard, wheat, and garlic, until the valley's end, when we climbed up to the village of Bungamati. I'd scarcely noticed we'd left Khokana behind.

We followed more Newari townhouses up along a path, trying to name the vegetables drying in bundles dangling from the roofs. Suddenly, we were surrounded—everywhere I looked, there were intricate wooden carvings of Hindu gods and goddesses, Buddhist mandalas, and local birds and flowers. A few paces away, a group of women were sanding down a piece of *sal* wood as wide as a car, which would be a door frame when finished.

Bungamati is a major center for wood-carving in Nepal, with shops and studios selling hand-carved prayer wheels and masks of Bhairab (one of Shiva's many forms) on every corner. Milan led me to a building nearby, and the women introduced me to Raj Bhai Shakya, a master carver.

This was no marble-floored showroom, but more like an artist's studio that's been opened to the public. Just-finished works still caked with sawdust lay about the studio, as the carver took us through the process involved in changing a chunk of wood into a high-priced work of art. (Shakya's work is sold internationally and is also on display at Kathmandu's luxury Yak & Yeti hotel.) Some of the larger pieces take months to sand and polish properly before they're ready for the market.

By the time we left, the sun was setting, so we stopped at an open-air restaurant overlooking the valley, watching a local volleyball game as we ate chicken chili and *momos*. I was impressed. This was a place I *never* would have thought to come to on my own, but everything about it—the fields, the houses, the sculptures and shrines, the regular people doing regular things—was eye-opening. On my trip to Nepal, I had been hoping to meet some locals beyond the rickshaw wallahs and Tiger Balm touts, and in Khokana and Bungamati, I found them, still engaged in the same honest work their ancestors had done centuries ago.

### *Newari villages outside Kathmandu*

Khokana and Bungamati are most easily accessed by taxi from Kathmandu, since the only buses there run from Patan, which itself is a bus or taxi ride from central Kathmandu. If your bargaining skills are good, it shouldn't cost more than 300 rupees each way in a taxi. Because very few people speak English in these villages, it helps to have a guide to interpret and add background to the sights. There are plenty hanging around Durbar Square or Thamel, although Devon recommends Milan, who can be reached at 977-9841-237836 or basuribadhak@hotmail.com.

## Lumbini

### *Srinidhi Lakhanigam follows his childhood dreams to Lumbini*

When I finally had the chance to spend two months riding through South Asia on my motorcycle, I was fulfilling more than one childhood dream. Several friends and I started out in India and headed for Nepal via the Sunauli-Bhairahawa border. I chose this crossing because it's the closest to Lumbini. This makes it busy, especially during summer months, when devout Buddhists arrive in droves to visit the birthplace of Lord Buddha.

Our first stop was the government customs and immigration office, so we could get our permits to travel by motorcycle through Nepal. The staff was courteous and helped us complete all the formalities for traveling on our Indian registered motorcycles. As this was my first time riding in a foreign country, I was thrilled to have achieved this first step in my goal to navigate the world on two wheels.

I was immediately charmed by the beauty of Nepal—the men and women in their traditional dress, the beautiful landscape, and the peaceful breezes. As we headed off on the dusty roads of the Himalayan kingdom, our first destination was Lumbini, where Buddha (Siddhartha Gautama) was born in 563 BC. The twenty-two-kilometer stretch from the border to Lumbini is narrow and not so smooth, but the rustic scenery and sparse traffic made the ride enjoyable, especially after the cacophony we experienced in the towns and villages of Uttar Pradesh in neighboring India.

As we entered Lumbini, a sense of joy overwhelmed me. I'd learned so much in school about the great prince who renounced everything to attain supreme knowledge, and now that I was in the very place of his birth, my happiness knew no bounds.

Given the popularity of Lumbini, I was surprised to find that this famous village was extremely quaint and nondescript. But because it seemed that Buddha would have wanted it that way, it felt like paradise to me. I was awed by the beauty and serenity of the Lumbini heritage park, a vast green area that is the main tourist attraction. Its highlight is the Maya Devi temple, which is said to be the actual place where Maya Devi gave birth to Buddha.

I entered the brick and mortar structure and followed a long pathway to the shrine that houses the nativity sculpture depicting the birth scene of Buddha. According to my local guide, this sculpture was installed by Malla kings that ruled throughout Nepal from the twelfth to the eighteenth century. Alongside the temple, I gazed at the crystal clear water in the tank (*pushkarini*) where it is said the infant Buddha was bathed immediately after being born. Adjacent to the tank, I stood at the *sal* tree under which Maya Devi rested just before giving birth.

Thrilled as I was to visit the monuments from Buddha's life, I was also captivated by those built to honor him. As I walked along the manicured lawns and colorful flower gardens around the Maya Devi temple, I was moved by the four stupas and stone pillar with a horse atop—gifts from India's Emperor Ashoka, who visited Lumbini in 249 BC. I tried to imagine what it would have been like to be a part of the emperor's royal entourage, traveling all that way to pay tribute to the birthplace of Buddha. But as much as I wished I could go back in time, I was grateful to be there today, where the spirit of Buddha lingered like a blessing over my long-awaited journey.

### *Getting to Lumbini*

Lumbini is situated in the Terai plains of southern Nepal and is easily accessible by road from India. The Sunauli border town of Bhairahawa, through which most visitors to Lumbini enter Nepal, is just over twenty kilometers away. Decrepit buses leave the local bus stand just north of Bhairahawa's dusty town center whenever there are enough passengers—this usually means twenty more than the bus can comfortably hold, plus another dozen on the roof. The journey takes about an hour and is a bumpy but enjoyable ride. The nearest airports in Nepal are located at Pokhara (105 kilometers) and Kathmandu (300 kilometers).

www.lumbinitrust.org

## *Lucy Corne trades shopping bags for prayer flags in Lumbini*

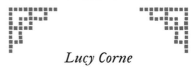

It was the eve of Buddha's birthday, and as I sat reading under a tree, I marveled at the silence surrounding me. I was fewer than fifty meters from the birthplace of The Enlightened One, and while celebratory preparations were under way, I couldn't help comparing the scene to Christmas Eve back home. Rather than witnessing scores of stressed shoppers rushing to buy last-minute gifts, I was watching small groups of pilgrims visit the exact spot where Siddhartha Gautama, the man who would be Buddha, was born around 563 BC.

The pilgrims started their visit by taking a few photos, the masses of vivid prayer flags providing a perfect backdrop. They then turned to the murky waters of the holy pond, bathing where the infant who would launch a whole new school of thought is said to have taken his first dip. Before heading to the birth site itself, the pilgrims paused to toss offerings of money, flowers, and even locks of thick black hair into a cordoned-off area surrounding the Ashoka Pillar.

Formalities taken care of, they headed into the Maya Devi temple. This temple is an unassuming red brick building, but it is also a much-revered landmark. Inside it, a piece of rock sits behind thick glass, and a simple plaque proclaims the marker stone as the exact birthplace of the Buddha. As Buddhists, Hindus, and tourists circled the excavated site, they talked in hushed tones. Then they wandered back out to the manicured grounds to contemplate the importance of this little-known religious destination.

Following some quiet time listening to the fluttering of prayer flags in the wind, I summoned a rickshaw and went off to explore the Lumbini Development Zone, a vast park behind the sacred birthplace. The unpaved network of roads took me on a kind of world tour of Buddhism, as I passed striking temples representing different nations. As well as discovering the different ways Buddhism is practiced around the world, I relished the chance to witness the varied Buddhist architecture, filling my camera's memory card with shots of an intricate, whitewashed Thai temple, a massive golden structure from Myanmar, and the immense offering built by Germany.

Silence prevailed over each temple, convent, and monastery I visited, despite the huge importance of the following day. And when I weighed the madness of Christmas Eve in the West against the tranquility of Lumbini, I knew that if I were forced to make a choice, I'd trade shopping bags for prayer flags without giving it a second thought.

### *Getting to Lumbini*

Go to the fact file in the previous essay.

### *Maya Devi temple*

The temple complex is a perfect place to spend an afternoon soaking up the silence and catching up on your reading. If you're planning to visit many of the temples, consider hiring a bicycle or a rickshaw and driver, since the complex is vast and it would take some time to get around on foot. Bicycles are available for rent in the village. If you opt for a rickshaw, prepare to haggle hard and then get your agreed-upon price in writing—drivers are not unused to dealing with unsuspecting tourists.

### *Staying the night*

Most people visit Lumbini on a day trip from Bhairahawa, but if you're keen to explore the pot-pourri of temples in depth, staying over is recommended. There are a few guesthouses in the village center offering rooms that are simple and cheap. Some higher-end options (ranging from $20 to $100) can be found just outside the Lumbini Development Zone.

## Pokhara

### *Joe Bindloss cultivates a love for Machhapuchhare*

It is hard to miss Machhapuchhare. This snow-capped pyramid of granite rises above Pokhara like a beacon. But even after a week in town, the first glimpse of it each morning can still take my breath away.

The mountain is almost too perfect, too triangular to have been formed by nature alone. In fact, what you see is an optical illusion. The mountain actually has two summits, rising side by side like a fishtail, the literal translation of *Machhapuchhare* in Nepali.

The gigantic mass of the mountain is also a trick of the eye. Although it seems to be the highest peak for miles around, 6,997-meter Machhapuchhare is one of the smaller peaks in the Annapurna range. Walk for a few days on the Annapurna Circuit trek, and the mountain will shrink to its real proportions, dwarfed by the far higher peaks of the four Annapurnas, particularly when viewed from the wild-strawberry-strewn meadow at Poon Hill.

Arriving from Kathmandu, back in the days when riding on the roofs of buses was de rigueur for any self-respecting traveler on the overland trail, I had the profound impression that the mountain was calling to me personally. As we wove in and out of ramshackle villages and whirled around hairpin bends, Machhapuchhare seemed to grow until it filled the entire horizon.

Most travelers head straight for the viewpoint at Sarangkot on the northern side of Phewa Lake, but I had been told that the best views of Machhapuchhare were actually from the south side. Renting a rowboat on the Pokhara lakeshore, I paddled my way through the morning mist to the Fewa Resort and struck up on foot through the scrub and maize fields. I later discovered there was a much easier way, but walking through small farms put me in contact with local farmers who smiled sagely or gestured in a good-natured way—probably trying to tell me that I was on the wrong path.

I finally achieved the ridge and found the worn track that I had been looking for, leading straight uphill to the gleaming white Nipponzan Peace Pagoda (World Peace Pagoda), built by Japanese Buddhists as a monument to world peace. From the steps to the stupa, the peaks of Machhapuchhare and the Annapurnas looked close enough to touch and were mirrored perfectly in the rippling waters of the lake below. I lost track of how much time I sat staring across at the peak, and how many pictures I took trying to achieve the perfect fishtail shot. Though I could hardly wait to climb it, my journey to the Nipponzan Peace Pagoda was an essential first step in cultivating a love and appreciation for the legendary peak.

### *Getting to Pokhara*

Yeti Airlines flies comfortable-sized planes from Kathmandu to Pokhara at higher altitudes that afford great mountain views—sit on the right side coming from Kathmandu. Buddha Air flies a smaller fleet at altitudes that barely get above the clouds. However, this "low and fast" method does cut the travel time nearly in half. As for facilities, don't expect much at the domestic airports. If you are going overland, Pokhara is a six-hour bus ride from Kathmandu's long-distance bus terminal. You can also take a faster minivan from Kalanki, several kilometers east of central Kathmandu on the ring road.

www.yetiairlines.com
www.buddhaair.com

### *Renting a boat*

Boatmen in the Lakeside District in central Pokhara ferry travelers across to the Fewa Resort for around 250 rupees. You can also hire a boat by the hour and paddle there yourself.

### *Taking it easy*

For views without the effort, take a local bus toward Butwal and get off at Kalimati, on the far side of the ridge from the World Peace Pagoda. Several obvious trails lead uphill from the road to the large white school building and on to the stupa.

### *Alternate route*

A third route to the stupa starts at the footbridge near the Phewa Dam in the Damside District of Pokhara. Just follow the path at the edge of the forest, then cut up on the main trail through the trees near the small brick temple. The peaceful forest scenery is quite gorgeous, but be sure to turn left and go straight uphill when you reach the ruined village just below the ridge—the other path peters out after a few hundred meters.

## *David Markus searches for mountain views in Pokhara*

Tourists returning from Mexico refer to "Montezuma's revenge." In India the same malady is known as "Delhi belly." Perhaps you will forgive the coinage "Kathmandoodoo," but whatever word you choose (*a rose by any other name* ...), it was 8 a.m. in the Kathmandu domestic airport, and I had it bad.

My traveling companion tried her darnedest to encourage me not to go to Pokhara, insisting that the chances of fulfilling my goal of seeing mountains in mid-April were nil. Setting off on the wrong foot, but with a secret stash of British-grade Kleenex and a packet of Imodium, I was ready to prove her wrong.

The descent on the flight into Pokhara, she had warned me, is the most stomach-turning ten minutes I would ever endure. But after winning my war in the stall of the men's room at the airport, this battle seemed a shoe-in. Moreover, I was met with a shimmering reward upon my debarkation—the very tip-top of Machhapuchhare, rising up, triumphant, above the clouds and a haze of brown pollution. As I hurried across the tarmac, I was overflowing with self-congratulation.

That afternoon I headed south along the endless line of Internet cafés, lassi stalls, and faux The North Face shops, eventually arriving at the boat rental stand just north of the former royal palace. For 400 rupees, a boatman would take me to and from the steps leading to the World Peace Pagoda, where the view, I had heard, was amazing. The alternate route is a two-hour trek through the southern part of the city, but the beauty of Phewa Lake is hard to resist for one who has just arrived in Pokhara, and being that I had planned to stay only a single night, there was no time to lose.

The ascent from the lakeshore to the pagoda, a calf-burning eleven hundred meters nearly straight up, took me through folds of shady jungle, past miniature temples, and alongside layers of rice paddies carved out of the verdurous mountainside. Several rest points along the way offered stunning views of the glistening waters of the lake stretching out far below as if in a fairyland. The walk can take between half an hour and an hour, depending on how much time you spend on the StairMaster back at home. But there is a reward at the top—a formidable stupa and a perfect Annapurna view.

But wait, where had the mountains gone? Vanished, it seems, behind midday clouds and the unrelenting atmospheric pollution. I was sadly discovering that I had a better chance of seeing snow-capped mountain peaks during a Stage 3 smog alert in Southern California's San Fernando Valley than on an April afternoon in the foothills of the highest mountain range on earth.

Fortunately, the serene setting of the Yeti Guest House, where I was staying, provided the perfect spot to drown my sorrows in locally manufactured "whiskey" alongside N.K., the sagacious owner, who has been supplying soul-searching Westerners with cheery accommodation and worldly wisdom for "only twenty-six years." Tucked away from the dusty main artery, with simple rooms, an island bar, marigolds along the patios, lychee trees, and a large weeping willow at the center of the courtyard, the Yeti made Pokhara an Eden to me.

N.K. likes to give the lowdown on every bar, café, and tour shop in town, including the raucous joint I was shortly to arrive at, a couple drinks and the most delicious plate of "chips" this side of London later: the Busy Bee. At this hotspot, passable margherita pizzas are the house specialty ("no *momo*"), and local acts play Western rock covers while hemp-clad Israeli girls swoon and throw back San Miguel into the wee hours of just before midnight—not bad by Nepali standards. The sudden jolt that I was not in Tel Aviv anymore came upon stumbling out onto the eerily quiet and almost pitch black-street, which, after a moment's disorientation, reminded me that I was also—bless Krishna—no longer in Kathmandu.

The following day I awoke at dawn determined to find the mountains for which I had come. The town of Sarangkot has the least obstructed views in the area and is an easy cab ride or motorbike trip from Pokhara. At 5 a.m., in any given Nepali town, one is liable to see more people on the streets than at the busiest hours of the day. The "morning walk" is an integral part of the daily routine in Nepal, a way to get one's exercise before it gets too hot. What I did not expect were the groups of joggers running up the switchback road to the lookout peak—nor the masses of British and Japanese tourists when I arrived, all of whom seemed as desperate as I was for a glimpse of the elusive mountains.

Through the haze, I could make out the perfect diamond outline of Machhapuchhare and several of its surrounding kin. Even more rewarding, however, was the experience of watching the sun rise from a valley horizon thousands of feet below. Mission mostly accomplished, I headed back to Pokhara and celebrated over a large breakfast amid the bamboo furniture, prayer flags, and laid-back elegance of Tea Time Bamboostan, a popular restaurant on the main drag. I couldn't wait to email my nay-saying travel companion back in Kathmandu, to brag about my achievement.

Yet despite my good fortune, the moral of the story remains: if you've come to look at the mountains, your best bet is to brave the crowds that flock to this area in the fall. Trekkers on the famous Annapurna Circuit will get close enough not to have the problems I encountered, but if you're not up for a hearty trek, and if a clear view is your priority, go in autumn—better safe than sorry.

*Getting to Pokhara*

Go to the fact file in the previous essay.

*Yeti Guest House*

The guesthouse is located in the central Lakeside District, also known as Pallo Patan. In this area David discovered a few other gems. For those travelers coming from India who find that Nepali tea doesn't quite satisfy their chai fix, there is a small chai shop on this northern end of town (on the lake side of the street just as the buildings start to become more sparse) that serves up a decent local equivalent. This part of town is also home to the Chhetri Sisters Guest House—the headquarters of a novel business, 3 Sisters Adventure, that offers female trekking guides for women travelers. For more information on this company, go to page 110.

yetiguesthouse@hotmail.com
www.3sistersadventure.com

*Up in the air*

Of her own experience viewing mountain peaks, Roberta Sotonoff adds: If trekking isn't your thing, or your stay in Nepal is limited and you don't have time to go to Pokhara, an Everest flight is a great way to see the mountains. Trust me, Everest's majesty is evident whether you are trudging to base camp or looking its legendary beauty in the eye from thirty thousand feet. While flights are offered year-round, the best views are typically seen from February to April and October to November. Numerous airlines offer this trip, with approximately twenty flights leaving Kathmandu each day, mostly in the early morning. You can make reservations online at Mountain Flights.

www.mountainflights.com

## *Joshua Esler pedals beyond the tourists of Pokhara*

My wheels hit dust and I rattle along, the handlebars shaking as I gather speed down the incline. The wind whips through my hair, and I lean forward, crouching down. The road turns uphill, and I stand up to pump the pedals again. I look to my left and see the edge of Phewa Lake a few meters down. To my right, the tip of Machhapuchhare, the sacred fish-tail peak, nudges up from behind the steep walls of the bank by the road.

I try the gears again, but they still won't change, and I lean far over the handlebars and pant up the hill. But when I reach the top, it all becomes worthwhile. The Annapurna range cuts the sky alongside majestic

Machhapuchhare, the winter snow stark against the deep blue sky.

The road takes me farther away from the town of Pokhara, and after an hour or so the dust turns to rock. I feel every rut and bump in the road, and I'm worried my bike will soon fall to pieces. Late in the afternoon, I stop for a well-earned break at a teahouse overlooking wide expanses of rice fields. The sinking sun is warm but pleasant, and the tea renews my strength.

As I sit and rest, I watch a few children walk along a path in the middle of the field, steering tires skillfully with pieces of wire. Monkeys chatter noisily and chase each other over the rice paddy fields and into the jungle. I try out my limited Nepali language skills with the elderly woman who brings me another cup of tea. There are a lot of blanks when she replies, but we manage a simple conversation. Her face is lined and drawn. She tells me she has to walk an hour from her village to the shop. She has lived here all her life.

Darkness envelops the mountains and lake behind me. I don't have a light, and although I should head back, I linger a bit longer. It's quiet here, and there are no tourists. A few houses in a distant village are lit, some with lightbulbs, others by candlelight. My stomach is growling, but it can wait. I gaze at the mountains and listen to the chirps of crickets in the fields. I let the peace of the moment sink in and breathe the fresh mountain air. Finally my stomach gets the better of me, and I crank the pedals, heading back toward town. The grinding of chain against metal teeth is the only sound in the still night.

### *Getting to Pokhara*

Go to page 51.

### *Renting a bike*

There are several small bike rental operations in Pokhara's Lakeside District, not far from the lake. You can also rent bikes in the Damside District, where the prices are lower. The cheapest rental places are those without an actual shop, stationed by the side of the road. Expect to pay from 50 rupees per day (cheaper, dodgier bikes) to 70-125 rupees per day (mountain bikes with gears). Prices are negotiable.

### *Riding out of town*

Head in a counterclockwise direction around Phewa Lake, following the road closest to the lake—it's difficult to get lost. Take the dirt road at the northeastern end of the lake after the bitumen road and the town of Pokhara ends. There a few teahouses and off-the-map villages along the dirt road, but they are few and far between, so take plenty of water and food. Allow for punctures and mechanical problems, especially with the older bikes, as it's a long walk home if you get stuck out there. The bumpy track also saps your energy quickly, so allow extra time for the ride back to Pokhara.

### *Lhasa Tibetan Restaurant*

The small teahouses along the bike route offer simple Nepalese meals consisting of a rather bland, watery lentil concoction—Joshua prefers the Indian version—and an equally bland curry and rice. Your stomach will probably suffer if you eat out on the road, so he suggests riding back to Pokhara, dropping off your bike, and stopping at the Lhasa Tibetan Restaurant in the Lakeside District. It's very close to the lake, a short walk from most Lakeside bike rentals places. The fresh naan bread served here is really something. The menu also offers a wide range of Western, Nepali, Indian, and of course Tibetan cuisine. Most meals are within the $1 U.S. range.

## Poon Hill

*Devon Wells gladly suffers for a view of Poon Hill*

It was 5 a.m., and my breath came out in foggy puffs in the cold of my room at the guesthouse. I answered a knock at my door to see Pradip, my guide, standing in his usual boots and pants, but now also wearing a thick jacket, gloves, and woolen hat.

"Shall we?" he asked, and he went down the stairs.

Once outside, we started on the path up to Poon Hill, which lies just outside of Ghorepani and is the highest point on the popular Ghorepani-Ghandruk trek in the Annapurna region. This was day 3 and I was in rough shape—never having been big on exercise—but I knew it had to be easier than day 2, which involved a vertical climb of more than three Empire State Buildings. Five hundred meters? A piece of cake.

The stars popped like rockets in the still-dark sky, and I realized I hadn't seen a night so clear in the fifteen years since I'd quit Boy Scouts. The smog really clutters them up in the city, even in a Kathmandu blackout.

Flashlights blazing through the pitch black, we staggered up the hill until reaching an entrance sign about ten minutes later. "Awesome! This is easier than I thought," I said.

Pradip just smiled at me.

Soon enough I knew why. Even though I'd left my backpack at the guesthouse, the walk was getting difficult. Really difficult. I had forgotten to bring water, but didn't think it would be a problem, since the climb was only an hour and there'd be hot tea at the top. I was wrong. With each step I took I could feel myself getting dehydrated—I needed water, stat!

We stopped at a resting place and I caught my breath. "How much farther?" I mumbled between gasps, making a mental note to get in shape when I returned home.

"About half an hour," said Pradip.

"I don't feel good."

"It's okay. Slowly, slowly."

*Damn Pradip,* I thought. *I'm about to keel over and he still looks like an Eddie Bauer model.* A few minutes later, I pulled myself together and stood up: *He's doing it, so I can do it.* We started off again.

The sun began cracking over the frosted leaves on the hillside as we approached the top, making it much easier to find my footing along the gravel path. At about one hour on the nose, we reached the viewing tower just as the sunrise was in full bloom.

The daybreak hike to Poon Hill is a major selling point of the trek I'd chosen. From the thirty-two-hundred-meter summit, the famous mountains of the Annapurna region look as close as a corner shop. Even the people I met who were doing seventeen-day hikes to Annapurna Base Camp, and had already spent two and a half weeks nestled in among Dhaulagiri and the other monoliths, stopped at Poon Hill, and for good reason. The view is outrageous, especially at dawn with a cup of *chai* in hand.

Pradip and I sat down on a log bench and soaked in the view. We weren't the only ones. About fifty trekkers and their guides snapped photos of each other smiling beneath their earmuffs as locals plied the exhausted ones with tea and Coca-Cola.

I had made it. The entire Annapurna region seemed to lie within spitting distance from the bench. Some of the biggest mountains and most stunningly gorgeous scenery ever were right there begging to be touched. And, as with every day on my trek, I sat thinking I was going to be sick, but grinning the entire time.

We stayed longer at the top of Poon Hill than I had expected to, even longer than the other trekkers, who were anxious to get down and have breakfast. I just didn't really want to go anywhere else, partly because I could hardly move, partly because I was dumbstruck by nature.

"This is totally worth how I feel right now," I said to Pradip.

He smiled. He knew it was true.

### *Getting to Poon Hill*

Poon Hill lies about an hour outside of Ghorepani in the Annapurna Conservation Area. Most people visit as part of an arranged trek booked through an agency in Kathmandu or Pokhara. Devon recommends Global Adventure Trekking. For solo travelers, the fastest way is to take a bus from Pokhara to Naya Pul and follow the path to Ghorepani with an overnight stay in Tikhedhunga. Guesthouses and camping facilities are widely available. A trekking permit is required and costs 2,000 rupees.

www.treksntours.com
www.globaladventuretrekking.com

### *Preparing for Poon Hill*

Wear a strong pair of hiking boots, despite what anyone says about sneakers being good enough. Bring water purification tablets, since bottled water is never around when you need it. And although you'll shed it by midday, a warm jacket is mighty nice in the early morning chill on Poon Hill.

## MANANG/ANNAPURNA

### *Sherry Ott takes a break in the village of Manang*

When I woke up in Manang, I didn't have to roll up my sleeping bag, repack my backpack, tend to my blisters, or put on my dingy hiking clothes. No, on this morning I rested. I lay in my bed listening to heavy hiking boots clomping back and forth on the wooden floor outside my door. I could feel the nervous energy that comes in the early mornings as trekkers get ready to depart yet again, while I dozed happily in and out of sleep.

Traditionally the village of Manang, at approximately 3,350 meters, is the resting spot for the Annapurna Circuit hikers. You don't necessarily stop here because you're tired. You stop here to let your body try to acclimate to the altitude. To slow down to adjust and fight off the ill effects of acute mountain sickness (AMS).

Manang was different from the other villages my dad and I had been through. It was designed to offer relief. There were little places showing movies at night, bakeries and cafés, laundry facilities, and tons of trekking supply shops. This was the last real "livable" village before we would reach Thorong La Pass and descend into Muktinath—four days away.

Even though Manang provided a rest day, as part of acclimatization people were strongly encouraged to do a day hike. Trekkers were advised to hike up a few thousand feet and then come back down to sleep again in Manang, thereby practicing the altitude acclimatization theory of hike high, sleep low. My dad and I weighed out our hiking options and decided to trek up to the local glacier, a 450-meter climb. The best part about this kind of day hike was that I didn't have to wear my backpack. I took just my camera and felt light as a feather.

The climb to the glacier was tough, since it was steeper than the Annapurna Circuit trail, but it rewarded us with spectacular views of ice blue lakes and golden valleys. Once back in Manang we celebrated our progress with one of the area's delicacies: cinnamon rolls. I have no idea how the cinnamon roll sensation started, but I was thankful that someone had brought fluffy bread filled with butter, sugar, and cinnamon to the Himalayas. From Manang, all along the trail, there would be places selling big cinnamon rolls, a completely guilt-free snack for energetic, long-term trekkers. At what other time in my life would I expend enough energy to justify eating a cinnamon roll every single day? I felt like I had landed on another planet—one where calories were nonexistent.

With our day of rest coming to an end, Manang had one more surprise for us. Word traveled around the village about a horse race, and the locals started to line up along the main drag, a long stretch of dirt road that served as a sort of rectangular town square. I could hear bells in the distance, and soon a group of locals trotted in on miniature horses. They paraded past and turned around at the end of the road. Then, without warning, the riders took off at full speed.

The crowd roared, the bells clanged, and Manang came alive. Back and forth they raced for about forty minutes—Nepal's version of 1950s drag racing down Main Street. There didn't seem to be any real winners or losers, and sometimes it got so wild that a rider lost control of his horse as it ran into the crowd of onlookers. Yet we continued to watch in amazement.

I kept an eye on the horses as much as I did on the spectators. No matter how absurd this event seemed to me, it was clearly well-loved in the village. Occasionally a herd of goats would parade into the road, stopping the whole race for a bit until the locals shooed them off to safety—after which the whole crowd, locals and tourists, would erupt in laughter.

By resting in Manang we also had a chance to socialize with other tourists. We bonded over beers, itineraries, blisters, fears, and the crazy horse race. This was the beginning of many trekking friendships for my dad and me. But my favorite thing about our stay here was that we had a chance to relax and take in village life and the trekking culture that we'd been passing by every day.

### *Exploring in and around Manang*

There is so much to see and do around Manang. The lower part of the village is very tourist-centric, but upper Manang is older and more authentic—the village as it existed before tourists started showing up on a regular basis. It's fun to wander around the upper village and see the "real" Manang.

Manang is an established stopping place on the trail, and you can do a number of short day hikes from here. There's a great little village nearby called Braga with a temple built into the mountainside. Another temple, Praken Gompa, sits up a cliff that rises above the village. A lama there conducts a short puja (blessing) on trekkers about to cross the Thorong La Pass, tying a piece of red ribbon around their necks for good luck—and for a price. (For more on this monk, go to page 148.) The climb up is difficult, but the views are stunning.

Ga Tso glacier lake is a short, easy hike and well worth it as the waters are an amazing turquoise color. You can view this lake from a distance and get great photos while on the trail to the glacier. The trail is a steep climb, but only takes about forty minutes to an hour. There are also many other lakes you can hike to in the area—with varying degrees of difficulty.

### *Resting up*

Sheri loved the little DVD movie houses in Manang—you pay a small amount to watch the movie being shown that night, and you even get popcorn! The movies are mainly about trekking or mountain climbing, but they're all good because they take your mind off your own personal trek and let you focus on something else for a while.

### *Mountain health*

Manang has a medical outpost (one of few along the trek) and offers free acute mountain sickness talks every afternoon at three. The outpost is manned by American volunteer doctors during the trekking months. It's a great place to get supplies or see a professional before going any higher onto the trail, where there are no medical facilities.

## Dolakha District

*Charis Boke meets friends old and new in Dolakha District*

We took the 8 a.m. bus from Dolakha Bazaar to Shingati, arriving thirty-five kilometers and three hours later. We hit the trail at noon after some quick *dal bhat tarkari* (lentils, rice, and vegetables) and a glass of hot buffalo milk with sugar. Buffalo milk is one of my favorite parts of going to rural areas in Nepal—it's really damn good.

The path was a diversity of green, with orchids, cacti, peepal trees, pines, hay fields, rice paddies, and vegetable gardens, not to mention grazing cows and goats. The Tamakoshi River flowed beside us most of the way, rustling down from the glacier melt of the Tibetan plateau toward the Indian Ocean. It's a beautiful river, a blue-white color because of the sediment carried in it. Its sound is soothing to walk near and to fall asleep by.

It took us about six hours to get to Jagat village that day on mostly flat trails, through scenery that felt familiar to me, at times reminding me of Vermont or California or Guatemala. But word to the wise: watch out for stinging nettles in this fecund and gloriously green place. On the way up the trail between Shingati and Jagat, we stopped at one point for a photo, and I accidentally stuck my hand in a nettle bush. Although my hand didn't fall off, it hurt! But it also gave us a good story to tell. When we got to Jagat and told the folks there about it, they had a good laugh.

Our destination had been Gongar, but by five thirty it was still two hours off, so we decided to sleep in Jagat, a little village that straddles the river. On the way to Jagat, we had to cross three "rope" bridges. These days, the rope bridges are by and large made of thick woven steel cables and welded steel slats. Not quite as romantic, but a heck of a lot safer ... until we reached the last one, in Jagat.

This final bridge was made of old wooden planks—or not. Some of the planks were missing, while others were broken. I thought to myself, donkeys walk over this bridge. Donkeys are far larger than I am. Through sheer willpower, I think I succeeded in convincing everyone watching (the whole of Jagat village) that I was not afraid of crossing the sixty-meter-long stretch. Thank God for theater classes.

Jagat is a favorite place for locals to stop for *chhang*, *raksi*, *tongba*, and *chai*—rice beer, rice liquor, hot fermented millet beer, and milk tea, respectively. I stuck with the tea, and I was glad I did. Judging by the state of some of the other travelers the next morning, the alcohols of Jagat are potent.

Our guesthouse had some unexpected amenities. A lightbulb had been fixed through a hole in the wall, providing two rooms with light. A raised bed with woven mat and Nepali mattress had a really thick cotton stuffed blanket and even a pillow. The simple plank walls of my room were covered in Nepali language newspapers—not for decoration, though. The paper stops the wind from coming through. As I fell asleep, the air smelled wonderful, like threshed wheat, whose sweetness I associate with haying, harvest, and square dances back in Vermont.

The next morning, as we walked toward Devlang village, we noticed that many people on the trail were headed off to work to build a new road. This road, which we were told would extend north from Shingati all the way to the Tibetan border, some forty kilometers away, was an exciting prospect here in the Dolakha District. During and since the civil war, many men of working age had found the need to move to Kathmandu—away from their families, homes, and fields—to find lucrative opportunities for income. This road work was about the only thing available for earning money in the area. So it was inspiring to watch everyone going to work, carrying heavy loads of wire and gravel on their backs. For many, it was a new day in Nepal.

Even in Devlang village, at more than five hundred meters above the Tamakoshi, you can hear the river flowing and fall asleep to the sound of rushing water. Devlang was our final destination, where there is a temple that I needed to visit for my work. The village is a steep hike up from Jagat—though probably only about three kilometers, it took us three hours to hike it. I was exhausted, with a cough from the intermittent fog. My local friends gave me hot water and tea, and invited me to join them on one of their millet terraces. We sat on a woven grass mat and chatted about Nepal, America, religion, and my research. As always, I was surprised at how open people are, how genuinely interested in my life. Although I really shouldn't have been after all the time I have spent in Nepal, I was, and it was a pleasant feeling.

There are no hotels in Devlang, but if you are intrepid enough to get up there, someone will likely give you a place to stay a night. My friends offered me a bed right next to the window looking over the steep river valley, and in the morning I could see Gauri Shankar Himal peeking up over the top of the hills. All up the valley other villages dotted the slopes, and I regretted that I had only a few days in the area. I sat in the chill at 6 a.m. with a cup of hot tea and watched the sun slide across the hills on the other side of the valley, accentuating the undulations of earth as it rose, and wondering as I so often did in that beautiful country, how I had gotten so lucky.

### *Getting to Dolakha Bazaar*

To reach the bazaar, the best option is to take the express bus from the Purano (Old) Bus Park in Kathmandu. It leaves at 6 a.m., and you'll want to be there at five thirty to secure a good seat. You can ask a travel service to purchase the tickets for you at least a day in advance for about 300 rupees. If you plan on exploring Dolakha District, it's a good idea to hire a guide to come with you.

### *Staying in Dolakha*

The bus dead-ends in Dolakha Bazaar. There are some good lodges, including Dolakha Lodge, near where the bus stops. There are also several in the older section of town (more picturesque with its traditional architecture), just near Dolakha Bhimeshwor (Bhimsen) temple. Walking straight down the hill from the bus stop will take you to the temple.

### *Getting to Shingati*

To get from Dolakha Bazaar to Shingati, you have two options: Walking will take you five hours or so and is fairly simple if a bit strenuous. To walk to Shingati, go back to the bus stop area and take the road that heads uphill—you can ask which road is for Shingati and anyone will gladly tell you. They will likely also tell you that you should take a bus!

To take the bus, you will need to go to the bus ticket counter a day before you want to leave and ask for the express bus to Shingati. On the way back, you will have to buy your bus ticket in advance again, which means spending the night in Shingati. There is no ticket counter in Shingati, so ask your guide, if you have one, to help figure the tickets out. If you're on your own, ask the manager at your hotel.

### *Where to stay*

In Shingati there are many hotels, some good and some not so good—you should ask to see the rooms before committing, and perhaps the toilet, too. The prices are fairly similar, from 150 to 250 rupees a night, with or without food. Jagat has about three guest-houses. Ask to see the rooms before checking in there, also.

### *Word of warning*

Many people get nauseated on these buses, due to the winding routes and road quality, as well as the heat and crowds. Vomiting is unfortunately common. If you get sick easily, you may want to consider taking medication to keep your nausea down.

### *Insider tips*

Charis recommends: Do try buffalo's milk and *tongba* at least once. Do bring earplugs if you're a light sleeper. Don't stick your hands in stinging nettles!

## Namche Bazaar

### *Jacqueline Sonderling hikes to a monastery outside Namche*

As I began to stir, the sunlight was just breaking across the sharp jagged cuts of the mountain. The morning was cold. I pulled myself out of my sleeping bag and went to the window. The lodge faced Kongde Ri, a peak that tops six thousand meters. The mountain, known as a difficult climb, rises southwest of the village of Namche Bazaar above the Bhote Kosi River. My view of it was impressive, toward the top of the peak that looks as if a bowl has been chiseled out of it.

A few days earlier, our group had gathered for our trek in Kathmandu, flying from the relatively low altitude of the Nepali capital (twelve hundred meters) to the lofty heights of Lukla (twenty-eight hundred meters), where life seems to center around the tiny landing strip. The flight is not for the faint of heart—hotshot pilots guide twenty-passenger prop planes among mountains that are often obscured by low-lying clouds. It's a little like flying through Arizona's Grand Canyon. You won't have a flight attendant offering peanuts, but one of the young pilots will offer you cotton balls for your ears.

From the landing strip in Lukla, it's a two-day trek to Namche Bazaar, the main Sherpa trading center in the area. Beginning easily enough, the trail is busy, even in late December, as it's the main road to Everest Base Camp. But the closer we got to Namche, the more difficult the climb—steep, with sharp switchbacks and rickety bridges high above the rushing river below. By the time we reached Namche, we were at 3,440 meters. We needed to stop to acclimatize. To help pass the three days this was going to take, our trekking guide, Kalu, planned a day trip for us to Thamo Monastery, about a two-hour hike away.

As we headed for Thamo, we began climbing again, passing the ochre-colored Namche Gompa, the monastery that rested on a tier above the town. A long line of *mani* stones (stone tablets carved with Buddhist prayers) stretched across the front of the *gompa*. The prayer flags fluttered in the gentle morning breeze, the prayer wheels at attention, waiting to be spun.

Our walk was on relatively flat ground, a relief after our steep climb to Namche. The trail was a traditional route to Tibet and used to be a busy thoroughfare for Tibetans heading to the weekly market in Namche. That day, though, we didn't pass anyone else—not a Nepalese villager, not a Tibetan merchant, not even a Western trekker. Our one constant companion was the mountain of Kongde Ri.

After a while, we came to an arch with brightly painted prayer wheels decorated with the "om" prayer set inside the concrete. Kalu told us it was built to honor Buddha and marked the entrance to Thamo. We spun the prayer wheels and continued up the road to the village, home to many of the Sherpas who have climbed Everest. It was small but quite clean, and the houses looked well tended.

We stopped for tea at a place called the Tashidele Restaurant. *Tashidele*, in its various spellings, is the Tibetan equivalent of *namaste*, which can mean "greetings to you and the spirit that dwells within." The view from the terrace outside the restaurant was a spectacular panorama of the Himalayas. We sipped our milk tea and relaxed in the warm sun for about half an hour before continuing another fifteen minutes or so through the village and up—always up!—to the monastery.

It turned out we'd come on a bad day. The lama was out of town, maybe in India, and so the monastery was closed. But after a few persuasive words from Kalu, the old nun who was serving as the gatekeeper allowed us to see some of the renovation work that was going on. Thamo Monastery is only about thirty years old, but it's already crumbling. Little by little, though, it's being restored, with help from Sir Edmund Hillary's Himalayan Trust, a charity established to aid the Sherpa people.

The nun led us into a small, dark room that had just enough light to let us see the magnificent paintings and murals that covered its walls. Various Buddhist stories were clear and vibrant. We all donated a bit of money, bid the nun farewell, and retraced our steps back down to the Tashidele Restaurant for lunch.

I ordered vegetable fried rice. From the terrace, I could see the restaurant's proprietress go into her vegetable garden, which was covered with a thick plastic tarp to shield it from the cold. She picked some fresh greens—the veggies for my meal! As I ate I asked Kalu the name of the mountains we were facing so I could write them down, and his reply sounded like a song, rolling off his tongue: Ama Dablam, Thamserku, Kusum Kanguru.

The return trip to Namche had some very memorable moments. Passing through the dappled sunlight and shadows from the pine trees felt like walking through a painting. A light green spruce tree was so bright it seemed to glow. The rushing water of the river far below provided a playful score to the afternoon. All too soon, we reached the *gompa* above Namche. I reached out and spun the prayer wheels as I passed and whispered, "*Om mani padme hum*"—my private thank-you for such a beautiful day.

### *Getting to Namche*

Following the flight from Kathmandu to Lukla, the trek from Lukla to Namche can be done in one long, difficult day; two days (one short and easy, one difficult); or even three days (one easy, one moderate, and one difficult). Because this trail is so well-traveled, there's no shortage of goods available along the way, including toilet paper, Cadbury chocolate, and bottled water, which gets more expensive as you climb to higher elevations—although it's still generally less than $1 for a liter.

### *The Himalayan Trust*

www.himalayantrust.co.uk

# Secret Gardens

*Where to hide away from the tourist crowds*

There are countries so hectic and overrun with tourists that quiet corners seem nearly impossible to find. But outside Kathmandu, all of Nepal is essentially a "secret garden"—a place where travelers can rest assured that they will find peace. Still, the capital city bustles, and the trekking routes can get relatively crowded during the high season, so we have rounded up this eclectic collection of suggestions for those times when you need to escape.

Some people stumble across their sanctuaries, as Devon Wells did when he wandered away from the Thamel tourist district into the Garden of Dreams. Others take a more determined approach: Caroline Martin keeps a list of Kathmandu restaurants and hotel gardens for her downtime needs, while Ellen Shapiro heads straight for the same hotel rooftop whenever she wants to rise above the overstimulating streets of Thamel.

Those looking to sneak out of Kathmandu for a short break don't have to go very far. From Boudha, home of Nepal's largest stupa, to Bhaktapur, where car traffic is not allowed, the outskirts of the city offer plenty of R&R. Much farther out, an impenetrable solitude beckons, as Anju Gautam discovers when she and her friends trek to the "gate to heaven" in the western part of the country. Equally enticing is the recommendation from Lonely Planet's Nepal guru, Joe Bindloss, who lets us in on his favorite secret hideaway: a rustic inn in Bandipur.

Of course, you can go to the most silent, untraveled place on earth and still not find peace if it's not quiet in your head. For this we offer essays by David Lee and Shannon O'Donnell, both of whom participate in meditation retreats in Pokhara, seeking a mind-set that matches the serenity of the surrounding mountain landscape.

*Sunset at Chitwan National Park*

## KATHMANDU

### *Ellen Shapiro finds a Thamel oasis in Kathmandu*

I am a regular at the Hotel Utse. In fact, it's become my home when I'm in Kathmandu. It's not the fanciest hotel—don't expect the Yak & Yeti. Nor is it the least expensive, though it's very reasonable. What it is: warm and welcoming.

I'm certain that I would never have found or stayed here many years ago had a friend not convinced me to book a room. It would be more convenient, he argued, than the hotel I was planning to stay at in Chhetrapati, the neighborhood just south of the Thamel District. So I checked in, and day after day I watched people arrive for relaxing meals in the hotel restaurant next door. Morning, midday, and evening, there were always diners enjoying the authentic Tibetan cuisine. Trekking groups came for posttrek celebrations, and locals chose the restaurant for evenings out.

My own first meal there was a safe one—breakfast. I had thick porridge and a spectacular pot of milk *chai*. The flavors were incredible. This wasn't just black tea with milk thrown in. This was the real deal, smoky black tea with a hint of green cardamom and other spices. My appetite was whetted, and other meals soon followed.

I savored buff and veggie *momos* with spicy, rough-chopped chili sauce and Tibetan bread. I ate *tuk* (Tibetan flat noodle soup) and *sha bale* (Tibetan fried meat pie). I was eager to share my "discovery," and I invited old friends and new to join me. At most every meal, the quiet yet friendly proprietors, who were Tibetan refugees, would stand at the bar, a framed photo of the Dalai Lama overhead, and give a brief smile or nod in welcome.

The hotel too was full of lovely surprises. When I went up to the cement roof one day to air out my sleeping bag, I found an oasis. Nowhere within a stone's throw of Thamel could one ever claim to find total silence on a rooftop, but here was peace and tranquility. Small coniferous trees were arranged in pots, and Tibetan prayer flags flapped in the wind. I threw my sleeping bag over one of the brightly painted cement benches and ran downstairs to grab my journal, a book, and a pot of milk *chai*. I later found a couple of empty beer bottles from previous guests. Clearly, I was not the only one to seek refuge on the Utse rooftop.

Whether starting my day quietly, watching and listening as the city comes to life, or sipping cups of smoky *chai*, waiting for the moon to rise, the roof and restaurant of the Hotel Utse draw me back again and again. They are my haven, and my first and last stops on any trip I make to Kathmandu.

*Hotel Utse*

The hotel and restaurant are located on Jyatha Road in Kathmandu's Thamel District. The hotel offers airport pickup if you are a guest. If you do stay here, tell the owners that Ellen sent you and give them her regards!

www.utsehotel.com

## *Devon Wells dreams up an escape in Kathmandu*

I needed a timeout. After a month of spotting rhinos in the jungle, hiking in the Himalayas, and riding around in rickshaws, Kathmandu was far too hectic for my weary bones. On every corner I was surrounded by music, people, motorcycles, and beggars. All of it was incredible, but completely overwhelming. There was no place for me to just stop and think in and around the alleys of the Thamel tourist district.

So, I started walking. I didn't know where I was headed, but luckily I didn't have to go far before I found what I was looking for: Swapna Bagaicha, or Garden of Dreams, just down Tridevi Marg about five minutes outside of Thamel.

The story goes that Field Marshal Kaiser Shamsher Jung Bahadur Rana built the garden in the 1920s with a heavy pot won in a game of cowrie shells. It later fell into disrepair until the Austrian government kicked in a million dollars for restoration. The garden reopened in 2006 and looked like just the kind of place I needed—full of trees, grass, benches, and no people, save the ticket agent!

The shift from Kathmandu's streets stunned me. No more battered pavement or overeager sadhus. Instead I found cobblestones and serene fountains. I instantly busted out my camera and shot everything in sight, from the central oasis filled with carp to the flowers hugging statues of elephants. Then, with the obligatory photo shoot complete, I began to unwind.

The garden seemed small at first, until I discovered little pathways, staircases, and underpasses all leading to hidden streams and secret hideaways within the greenery. It's no wonder this was a popular spot for lovers before the renovation took place. In each of the six pavilions, named for the six Nepali seasons, there are antique sculptures of Western design that have been retooled to keep with local culture. For instance, stick a lotus flower and some coins on a Greek goddess and she becomes the Hindu goddess Laxmi. Inside one building I found a photo gallery. Along with pictures that detailed the restoration process, there were images that made me wish I was visiting at night, with everything lit up by hundreds of lanterns.

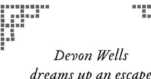

Feeling more relaxed, I ambled around in bliss for half an hour before I noticed the café. The wrought-iron and marble tables flanked the central carp pond. I knew immediately that this place demanded a sit-down. I checked the chalkboard menu advertising a 1,000-rupee set meal. It was a bit out of my budget. If nothing else, I decided, this would prove the perfect place for a leisurely drink.

The waiter grinned and brought me a Carlsberg beer. I eased back, waiting for the foam to settle, and watched a squirrel scamper across the walkway. Just minutes from the constant buzz of Kathmandu, I sat, craned my neck to the sky, and let the silence roll in. I spent the afternoon flipping through a book and topping up my glass.

A few hours later, when I headed back to my guesthouse, I was once again dodging motorbikes and flute salesmen, but now I had a mile-wide grin on my face. Only a small part of that was due to the beer!

### *Swapna Bagaicha*

The Garden of Dreams is located at Kaiser Mahal at the corner of Tridevi Marg and Kantipath, opposite the Fire and Ice Pizzeria. Admission is 160 rupees for foreigners and 80 rupees for locals. The garden hosts cultural events; check local listings.

www.klib.gov.np
www.fireandicepizzeria.com

## *Caroline Martin seeks peace in Kathmandu*

Written by Kim Stanley Robinson, *Escape from Kathmandu* is a novel that I come across often, but I've never read it. Instead, it's something I yearn to do frequently while living and working in Kathmandu.

The city has its share of magic, but also more than its share of air and noise pollution. The Mountain 'Du is a perfect example of how increased "prosperity" can actually make a place less livable. Like thousands of travelers, I arrived in the Gateway to the Himalayas expecting a refreshing climate and mountain views. But what I found was a growing number of personal vehicles on the road, paired with no emissions laws and aggressive "horning" habits. The pagoda-filled valley has turned into a smoggy cauldron.

Then there are the garbage strikes. Thanks to Nepal's Maoist revolution, greater political awareness and labor organization mean more frequent sanitation *bandhs*. Within a day of an announced work stoppage, mini-Mount Trashmores accrue on every other corner. Negotiating the obstacle course of a Kathmandu street becomes great practice for rural trekking. In the monsoon's daily rains, the sodden heaps quickly fester into reeking flytraps.

Dreaming of the legendary "Valley of Shangri-la"—thought to be a hidden paradise amongst arid, craggy mountains—I find respite in urban oases. Behind its traditional brick-masonry walls, Kathmandu conceals gracious courtyards where soothing fountains flow, sunlit flowers buzz with butterflies, and iced drinks are served in the shade.

Among these secluded gems are Babar Mahal Revisited (a collection of boutiques and cafés in renovated Rana palace outbuildings in southeast Kathmandu); Imago Dei Café and Gallery (with excellent spinach-artichoke dip, real ricotta cheesecake, and the best service in town; see page 36 for more about this café); Mike's Breakfast (founded by a former Peace Corps worker in the 1970s, in the Naxal District); and the gardens of the Hotel Vajra (www.hotelvajra.com). These places are evidence that the idylls of Shangri-la Valley survive beyond mountain mythology, and while I enjoy them all, there are yet a few others that serve as my favorite ways and means of escape:

**Shangri-La Hotel's Shambala Garden**
www.hotelshangrila.com/kathmandu

I've been accused of having moved to Lazimpat, Kathmandu's diplomatic district, strictly for the sake of proximity to the Shambala Garden. Along with the Yak & Yeti, Shangri-La is the old, established face of genteel, high-end Kathmandu tourism. The garden, designed by the late artist and Nepalophile Desmond Doig, features illy coffee (imported from Italy) and seemingly endless sunny days. Spotless white parasol tables dot the green grass, though during hotter months I take refuge from both sun and mosquitoes in the glassed-in terrace. On a recent visit, I befriended a tour group of Paraguayans lounging on the lawn, swapping trekking tales and their traditional yerba mate drink served in calabash gourds. Shangri-La's swimming pool and tennis court are available to outsiders on weekends, and the restaurant serves decent Indian, Nepali, and Continental food.

**Dwarika's Hotel**
www.dwarikas.com

I discovered Dwarika's heritage hotel following an exhaustingly hot morning at the cremation ghats of the Hindu temple Pashupatinath. Stepping off noisy Battisputali (the road's name means "32 butterflies") to slip behind the dark wooden doors laden with detailed carving, I entered an elegant city within a city. Dwarika Das Shrestha devoted his life to collecting the intricate hand-carved wooden pieces discarded by Kathmandu's modern property developers, not knowing what he'd ever do with them, but sensing their innate value. His hobby eventually became this hotel, which doubles as a museum for Newari art heritage. The complex manages to be enormous and intimate simultaneously, and each handcrafted room is individually appointed.

Dwarika's location is rather out of the way, unless you are en route to either Pashupatinath or the airport, but it is well worth the taxi ride. It offers no less than three restaurants—the main terrace with its adjoining (and icily air-conditioned) library, Fusion Bar (serving a mean, lychee-flavor frozen margarita), and Krishnarpan, where traditional maharaja meals (ranging from six to twenty-two courses) can be ordered. My favorite treat at Dwarika's is the lemon cheesecake and iced tea, laced with essences of cinnamon, lemon, and mint.

**Kantipur Temple House**
www.kantipurtemplehouse.com

Though this place is less illustrious than Dwarika's, its location, in the Thamel tourist district, makes it a more convenient stop during a casual walk. A stroll from Thamel's main drag, down labyrinthine streets, will take you away from beggars and hawkers, toward the Chusya Bahal Buddhist temple and refuge in the Temple House courtyard. I alternate between the cool interior shade and the soothing sun of the garden, depending on the seasons and time of day. KTH prides itself on being an eco-hotel—it uses no disposable plastics and is furnished entirely with locally crafted products such as handmade paper and woven baskets. It is perfect walking distance from the busy Kantipath main road and the historic locations of Durbar Square, Hanuman Dhoka, Swayambhunath temple, and Asan Tole's ancient open-air markets.

**Nirvana Garden Hotel**

This hotel is another pleasant surprise within Thamel, all the more so for its proximity to the hustle and high-decibel rock music that pervades the area from twilight into the wee hours. The lush garden's waterfall and noisy frog pond never fail to soothe my traffic-abused ears. It's located around the corner and down a back street from the world-famous Kathmandu Guest House.

**New Tushita Restaurant**

*Tushita* translates into "place of contentment," and this particular contentment can be found round the corner from my flat, on Lazimpat Road just north of the French Embassy. The coffee is good, and although the food is mediocre, the traditional Brahmasthanam architecture offers space, with plenty of cool corners to hide in. Better yet, the Wi-Fi is free. The real heart of Tushita is Dai, a senior Newari gentleman unfailingly attired in flawless topi *daura-suruwal*, who performs Buddhist *pujas* daily in the lower courtyard. Tushita also has an unadvertised guesthouse with a loyal following in the garden behind the restaurant.

# BOUDHA

## *David Lee trades Thamel for leisurely Boudha*

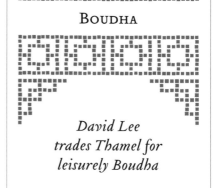

After a few nights at the historic Kathmandu Guest House in Kathmandu's Thamel District, I was ready to escape the live cover bands and honking taxis for some peace and quiet. I put my main backpack in storage and grabbed a taxi east toward Boudhanath Stupa. Since rioting Tibetans and the iron fist of the Chinese government meant I would have to skip Tibet on my trip through Asia, I wanted to soak up as much Tibetan culture as possible while in Nepal. Nowhere was it more vibrant than around the stupa, the fifth World Heritage Site I visited in the Kathmandu Valley.

Upon catching my first glimpse of the all-seeing Buddha eyes atop the massive monument, I knew that I was going to spend my last few nights in Nepal beneath their gaze. I checked in to the P.R.K. Guest House, run by Sakya Tharig Gonpa, an adjacent monastery. My room overlooked their well-manicured garden and a large school courtyard. For $6—half the price of my Kathmandu lodgings—I had a fantastic view, better decor, and a sparkling clean bathroom. I was a very happy camper.

In Boudha, monastery bells begin ringing each morning at five thirty. Curiosity trumped my normal penchant for sleep. I rolled out of bed, threw on some warm clothes, and stepped outside into the predawn darkness. Residents were walking down the various alleys toward the stupa, counting their mantras on *malas* (prayer beads) hanging from their hands. I quietly joined the procession and walked around the stupa several times to generate good karma. As most tourists tend to spend only an hour or two (usually later in the day) at Boudhanath, I felt fortunate. Aside from myself, there were only a few other Westerners; the remainder of the crowd was predominantly Tibetan, distinguished by the traditional dress worn by the women.

Boudhanath is the largest stupa in Nepal, and among the most important Buddhist Tibetan pilgrimage sites outside of Tibet. Life literally revolves around it. From sunrise to sunset, and well beyond into the night, Nepalese, Tibetans, and tourists circumambulate the stupa in a clockwise direction, spinning the 108 prayer wheels ensconced in the outer walls, repeating mantras, and catching up with their neighbors. With so many people praying and moving in the same direction together, there is a palpable sense of spiritual energy being generated.

On my second early morning, I stepped into the courtyard of the monastery that runs my guesthouse, where one of the monks indicated I could enter the *gompa* (meditation hall). The morning *puja* (worship) was in session, and I quietly took a seat in a back corner so I could listen to the prayers. Every ten minutes, cymbals crashed, small kids blew on horns made of giant white shells bigger than their heads, and two massive drums were banged. When the instruments were played, I closed my eyes, and it felt as though I was in a scene from the movie *Kundun*, or in an old monastery on the Tibetan Plateau. It was exactly as I imagined Tibet to be.

Moving out of Kathmandu's brash and hectic tourist district to the serene, traffic-free area around the stupa was one of the best decisions I made on my trip. I was able to photograph daily life around the stupa in all manners of light, from every angle. I captured everything from the warm, golden glow of butter lamps to a marching band accompanying a wedding party around the stupa. And while I may have been woken up every morning before dawn by the reverberating drums and Tibetan chants from the monks next door, I much preferred that over being kept awake every night by the harsh sounds of Thamel's bands playing the same rock-and-roll classics I'd heard all my life.

### *Getting to Boudha*

Go to page 21.

### *The benefits of Boudha*

While David had to make the trip between Boudha and the Thamel District a few times to pick up his main backpack, organize his Indian visa, and bargain for a new camera, he felt the extra cab fares were well worth the cost of being able to spend the majority of his time among Boudha's Tibetan community.

### *Where to stay*

The P.R.K. Guest House is located a short walk down one of the alleys radiating from the stupa. Once you arrive in Boudha, you can ask any local for directions to the guesthouse or the adjacent Sakya Tharig Gonpa monastery.

www.sakyatharig.org.np

### *Dining with views*

The stupa is surrounded by monasteries, restaurants, Tibetan souvenir shops, and *thangka* schools. For dining, David recommends the tourist restaurants that occupy rooftops, as they enjoy fantastic views of the stupa and surrounding area.

## Bhaktapur

## *Janelle K. Eagle prefers the alternative of Bhaktapur*

"*Chai khane ho*?" asked the young man working at the Pagoda Guest House in Bhaktapur.

In response, I accepted a cup of tea from him, as I did each morning, looking out from the rooftop balcony. At this restaurant atop my home away from home, I filled my belly with fresh eggs and my eyes with the sights I'd dreamed of finding in Nepal. The snow-capped Himalayas hiding behind clouds, smaller mountains covered in green grass hugging the surrounding fiefdom, and a pagoda being visited by gracious locals.

When I arrived in Bhaktapur, just twenty kilometers away from Kathmandu, I felt an immediate connection. I had come there to film a documentary about thirteen adorable girls living in the Unatti (Progress) House. Immediately, they called me *sister*. Along with the adults we met, they took pride in their culture and loved to ask questions and practice their English. These children of poverty took my breath away as they bounced down five flights of stairs each morning to go to school, paid for by the generosity of the Unatti Foundation and its donors.

While I was in Kathmandu, it had often felt like I had a neon sign over my head that said, "Ask me to buy something." In Bhaktapur everyone was more interested in learning, sharing, and living in harmony. I felt like family, and it was my honor to wake every morning, head to the orphanage, and walk the girls to school. When they came back in the afternoon, I was there to greet them and help with homework. What a pleasure to directly witness a transformation in their knowledge, language skills, and confidence.

While the girls were in school, I had my morning *chai* and fresh eggs and then went to the cyber café in the adjoining square. It looks out directly at the five-tiered Nyatapola temple. Throughout the day, the residents of Bhaktapur ebb and flow around this structure, lighting hundreds of oil lamps and incense sticks for offerings. Both individually and as a community, they gather on the steps, chant, and pray. I often checked my email, sipped tea, and people-watched here for hours.

When I finally left the café to return the orphanage, I always appreciated how walkable Bhaktapur is. The small town is closed to outside traffic, and this means that the only methods of transportation are by foot and motorbike, although occasionally I would see a taxi or tractor driving through. Considering that most roads in Nepal are shared by cars, buses, motorbikes, dogs, cows, and pedestrians, the lack of automobiles in Bhaktapur is a rare treat—as is the resulting lighter pollution. As we navigated the cobblestone streets, we were surrounded instead by townspeople, the incense smoke of their morning offerings, and the distinctive architecture of Bhaktapur, with its breathtaking stone and woodcarving, much of which is done in the open as you walk by the small storefronts.

I liked to reflect on the tall, thin structure of the buildings as I walked. Layer upon layer, they seemed to reach up into the sky, just like the mountains that surround this cultural treasure. The same buildings have been in the area for centuries, and even today, if a person buys property or wants to build onto a house, they have to do so in the ancient style. This renders many places unfriendly toward the physically disabled, but the ardent connection to tradition feels meaningful and makes everything stunning to look at.

While I am drawn to Bhaktapur's pace and architecture, what I like most about the town are the people who live there. More than half are ethnic Newar and come from centuries-old family lines. They speak a different language and embrace a culture that encourages you to slow down and eat a meal with your neighbor. In fact, they *love* feeding each other—and visitors. They seem to show their love by forcing others to eat yet another buffalo *momo* or sip another small glass of *raksi*.

In theory there isn't much to do in Bhaktapur, but it's near everywhere you want to be, including Nagarkot for great sunrise views. The town is the same distance from the airport as downtown Kathmandu and offers most of the goods you'd want or need to buy. The difference is, in Bhaktapur you can relax. I never expected to feel as comfortable or welcome as I did there. I now know from the many other travelers I met on the road that this is not a unique experience, which is just one of the many reasons you should take a detour through this enchanting town.

### *Getting to Bhaktapur*

Go to page 23.

### *Unatti Foundation*

As Janelle walked through town, many young children asked for money or offered to give a tour for a couple rupees. It was hard to say no to them, but she was comforted knowing that when she arrived at the orphanage, she was making a more long-term difference than if she simply handed over some coins.

www.unattifoundation.org

### *Pagoda Guest House*

Rather than staying in the touristy Thamel or Lazimpat neighborhoods in Kathmandu, Janelle suggests getting a room in a guesthouse in Bhaktapur. Her stay at the Pagoda Guest House cost a whopping $9 a night. She says that the rooftop café has the most gorgeous view of the pagoda and surrounding hills and mountains. The staff is amazing and really did become her second family during her few-week stay— a shout-out to Sharmila and Robindra!

www.pagodaguesthouse.com.np

### *Palace Restaurant*

On her way to the orphanage, Janelle passed through Durbar Square and by the Palace Restaurant, which serves incredible *dal* meals along with more Westerner-friendly cuisine like grilled cheese and chow mein. The only kind of cheese available comes from yaks, however, so she always skipped the sharp and odiferous pizza in favor of a traditional *dal bhat, takari,* and *achar* (lentils, rice, veggie, and pickle) platter. The locals eat this meal three times a day, every day, using their right hands to scoop the mixture together, and she says it's an art—really!

http://palacerestaurantbkt.com

## Swargadwari

### *Anju Gautam Yogi rings in the new year at Swargadwari temple*

I wanted to do something special to celebrate the Nepali New Year, so I gathered a group of fourteen friends and we decided to trek to the Swargadwari temple in the western part of Nepal.

Like so many Hindu temples, Swargadwari is shrouded in myth. According to the epic *Mahabharata*, Pandyas (five royal brothers) reached heaven from the hill where the temple is now located—hence its name, which means "gate to heaven." It is believed that a sage named Swami Hansananda later performed many miracles here. After he was buried, the temple became an important pilgrimage site. Some say he built the present temple, others that it was built in his honor.

To reach the temple really did feel like a trek to heaven. The hill is a steep and challenging culmination of the journey, which began for us as we walked east along the banks of the river near the city of Ghorahi in the province of Dang. The heat was scorching that day, and I remember the great relief when we stopped to play in the water. But we wanted to reach the temple before dark, so we were soon on our way again.

Although many people, both locals and foreigners, visit the temple each year, the area still lacks good hotels, restaurants, and modern amenities. However, there are a few *dharamshalas*— a type of rest house provided for pilgrims and other travelers along pilgrimage routes. And we were touched when several locals appeared on our path and offered us some simple food. We drank lots of cold water, curd, and buttermilk.

Sometimes we had to ascend the steep hills, while other times we had to descend perilous, small paths. But the scenery was varied and beautiful, with radiant streams and green, lush meadows. Finally, after about six hours, we reached the hill where Swargadwari is located. It was covered with trees full of red and blue flowers, at the center of which was a temple dedicated to Lord Shiva.

After we climbed the final steps to reach the top, we were exhausted, but we weren't too tired to be amazed by the simple beauty of the temple. At a time when so much of Nepal was suffering from the ills of the civil war, this place was completely untouched by it. We all felt as though we had truly escaped the violence and problems of our country and our own hearts.

We were further rewarded by the temple's *dharamshala*, since travelers who reach the top of the hill and pass through the gate to the temple are offered food and a place to stay. After our long day of trekking, the meal of rice and *gundruk* (similar to sauerkraut) was the most delicious we had ever tasted.

That night, we lay on the wooden floor of the *dharamshala* and fell asleep to the melody of religious hymns. We were woken in the morning by the chirping of birds. As we got up and wandered out to enjoy our surroundings, we decided that this was the very best way to ring in a new year. Swargadwari truly was a gate to heaven, for we had all found peace, even if it was just for a little while.

### *Getting to Swargadwari*

The temple is located in the Pyuthan District, about twenty-five kilometers south of the district headquarters of Khalanga Bazar. Travelers can reach Khalanga Bazar by taking a comfortable microbus (about ten hours from Kathmandu). Forty-five-minute flights can be booked to this area, but there is not a regular flight schedule for the region. The temple can also be reached from the neighboring Dang District—this is the daylong trekking route Anju took. Most travel agents in Kathmandu can arrange either option for you.

### *Where to stay*

The trail to Swargadwari has a few *dharamshalas*. At these places there is no charge for food and lodging, and visitors generally stay no more than one night. Keep in mind that you will be expected to participate in group songs and dance while there. All food is provided by temple income, so donations are always appreciated.

## Bandipur

*Joe Bindloss discreetly reveals the secrets of Bandipur*

Every traveler has his own list of secret hideaways. Those places that you discover off the beaten track and claim as your own. Mentioning these places to others is subject to a rigorous selection process. Are the people you are telling the right kind of people? Will they enjoy your secret hideaway for what it is and not try to change it? Can they keep the secret?

I'll assume that you are the right kind of person and reveal my own secret hideaway in Nepal. Bandipur is set high on a ridge above the Prithvi Highway between Kathmandu and

Pokhara. Unlike many villages in Nepal, Bandipur has opened to tourism on its own terms. There are no travel agencies or souvenir shops; instead, just a few guesthouses overseen by the Bandipur Social Development Committee. Getting here involves leaping off a Pokhara-bound bus at Dumre and a bumpy jeep ride uphill on a pitted dirt road.

As the jeep rumbles into the main street in Bandipur, it's hard to believe somewhere this perfect could still exist in rapidly changing Nepal. Most of the buildings are nineteenth-century Newari mansions, with wildly overhanging eaves, precarious balconies, and ornately carved wooden doors and windows. A handful of these old village houses have been converted into guesthouses, most notably The Old Inn, run by Himalayan Encounters, one of the oldest and most professional rafting and trekking companies in Nepal.

Himalayan Encounters finds most of its clients by word of mouth, ensuring that the inn is not overrun with tourists. Inside, narrow wooden stairways lead to comfortable but endearingly rustic rooms with warped floorboards and leaning wooden balconies, facing a magnificent vista of Himalayan peaks. Staying here is like visiting a stately home. Rooms are full of Nepali heirlooms, and everyone eats together in the evenings at huge wooden tables, either inside or out on the rear terrace, with the moonlight glinting off the snow on the Annapurnas.

Refreshingly, the money from tourism is reinvested in the local area, helping to preserve the fabulous Newari buildings on the main street and paying the fees of local guides who lead guests on treks in the hills around Bandipur. The town is full of wooden temples, and paths wind through the surrounding mustard fields and orchards to Gurung tribal villages, eroded limestone caves, and exposed hilltops with giddying views over the Marsyangdi Valley and Himalayas. On clear days, you can trace the path of the river most of the way to Mustang.

Added to this are the residents of Bandipur, who are astoundingly polite—maybe a consequence of the education provided by the Notre Dame School, founded by Catholic nuns in the 1980s. Begging and touting is unheard of here. Most villagers are happy to stop and talk to visitors, but there is no ulterior motive. People just want to practice English and show off their understandable civic pride. Treat Bandipur with that same respect, and it could stay like this for decades.

### *Getting to Bandipur*

Bandipur is a seven-kilometer walk or jeep ride uphill from Dumre, on the Prithvi Highway. Any bus between Kathmandu and Pokhara can drop you at Dumre, where you can charter a jeep or wait for other passengers and split the fee. The journey to Dumre takes about two and a half hours from Pokhara and four and a half hours from Kathmandu.

### The Old Inn

Bookings for the inn are made through Himalayan Encounters. Accommodation starts at $20 per person per night, including meals and guided walks. A description of the inn can be found on the Himalayan Encounters website in the "dossier" section.

www.himalayanencounters.com

### Around Bandipur

Destinations for walks from Bandipur include the easy, half-hour, uphill stroll to the Thani Mai temple and the hike downhill to the caves of Siddha Gufa and Patale Dwar—both crammed with stalactites and stalagmites. For more information on what to do in Bandipur, see the official village website.

www.bandipure.com

## Pokhara

## *Shannon O'Donnell survives solitary confinement in Pokhara*

Now that I'm on other side of the ten-day meditation course at the Pokhara Vipassana Center, I can only wonder what prompted me to take this intense spiritual boot camp of sorts. I'd never really meditated before. Maybe it was because I didn't know what I was getting myself into—a realization that only began to dawn as I signed a contract agreeing to stay for the whole course and learned of the many restrictions, including "Noble Silence" and no writing. I cracked on that last one on day 4, which is how I am able to share this account of my time in solitary confinement.

### Day 1: Oh, the Endless Pain

The sole task for the day is to focus on my breath—the air naturally coming in and out of my nostrils. For ten hours and forty-five minutes I do my best to focus as much of my attention as possible on my nose, despite the traffic of thoughts racing through my mind. The day's main discovery: my left nostril is working overtime, doing most of the work. Another discovery: Nepali songs are annoyingly catchy. Although I am determined to keep all trekking songs out of my head, "Chati Ma Mero" echoes through my mind for hours. As for sitting on a cushion on the floor for eleven hours—not pleasant!

### Day 2: Goodbye, Cousin of Mine

The bulk of the course is taught via a video by the spiritual leader S. N. Goenka. Teacher, who leads our class, is essentially just an assistant. Goenka has a *really* slow voice, making it hard to stay awake and watch his hour-and-a-half discourse in the evenings.

And now, as a cruel joke, we have to listen to tapes of his singing during morning meditation. Worse yet, Goenka is competing with Madonna's "Like a Prayer"—the new song stuck in my head. My cousin Helen can't take it and leaves; I'm left on my own, focusing once again on my nasal cavity ... oh, and that left nostril of mine is *still* doing all the work.

**Day 3: It Never Ends**

Who knew there could be so many interminably long hours in a day when you're doing nothing but observing the air as it passes in and out of your nostrils? Today's new task is to focus on the sensations in the nose area ... I am *seriously* contemplating leaving. The thing is, I'm trying to get over my self-defeating belief that I'm a quitter. Today's winning song: the Red Lobster version of "Happy Birthday" because the universe really is just that funny. As for the upside of the day? No more falling asleep during meditation!

**Day 4: Totally Cracked**

Like a cosmic joke, at 4:30 a.m. "Don't Stop Believin'" blares into my head to accompany all of my weighty thoughts and our entry into actual Vipassana techniques—apparently everything else so far has been just a warm-up. For one hour three times a day we have to sit perfectly still without shifting or moving. More groaning/moaning/singing from Goenka all day long has me fantasizing about meeting up with Helen, and I am ready to get the hell out of here by the day's last question session.

I wait my turn to talk to Teacher after the evening meditation and video lesson, and when he prompts me for my question, I bluntly inform him that Goenka's singing is slowly killing my soul. I plead with him to let me go and save me from the urge to kick puppies that comes every time I hear Goenka's voice. Teacher merely prompts me to get some sleep and laughs good-naturedly as I literally drag myself off the question cushion and crawl back to my own.

**Day 5: Still Here**

I make one last desperate plea to leave today, but Teacher shuts down all of my arguments. He says I can go if I can give him one good reason. I state my case; I even bring the Dali Lama into it—His Holiness says that Buddhism isn't necessarily the right path for all Westerners. My teacher's rebuttal: How can I say that Vipassana meditation is not for me after just four days of a ten-day course? I guess he has a point when he puts it like that.

**Day 6: Relieving Tedium**

Today we are asked to take all sensations—pain and pleasure—and merely observe without a reaction of craving or aversion. So as intense pain shoots up my legs and pulsates through my butt and then up my spine, I am expected to merely observe and go, "Gee, there is a sensation of knifing pain in my knee ... now what other sensations are there?" Um, well, not a whole lot other than the pain, actually.

### Day 7: Not Too Bad, All in All

Nothing too exciting to report meditation-wise. Goenka's singing isn't driving me as nuts as usual. I guess it's true what he's teaching—everything in life is impermanent, which is why we are training ourselves to stop reacting with craving and aversion.

### Day 8: A Pretty Positive Day

I have to admit, this whole thing has gotten easier over the past couple days. Either that or I'm finally resigned to staying the whole ten days. It's no longer as hard to sit still for the full hour; I've found that position is the key to lasting. I can actually sit in the Dhamma hall for the entire eleven hours and meditate without feeling the angst and drama of day 4. It's sinking in that I'm glad I stayed. A certain balance is creeping into my thoughts, and I kinda like it! I don't know if everyone else feels the same though. I seem to be one of the few still smiling ... although I'm not supposed to notice since we're not supposed to look at each other.

### Day 9: One Day until Freedom!

Praise be, this is almost over! Today is more "very, very serious" meditation, and although I have actually grown to like the technique, ten-plus hours every day is a bit more than I can handle. Our Noble Silence ends late tomorrow morning, and then it's discourse for the rest of the day. I'm proud of myself for sticking it out, even though I'm ready to leave—or at least talk. The end is in sight ...

### Day 10: A Breath of Fresh Air

Once we are able to break Noble Silence, we burst. If you want to hear some motormouths, just meet up with a group of Vipassana students at the end of their course! We're all proud of making it and understanding—not in theory but in practice—the principles of Vipassana. Craving and aversion are the root of all personal suffering because of the law of impermanence. Nothing in this world is permanent, and if you crave anything then you are bound to suffer when it is gone. But you can take personal responsibility by practicing meditation techniques that limit reactions to pleasure and pain. According to the Buddha, this is the first step on the path toward Enlightenment. As for me, I feel lighter and able to cope with both positive and negative situations in a balanced way.

*Getting to Pokhara*

Go to page 51.

*Pokhara Vipassana Center*

www.pokhara.dhamma.org

*Discipline*

Along with signing the contract agreeing to stay for the full course, participants are also asked not to read or write and to refrain from speaking and nonverbal communication with anyone other than Teacher and the server, a previous Vipassana student volunteering to assist during the course. Additional precepts include: no killing of any living creature, no lying, no stealing, no sexual activity, and no intoxicants. Religious people are asked to suspend all practices such as prayers and mantras.

### *Fasting*

Students are given a full breakfast and lunch. They then fast from noon until breakfast the next day, with the exception of lemon water for returning students at the evening tea break and a small dish of puffed rice with a few peanuts and milk tea for new students. Shannon requested a special snack every night at nine for personal health reasons and was obliged with milk and biscuits.

## *David Lee forges bonds at a weekend retreat in Pokhara*

During evening meditation, I purposefully opened my eyes and peeked around the *gompa* where I was trying to remain free from all thoughts and distractions. The room was dimly lit by flickering candles fastened to the floor with dabs of their own melted wax. The front wall was draped with *thangkas*, traditional Tibetan cloth paintings, depicting common Buddhist themes. A simple, smiling image of His Holiness the 14th Dalai Lama hung large, with an altar hosting a variety of small offerings beneath it.

I closed my eyes again, tucking a mental snapshot of the scene away for further reflection. My focus returned to my breath and the endless cycle of acknowledging thoughts as they occurred—and promptly letting them go—just as I'd always been taught. After all, this wasn't my first meditation retreat. It was my longstanding interest in Buddhism that had brought me here.

A week to the day after completing my Annapurna Sanctuary trek, I had walked into the Ganden Yiga Chozin Buddhist Meditation & Retreat Centre in the northern section of Pokhara's Lakeside District to inquire about their three-day meditation course. My timing couldn't have been better. The next weekend session was set to begin within thirty minutes.

The residential course was taught by an American monk, Venerable Losang Yeshe. Participants stayed in basic rooms from Friday afternoon through Monday morning. With thirteen people, my class was unusually large, and since I was the last to join, I was told that I wouldn't be able to stay overnight on the property as there were no more rooms available. But I was willing to live off-site in order to learn more about Buddhism in Nepal.

As with monastic life, we adhered to a strict schedule. Each day began at six thirty with a half-hour breathing meditation, followed by breakfast, Hatha yoga, a Dharma teaching, lunch, a group discussion, a second meditation, dinner, and a third and final meditation at seven thirty. After our evening meditation, we were to remain silent until the completion of the following morning's meditation. In addition, we were to refrain from listening to music and using the Internet. This quiet time was intended to allow us a chance to reflect on the lessons and conversations from earlier in the day.

On the first night, while everyone retired to their rooms, I headed back to town. If someone said "hi" to me, I was unable to return the pleasantry. The potential to be viewed as impolite weighed on my mind as I walked along the dirt road, under the light of a full moon and a sky speckled by bright white stars, but I did my best to stay disciplined.

Unfortunately, my good intentions did not last long. Once within the bounds of the central Lakeside District, before I had even reached my hotel, I impulsively ducked into a tour company's shop and looked at my email. I had been checking my email every morning on this trip, so I knew the likelihood of a vaguely interesting, let alone urgent, message waiting for me was minimal. Almost immediately I had broken the retreat's rules.

The next day, I returned to the meditation center and instinctively said "good morning" to one of my classmates. The resulting glare was all it took to bring this second mistake to my attention. Needless to say, I was not the only one excited to complete morning meditation, after which we were allowed to talk once again.

As a practitioner of Buddhist principles and meditation for several years, I found that the introductory teachings we received each morning served as a wonderful refresher. The majority of other participants, hailing from Switzerland, Holland, Israel, England, and the United States, were being exposed to the Mahayana Buddhist ideology for the first time. It was fun to watch them grapple with concepts like reincarnation and karma while learning about the life of Buddha. And Venerable Yeshe's sense of humor always added levity to our afternoon discussions.

During the communal meals, which were strictly vegetarian and always tasty, we shared our experiences from the retreat. We were all unaccustomed to sitting in one place for thirty minutes at a time, let alone meditating like that three times a day, so our inability to sit still was a popular topic. One of the couples even admitted to speaking in their room after the evening meditation, which made me feel a little better about my own transgressions. We also used the time to get to know each other better—which treks we had done, how each of us came to be in Nepal that April, and where we were headed next.

It was intense spending so much time with people I had just met. We did everything together for thirteen hours every day—meditation, yoga, classes, meals. Aside from bathroom breaks, there was no real occasion to leave the group until the completion of evening meditations. Naturally, frictions occurred, but overall, by the time the retreat came to a conclusion, it felt as though we had undertaken a collective spiritual journey together.

Bonds had been formed, and many of us went out to celebrate that night in town over dinner and drinks. Those who had time to spare lingered several weeks longer in Pokhara to take advantage of the relaxed atmosphere and local activities. As for me, the experience continued long after I left Nepal. Several months later, I reunited with two of my classmates in northern India, and I even visited one of the Swiss students in Bern the following year.

### *Getting to Pokhara*

Go to page 51.

### *Ganden Yiga Chozin Buddhist Meditation & Retreat Centre*

The retreat is located in Pokhara's Lakeside District near the Chhetri Sisters Guest House.

www.pokharabuddhistcentre.com

### *What to bring*

The first item David suggests bringing with you to the retreat is an open mind. He had little experience with yoga but was curious to learn more. And he is not a vegetarian, but he accepted that such food always comes with the territory at Buddhist retreats. He says that when you surrender control, it can open you up to a different way of life. At the very least, you learn that refraining from meat for a few days isn't the end of the world, and maybe, just maybe, you are more flexible than you once thought.

He also recommends bringing a journal so you can write about your thoughts and experiences during the retreat. This is especially handy if there are periods of silence in the evening when you not allowed to talk, listen to music, and/or use the Internet. Because rolling power outages are common (up to eight hours a day without electricity in Pokhara), a headlamp is also helpful. It allows hands-free use for journal writing.

### *Breaking the rules*

All of the restrictions can seem impossible to adhere to at a meditation retreat, so if you find yourself breaking a rule, don't be hard on yourself. Just do what David did: move on and don't do it again. He admits that he checked his email that first night of the retreat "because I could." He says residential retreats help maintain a sense of order and community, and when he walked off the property and back to his hotel, the physical distance created a mental disconnect from the experiences he'd had earlier in the day. That said, he felt bad about it and didn't check his email again until the end of the course. Rather than chastising himself, he considered it a lesson learned.

# Retail Therapy

*Discovering local markets, boutiques, and artisans*

As with the restaurants of Nepal, boutiques are not what draw travelers to the country. But for shoppers, just as for foodies, treasures can be found—you just need to know where to look.

For the most part, shopping experiences in Nepal come in two basic types: sacred and "for a cause." The former does not mean that you will have a spiritual epiphany every time you buy an item, but rather that popular items for sale include traditional Tibetan Buddhist objects. For a mandala or prayer flag to take back home as a reminder of your journey, follow Joe Bindloss in Kathmandu or Ellen Shapiro and Jacqueline Sonderling as they track down prayer beads and mantra wall hangings in Boudha.

Those who want their purchase to benefit others will find a good starting point with the list of fair trade outlets compiled by Rex Turgano. From hand-knit bags to CDs by local musicians, these shops have something for everyone, while at the same time contributing to the welfare of disadvantaged groups and marginalized communities. Also of note is the women's cooperative written about by Elizabeth Sharpe. Located in Janakpur, it produces (and preserves) the traditional folk art of the ancient Mithila kingdom.

Whether you're seeking ceremonial drums, carpets, or even trekking gear, this chapter offers a modest, and reliable, set of recommendations from expatriates and travelers who have scouted the streets for the best bargains and highest quality products the country has to offer.

*Woman lighting butter lamps at Boudhanath Stupa in Kathmandu*

# KATHMANDU

## *Joe Bindloss flags down Buddhist souvenirs in Kathmandu*

Few Kathmandu residents know the address of their nearest supermarket, but every self-respecting Nepali Buddhist can tell you exactly how to find the closest Buddha shop. Decked out with prayer flags, wall hangings, cast metal bells, polished brass *dorje* (celestial thunderbolts), and rolls of iridescent silk patterned with dragons, snow lions, and other characters from the Buddhist bestiary, these shops are a way of life in Nepal.

I first discovered the shops around Thahiti Tole while walking from Freak Street to Thamel as a young backpacker in the early 1990s. Shopping on a shoestring, I was thrilled to discover stores that catered to locals rather than tourists, with exotic Buddhist objects at prices I could afford. It was in one that I bought my first hand-held prayer wheel—part of a growing collection—and where I found the bundles of multicolored prayer flags that still flutter from the trees in my garden at home, block printed with images of the Wind Horse, the spirit being that carries prayers to heaven.

Tibetan Buddhism is a fascinating religion. Certain people—and I count myself in this category—become obsessed with the color and ritual, the crowds circumnavigating Buddhist stupas, the masked dances and honk of Tibetan horns at festivals, the ringing of cymbals fading to silence in the dusty halls of ancient monasteries. As well as places for buying items to liven up the living room back home, Buddha shops are wonderful for people watching. Monks drop in to purchase new robes and ceremonial drums. Tibetan refugees come for incense and fabric. Sherpas stock up on prayer flags to drape over high mountain passes.

At the shops around Thahiti Tole, prayer flags are bundled up into bulk packs of ten or twenty. The average Buddhist family hangs up dozens of strands of prayer flags every year, and stupas are choked with them. They flutter triumphantly above hidden courtyards in the backstreets of Chhetrapati, while the bridges over the Bagmati River are a riot of flickering fabric. Anywhere the wind blows, you'll find these statements of goodwill to mankind sending prayers to heaven. This custom, combined with warmth toward all of humanity, is perhaps the defining characteristic of Tibetan Buddhism, which is why prayer flags are an ideal way to remember the spirit of Nepal once you have returned home.

### *Thahiti Tole*

Thahiti Tole is south of the Thamel neighborhood on the small street leading south to Indra Chowk and Asan Tole. You may have to fight through crowds of shoppers and motorcycles to get there, but once you arrive it's much calmer than Asan Tole. There is no public transport, but a cycle rickshaw will cost around 30 rupees from Durbar Square or central Thamel, and will give you a perfect vantage point for taking photos of the medieval streets.

### *Something to smile about*

While in Thahiti Tole, continue south along the same road to the intriguing toothache shrine at Bangemunda. Dedicated to Vaisha Dev, the patron saint of toothaches, the shrine consists of thousands of rupee coins, nailed to an ancient block of wood by pilgrims seeking relief from the agony of abscesses and rotten teeth. Appropriately, several dentists have set up shop in nearby streets.

## *Brian Smith gears up in the shops of Kathmandu*

In the tourist-filled streets of the Thamel neighborhood, a huge number of shops sell trekking gear at what seem to be really low prices. To even a casual observer, though, it soon becomes clear that Mountain Hardware and The North Face logos (sometimes both on a single product!) are not authentic. Almost all of the supplies in these shops are Nepali made, and much of it is of dubious quality. The trick is to know what you can get and what you can't—what will stand the test of time, and what will fall apart.

Many of the items bought here will last you a single trek, which is fine if that's all you need. That said, equipment of great importance that will be in constant hard contact with your body, i.e., shoes and backpacks, should be avoided altogether, as you're just asking for sores and blisters. Zippers are the components that I have found often break, while straps lack the correct adjustability and usually fall apart after a limited number of uses as well. The key when shopping is looking to minimize the number of seams, zippers, and straps, since these are where the Nepali products are the weakest.

This does not mean that absolutely everything sold in these shops should be avoided. I bought a "Polartec" headband back in 2002, and nearly a decade later I still use it, as the fabric keeps my ears warm and the Velcro attachment in the back works fine. Other items that stand up a little better to time are fleeces, sleep sacks, water bottles, hats, and travel towels. Be aware when making your purchases that the advertised GORE-TEX or other specialized fabrics are not genuine, and many products claiming to be waterproof are not. In the instance that an item is actually waterproof, you can almost be certain that it will not be breathable.

Recently a couple of official outdoor shops have opened in Kathmandu, and this is where I go if I really need dependable gear. The North Face and Mountain Hardware have stores on Tridevi Marg, heading toward the Garden of Dreams east of Thamel. These stores sell the real deal, but you will also pay real prices for their products, often equal to what you would in stores back home. Another quality retailer I've bought from is Sherpa Adventure Gear, which has a location just south of the Royal Palace Museum area on Narayanhiti Path.

Over the years I've discovered that the key to gear shopping in Nepal is to be aware of what I'm buying and to adjust my expectations accordingly. And of course it helps that between these three shops I have a reliable choice for shoes, tents, and clothing—essentially, anything that is going to take a beating or has zippers.

**Quality gear in Kathmandu**

*The North Face*
Tridevi Marg
Thamel District

www2.thenorthface.com

*Mountain Hardware*
Tridevi Marg
Thamel District

www.mountainhardwear.com

*Sherpa Adventure Gear*
Lal Durbar Marg
Next to Jai Nepal Cinema

www.sherpaadventuregear.com

## *Rex Turgano promotes fair trade shops in and around Kathmandu*

In Kathmandu and Patan, there are numerous fair trade shops that sell locally made products and support small community groups, especially those working with women. Traditionally, women in Nepal are brought up to manage the household, raise children, work in fields, and cook meals. They don't have many other options, and fair trade shops often fund programs such as literacy classes, lessons on managing finances, and even workshops for how to start a small business. Following are some of the most popular shops, as well as my favorites, both big and small.

**Dhukuti**
www.acp.org.np

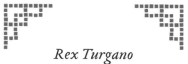

Located in Patan's Kupondole neighborhood, Dhukuti is a member of ACP (Association for Craft Producers). With a goal to employ and empower women from severely disadvantaged backgrounds, ACP provides training, employment, access to health care, and other benefits to more than twelve hundred women. This multilevel store pretty much has everything to decorate your home and to remind you of your visit to Nepal.

**Fiber Weave Nepal**
www.fiberweave.com.np

Not only did I have the good luck to stumble upon this store in the Kupondole neighborhood of Patan, I stumbled upon its workshop, as well, where the owners were teaching Nepalese women how to weave. This shop sells interesting and beautiful hand-woven products.

**Jawalakhel Handicraft Center**
www.jhcnepal.com

Also known as Tibetan Refugee Camp, this center in the Jawalakhel District of Patan is one of Nepal's largest carpet manufacturers. The huge selection includes contemporary, traditional, and Persian designs. This is a friendly place, and you can even walk through the carpet-making facilities. However, it's a little on the pricey side.

**Kumbeshwar Technical School**
www.kumbeshwar.com

Located in Patan, this school provides vocational training in hand knitting, carpet weaving, and furniture making. To fund and sustain these programs, the school sells products made by students. I've been told that they offer a great deal on carpets.

**Mahaguthi**
www.mahaguthi.org

Billing itself as "craft with a conscience," Mahaguthi has shops in the Lazimpat District and Patan's Kupondole neighborhood. With its wide range of heritage and cultural products, it's often one of my first stops when I'm shopping for gifts.

**Third World Crafts**
http://thirdworldcraft.com

Although Dhukuti and Mahaguthi are the best-known fair trade shops in Kathmandu, my favorite is the small Third World Crafts on Lazimpat Road. This store has lots of gems, from unique little singing bowls and diverse *thangka* paintings to grand prayer wheels and CDs by local musicians. On my most recent visit, one of the owner's nephews took the time to help me find the souvenirs I needed, and then offered me a discount off my total purchase. It's the shop's friendly one-on-one service that makes the difference for me.

*Fair Trade Group Nepal*
www.fairtradegroupnepal.org

FTG Nepal is a consortium of fair trade organizations focused on underprivileged and marginalized producers in Nepal.

*Women's Skill Development Project*
www.wsdp.org.np

Located in Pokhara, this organization was established in 1975. It is committed to providing Nepalese women with vocational skills training. Keep an eye out for their products, which can be found in nearly every fair trade shop in Nepal. Rex's father-in-law purchased an excellent side bag made by this group.

## Boudha

### *Jacqueline Sonderling bargains for beads in Boudha*

The cramped, crowded shops that surround Boudhanath Stupa are stuffed with goods, from rare and beautiful trinkets to kitschy tourist souvenirs. During my visits, I've found such treasures as a necklace of carved yak-bone beads and a hand-hammered Tibetan singing bowl. I've also purchased good-quality pashmina and unique Tibetan items like puppets and textiles. This truly is some of the best shopping the Kathmandu area has to offer.

My favorite shop is one that sells nothing but prayer beads. I'm always mesmerized by the beads on display outside. They hang on hooks on a peg board—all shapes, sizes, colors, and lengths. The *mala* strings have tassels of yellow and red, pink and blue. And that's just for starters. Wait until you step into the shop.

What seems like millions of strands of beads cover the walls of this narrow space, which is barely wide enough to move through single file. Every inch is draped with strings of the *mala* prayer beads made of every material you can imagine. Do you want lotus seeds? Or perhaps you prefer beads carved from a local wood. How about yak bone? Precious stones or glass or ceramic? Are these beads too small? Try the same style but a size or two larger. And if this strand is too short, here's a longer one. It's almost impossible for me to narrow down my selection. I've never walked out with fewer than half a dozen strands.

The minute I start looking at the beads, the owner of the store silently appears ... and hovers. Up and down the store he follows, like a shadow, until I've made my decision. I hand my carefully selected strands over and follow him to a small room in back that doubles as his cashier's corner and a storage area. It's time to negotiate and complete the deal.

"How much?" I ask, beginning the ritual dance.

He examines my selections and then pulls out a small brocade drawstring pouch and stuffs the *mala* strands in. He makes his first offer. As expected it's more than I'm willing to pay.

I take the next step in this carefully choreographed tango—a counteroffer.

He grumbles and refuses to budge from his price. I shrug and repeat mine. He grunts and doesn't negotiate. I do a pseudo-turn to walk out of the store. He stops me. "All right," he grouses and meets my offer. I hand him the rupees, and he gives me the brocade bag. I thank him. He nods. This is the same routine we perform every time I come to the store. Some might call it a pain, just to obtain some beads. As for me, it's tradition, and I wouldn't have it any other way.

### *Finding Jacqueline's favorite shop*

Jacqueline adds: So few shops here have names or signs out front, and while there are many in the circle around Boudhanath Stupa that sell prayer beads, "my shop" is a must-see. If you think of the stupa as a clock, and you enter at six o'clock, the shop is at eleven o'clock. Since it's right on the main drag, you can't miss it.

### *Stupa View Restaurant*

Because heavy bartering always makes Jacqueline hungry, once she tucks the bag with her prized *mala* strands safely away, she continues her circumambulation until she reaches her favorite lunch spot, the Stupa View Restaurant. For more on this restaurant, go to page 20.

### *Bag lady*

The gorgeous little brocade pouches that shopkeepers put the beads in are a staple in Nepal. They are ingeniously simple to use, so Jacqueline hates admitting how long it took her to figure them out. There are two short strings and two long strings. Pull the short ones—the bag opens, and the short strings become long. Pull the now-long strings, and the bag closes. Duh!

## *Ellen Shapiro shows no restraint in the shops of Boudha*

I've never made a trip to Nepal when I didn't begin and end my journey with a visit to Boudha. If you haven't been there, it should be at the top of your list. If you have, well, you know what I'm talking about.

There's something so spiritual about the town. Perhaps it's the devotion of the people, young and old, counting their circuits around the giant Boudhanath Stupa. Or maybe it's because I can't imagine how this place could be anything more than it already is. For whatever reason, as cynical as I am (and I *am* cynical), Boudha holds a very special place in my heart.

Because I have such a fondness for Nepal, I've made my home into a bit of a shrine to the country and its people. In my son's doorway hangs a Tibetan "endless knot" door curtain. Above the door to my bedroom is a multicolored mantra with a rainbow of tassels draping down. Nepali and Tibetan carpets are scattered throughout, and to keep things from getting out of hand, I display only a single favorite photograph from Nepal. At least I restrained myself and didn't hang the prayer flags!

Many of these treasures came from Boudha, where there's a great variety of objects to choose from—and a great variety of quality too, but that rule is universal. It's hard not to get caught up in "acquisition mode," which, of course, is extremely un-Buddhist-like. Still, I can't help seeking out my favorite mementos, including the aforementioned door curtains. The endless knot design is just one option. The eight auspicious symbols of Buddhism is another popular style. If I had more doorways, I'd have both.

I also like the prayer flags, prayer wheels, and wall hangings, which also depict the eight auspicious symbols, as well as variants of the mantra *om mani padme hum*, stitched in bright colors with tassels hanging down. These are by no means the only items available in the shops around Boudhanath Stupa. They are simply the things that speak directly to my heart. Whatever bond you make with Nepal and Tibetan culture, Boudha is an excellent place to find tangible reminders of that connection to take back home.

### *Getting to Boudha*

Go to page 21.

### *Shopping in Boudha*

All around the stupa are shops selling religious items, Tibetan CDs (mostly chanting), and a selection of souvenirs. The paths leading to and from the stupa are also lined with shops. It's important to remember that while this is a religious site, it is also a major tourist destination, so be prepared to bargain hard. If that feels too daunting to you, look around at what's available and make your purchases at a monastery (most have shops). You will accomplish two things at once: you won't have to bargain, and you'll be supporting a good cause.

## Tansen

## *Elizabeth Sharpe shops with spirit in Tansen*

I peer into a narrow shop in Makhan Tole, the main bazaar in Tansen in the Palpa District. I've come to buy *dhaka*, a brightly colored textile that distinguishes itself in Nepal, namely in the signature men's cap (topi) that is part of Nepali native dress.

The topi is not the only item the store sells. Above my head and framing the wide doorway are folded shawls (*labeda suruwal*) hung side by side in vivid, contrasting colors and distinct designs. There are also blouses (*chaubandi cholo*) that in the colder months become thicker and warmer, as do the shawls, each lined with an extra layer of white cotton.

I want to leave Nepal with a *dhaka* shawl, carrying home with me a piece of Nepali culture I've long admired on many beautiful local women, with their dark hair, cinnamon-brown eyes, tan skin, and curious smiles that have beckoned to me on countless occasions. Over cups of tea, we would sit cross-legged, asking questions of each other and about the worlds we come from, while the women wrapped their shawls more tightly around themselves against the cold. Now I want a shawl to keep these memories of the country near to me when I return home—to keep the part Nepali culture I have come to know while living in the country for two years close to my heart.

But how can I possibly choose just one? There are too many beautiful shawls. To make my decision more difficult, the shopkeeper pulls out even more from the shelves for me to see. I decide that I want to share the beauty of this cloth and where it comes from with as many friends and family members back home as I can. I want them to know how *dhaka* embodies the spirit I have come to admire about the Nepalese people, that beauty that comes from hard work and meticulous attention to an age-old craft.

In Palpa, women weave the *dhaka* cloth on giant looms that the men have made from wood and bamboo. The female weaver sits on a wide bench, almost as though she's seated at a church organ. Lined up before her are symmetrical, spiderweb-thin threads. As her nimble fingers weave paddles of colorful thread through lengths of spun cotton or muslin, the bright geometrical designs grow larger. A single *dhaka* shawl can take up to a week or more to make. All that work for a mere $20.

Finally, I tell the shopkeeper, "I'll take two of these." I have not changed my mind and decided to limit my purchases. It's just that I know I still have more *dhaka* shops to browse through down the road.

### *Getting to Tansen*

Go to page 24.

### *Shopping for dhaka*

*Dhaka* shops are not hard to find in Tansen. Elizabeth suggests browsing among the many in the main bazaar. To reach the main bazaar (Makhan Tole) from the bus park, walk west toward the Tundikhel neighborhood. You'll see *dhaka* shops on the corner as you take a sharp left up a narrow cobblestone street that comes out above Makhan Tole, which is just opposite Tansen Durbar, the old palace. As well as *dhaka*, the shops in the bazaar also sell kitchen wares, spices, fruits and vegetables, and other fabrics. To learn more about *dhaka* weaving, search "*dhaka*" at the website for The Women's Foundation of Nepal.

www.womenepal.org

### *Coffee break*

Rest your tired feet and take a break from shopping at Nanglo West, a Newari-style restaurant that serves Nepali, Indian, Chinese, and Western dishes. And make sure to order a cup of coffee—it's Palpa-grown. Ask to sit upstairs, rather than in the patio. From the *dhaka*-covered pillows scattered on the floor, you can sit and view the bazaar just outside the windows. For more on Nanglo West, go to page 23.

## Janakpur

### *Elizabeth Sharpe seeks a blessing in Janakpur*

Swaddled in a dark pink cloth, the baby was curled against the mound of his mother's crimson-draped calf, his small head turned slightly to rest on her knee. As he slept peacefully, she seemed oblivious to his presence, her attention fixed instead on the small mug in one of her hands. Her other hand held a brush, and female figures were slowly emerging in glaze on the mug's surface.

She was working alongside three other women in the courtyard of the Janakpur Women's Development Center in Kuwa village, just outside Janakpur, a historic city about 180 miles southeast of Kathmandu and just shy of the Indian border. I was transfixed, watching as she carried on a tradition of painting ritual designs that has been part of Mithila culture in Nepal dating back to the seventh century.

Famous for the Janaki temple, Janakpur was once the ancient capital of the Mithila kingdom. According to the *Ramayana*, it is also the birthplace of the goddess Sita, considered to be the epitome of all that is virtuous and beautiful in women. Mythology and religion reign strong in Mithila culture, and the artwork that Mithila women paint on the walls and floors of their homes is part of the rituals to celebrate holy days and marriage ceremonies and to honor the house deities. The end product—the painting itself—is said to be a charm.

I was first introduced to the work of the Mithila women in Kathmandu, where many shops displayed and sold their distinctive artwork: folk paintings on homemade paper, colorful cups and mugs, brightly designed felt bags, and papier-mâchéd mirrors. With my sister soon to be married, I wanted to share with her and her husband-to-be this unique aspect of Nepali culture.

I commissioned a *khobar ghar* painting on homemade paper—it would include the images to signify prosperity, fertility, and happiness that were traditionally painted on the walls of the nuptial chamber of the bride and groom. Because I found the Mithila tradition so fascinating, I decided that I wanted to meet the women who made this exceptional art. I wanted to see where they worked, so I went to Janakpur to pick up the painting myself.

When the Janakpur Women's Development Center was built, the artisans learned to translate their technique to homemade paper and pottery with acrylic paint and glaze that matched the red, blue, green, and yellow designs they used to paint the walls and floors of homes. The women sell their work around the world, and their talent earns them an income their families greatly need. Some scenes they paint are of everyday life: planting rice, cooking, or caring for a child. Others feature Hindu deities, such as Shakti, Vishnu, or Shiva. There are also more fanciful designs, and my favorite depicts an elephant walking alongside beak-nosed women with dark, flowing hair. Peacocks flew above their heads, while lotus flowers danced at their heels.

When the center's manager brought out the finished *khobar ghar*, there in familiar colors and designs were a man and woman being married, surrounded by lotus flowers while fish, turtles, and peacocks danced in celebration around them. Admiring the piece, I knew that my sister and her marriage would be blessed, for I was bringing home an artist's genuine prayer, wishing the bride and groom a life full of love, children, and good fortune.

### *Shopping for Mithila handicrafts*

Many shops in Kathmandu sell Mithila products. The organizations listed below have offices in Kathmandu and work with women's cooperative groups all over Nepal. All belong to the Fair Trade Group Nepal.

www.fairtradegroupnepal.org

**Sana Hastakala**
www.sanahastakala.org

**Mahaguthi**
www.mahaguthi.org

**Manushi**
http://manushinepal.org

### *Janakpur Women's Development Center*

For information about the center and visiting the artisans of Janakpur, go to the following website.

www.sunavworld.com

### *The Mithila in Janakpur*

The Mithila is one of many ethnic groups in Nepal. Their culture is distinctive, and they are proud of their melodious language. Janakpur, too, has a rich history and is visited by pilgrims each year during religious festivals. The city is well worth visiting for the Mithila artisans and the Janaki temple, one of the most beautiful temples in Nepal.

www.janakpur.com.np

## General Nepal

### *Jacqueline Sonderling schleps carpets home from Nepal*

I live in a typical one-bedroom apartment in New York City, so you might be surprised to learn that I own not one, not two ... but five authentic Nepali rugs—all strategically placed for maximum effect.

I bought my first carpet in the village of Namche Bazaar on a trek in Solukhumbu. Namche's market day (every Saturday) is a wonderful opportunity to witness Nepal's rural lifestyle. But the wares are geared toward the locals who come to stock up on essentials, so don't expect to find keepsakes here. In the mood for air-cured yak leg? You get the idea.

In the center of town down by the stupa, however, there is sometimes another market. I was in luck when I was there. The Tibetan traders were "in town." They come periodically to Namche, walking through the mountains to bring goods from Tibet. While they do sell to locals, curious travelers often browse through the rows (mostly set up on tarps that double as makeshift tents for nighttime sleeping) hoping to find treasures.

As I wandered back and forth through the traders' camps, a few Tibetan carpets caught my eye. They were the traditional variety, about one by two meters, that are often used in homes as the top layer on a couch and for sleeping. I was drawn to a pair, one of which had a dark blue background with peach-colored lotuses, while the other had the reverse pattern. I wasn't sure about the color scheme, but I liked the style and entered into a negotiation.

Before I knew it, other tourists and traders gathered around to observe the exchange. In the end, we settled on a price, and I walked away with two new authentic Tibetan carpets—after all, they had been brought from Tibet on the backs of yaks by Tibetans. They even had the dirt (and smell!) to prove it.

My other carpets came from the Jawalakhel District in the town of Patan. From a purely aesthetic standpoint, I like them better. The designs are taken from ancient patterns, very different from those I bought in Namche and the run-of-the-mill designs I saw in every store I passed.

Most of these stores "on the strip" hang carpets out front to excite interest, and often the selection is not just in the "showroom" but also in what seem to be secret rooms behind the stores. If you don't see something you like, you can ask if there are any other styles. Don't be surprised if you are ushered through dark, cement corridors, out the back of the shop, and into another room in an adjacent building.

As I discovered, while traditional Nepali and Tibetan carpets can be a heavy load to cart back with you, they will bring an unusual and memorable touch, no matter how big or small your home.

### *Getting to Namche*

Go to page 65.

### *Shopping in Patan*

Jawalakhel is a Tibetan enclave in Patan, about five kilometers south of Kathmandu. You can take a taxi there—just tell the driver to drop you at the carpet shops (one long street of vendors, most selling carpets), and be prepared for him to try to take you to his favorite shop. If you are feeling ambitious, you can even walk from the Thamel District, although Jacqueline recommends getting your hands on a good map if you do. If you find a carpet you like, most shops will pack and ship.

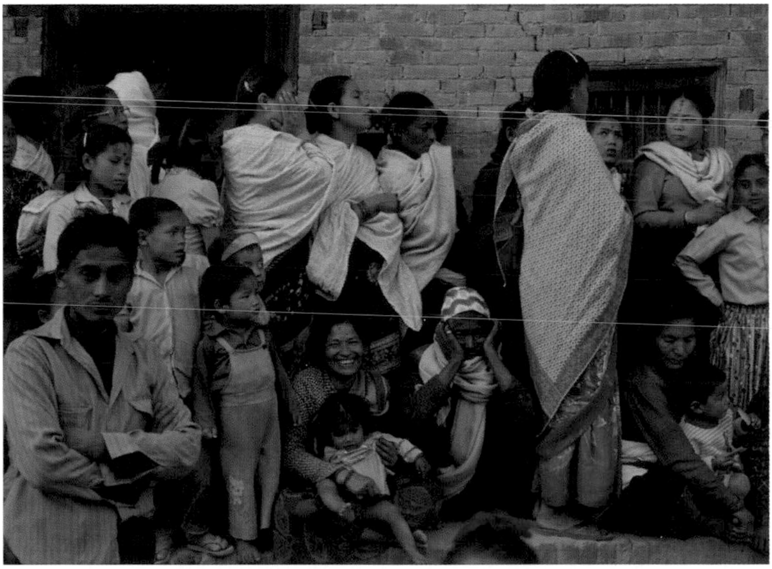

*A local gathering in the Kathmandu Valley*

# Into the Wild

*Tales of trekking and beyond for adventurous travelers*

From the savannas of Africa to the national parks of the United States, few (if any) places compare to Nepal's Himalayas when it comes to jaw-dropping grandeur. No one who visits these exhilarating mountains goes home unchanged. That's why the essays in this chapter focus on emotional *and* geographic landscapes. It's one thing to describe the way this region looks, and another to describe what it feels like to push yourself to the limit while you're there.

For extremists, David Hammerbeck travels to the far reaches of Western Nepal, where he triumphs over heavy rains and raging rivers. On the other end of the country, Cameron Burns discovers the value in not exerting oneself too much as he accompanies a marathon along the Singalila Ridge. And in between, numerous writers face their fears and find their own pace in the country's two most visited areas, Everest and Annapurna.

Although trekkers, for the most part, tend to follow common routes, every experience is unique because of what each person brings to it. Renee Robertson and her husband up the challenge ante by trekking with their seven- and eight-year-old daughters, while Laurie Weed adds an element of gender empowerment by choosing her guide from an all-female trekking company. As for those who want to get away from the Everest and Annapurna trails, but aren't quite ready to risk life and limb to go off the beaten path, Brian Smith suggest the Tamang Heritage Trail, which offers beautiful vistas and a taste of old Nepal.

While Nepal is best known for its mountains, huffing and puffing your way to their peaks isn't essential for getting to know the country's great outdoors. Rex Turgano finds his adventure at a resort on the way to the Tibetan border, while Kristina Wegscheider enjoys a leisurely escape with the elephants in Chitwan National Park. And if you can't decide how you want to explore the country's natural beauty, follow Roberta Sotonoff's lead as she samples the mountains, rivers, and jungles, all in one tour.

*One-horned rhinos at Chitwan National Park*

# Dolpa District

*David Hammerbeck passes through the Dolpa District*

On popular trekking routes, such as Everest Base Camp or the Annapurna Circuit, amenities and support are never far away. Even going over the Thorong La Pass on Annapurna's main high route, you are never more than three hours from a hot cup of tea. But some areas in Nepal are less forgiving. Take the Dolpa District, for example, where it pays to be prepared, even if you are just passing through.

Last summer during the monsoon season, I trekked to Phoksundo Lake from Dunai. Dunai is the administrative center of Dolpa, Nepal's largest but least populous district, immediately west of the Mustang District and abutting Tibet to the north. The rainy season is considered the perfect time to trek in Dolpa, as it lies in the rain shadow of the Himalayas. The district typically escapes the brunt of the annual onslaught, while the usually arid landscape blossoms and bursts with life. This, of course, also means that there is more water hanging around than the ecosystem normally accommodates.

I was trekking with three Nepalese friends: two government employees and a karate instructor. Part of our trek would follow Thulo Bheri Khola, the main river that drains from the highlands through Lower Dolpa, running through a deep ravine that is like a larger-scale version of the Grand Canyon, lined with primeval pine forests and a two-hundred-meter waterfall. The rains had been considerable, and the river raged past Dunai, black with silt, churning and thick.

Accommodations on the way to the lake are sparse to nonexistent. We spent two nights sleeping in a small village one hour south of Chepka in a granary on the floor, and another two in a semideserted inn in Sumduwa, where no food was available. My friends traveled Nepali style—wearing everything they had and sharing a small pack between the three of them. I carried a full pack, and we joked that I looked like a foreign porter for three Nepalese tourists.

Rain fell constantly, and by the time we reached Phoksundo Lake, time was running short. We heard rumors that the rains were causing problems down the trail. Several bridges had been damaged—one verging on collapse—and in several places the trail was already being swallowed by the river. So we headed back down quickly, but soon reached an impasse. An area of the trail where previously we had waded up to our knees was now much deeper, submerged in swift waters. If we waded any farther we would risk being swept out into the main current. There were no other trails for a detour, and retreating would add two days to our itinerary. We did not have extra food, so as the rain eased, we decided to wait for the river to subside.

Five hours passed, and the river raged on. Another expedition approached from the south. We communicated via hand signals and decided that both groups would try forging a path up the hill after wading as far as we could. Over the next hour or so both parties hacked, slipped, and clawed up and across the tangled, sheer hillside. The other group's eight porters did the lion's share of the work, dragging along four extremely distraught, middle-aged German hikers. We finally made it across and proceeded down the trail at a breakneck speed. Our goal was to make it to the same granary floor we slept on that first night. We arrived soaked and well after dark, but there was food and plenty of *raksi* to warm us up.

We left early the next morning. A bridge only twenty-five meters north of the granary vibrated ominously as we departed—one end of it was built on top of a two-ton boulder, which was in danger of being dislodged by a raging side stream. Fortunately we were headed in the opposite direction. But rumors persisted that a bridge farther down the river toward Dunai was on the verge of collapse. When we reached it, I was sickened by the look of it. It sagged and dipped to one side, but what choice did we have? One by one, as lightly as possible, we sprinted across.

We reached Dunai late that evening. The next morning the bridge collapsed into the angry torrent. No one was crossing at the time, but the lives of the locals were disrupted indefinitely. We were luckier. Not only had we made it across just in time the day before, we were just passing through.

### *About Dolpa*

Very few foreign visitors come to Dolpa, a remote area that was made famous by Peter Matthiessen in his book *The Snow Leopard*, the story of his trek with renowned zoologist George Schaller in search of the region's rare snow leopard. High and dry, lying on the north side of the Himalayan crest, Dolpa is also known for its ancient and difficult to reach Bon-Po and Tibetan Buddhist temples and small monasteries, as well as wildlife, such as the rare Himalayan blue sheep. Entered by way of Phoksundo Lake, Inner Dolpa is right next to Tibet.

### *Getting to Dolpa*

The administrative center of Dunai is the starting point for some, but not all, treks in the Dolpa District. The village is a three-hour trek (all downhill) from Juphal, which is a forty-five-minute flight from Nepalgunj. You can also fly from Jumla, around forty-five minutes as well.

To trek from Jumla, west of Dolpa and on the way to Rara Lake, to Dunai takes around six days. You can also trek to Dunai from Beni, one of the end points for the Annapurna Circuit trek (in the Kali Gandaki River Valley). This takes around twelve days and is the route taken and described by Matthiessen in *The Snow Leopard*. It will lead you over several high passes to the west of the Dhaulagiri Massif. A guide and porters are necessary for this trek, as what accommodations can be found are rudimentary.

Another possible point of entry would be to trek up the Kali Gandaki River Valley from either Bedi or Naya Pul to Jomsom or Kagbeni. Here you take one of two high routes: one goes from Kagbeni into southern Inner Dolpa, and the other travels farther up the Kali Gandaki River into far Upper Mustang, then heads west into Inner Dolpa.

### *Roughing it*

Lack of facilities and difficulties in obtaining food in this area are a real issue here. This is a region (like Mustang, Manaslu, Kanchenjunga, or Makalu) where going with an experienced trekking company is strongly recommended. Many companies can assist you, including David's Alta Vista Treks & Expedition, which is located in Pokhara.

www.altavistatrek.com

### *Plan ahead*

If you decide to go to Dolpa, you must be prepared with proper documents. David witnessed a French couple, who didn't have all the necessary permits when they arrived at park headquarters between Juphal and Dunai, get refused entrance. This was after they waited for a flight to Juphal for five days in Nepalgunj, due to inclement weather—another very real possibility when flying to Dolpa. Imagine their frustration. Fly halfway around the world, only to wait in Nepalgunj, not one of Nepal's garden spots, for nearly a week, then finally make it to Dolpa only to have a government functionary deny you entry because he deems your paperwork to be insufficient.

### *The high cost of trekking*

Most Dolpa treks pass through or are entirely in Shey Phoksundo National Park. At the time of publication, the basic park entrance fee was around 2,000 Nepali rupees (about $25). Permits for Inner Dolpa are expensive, about $700 for ten days, with $70 per day for each additional day.

## Chitwan National Park

*Kristina Wegscheider befriends the elephants of Chitwan*

India left us in a state of complete sensory overload, so we were thrilled to spend the second half of our two-week holiday in Nepal. Following a brief stay in Lumbini, birthplace of Buddha, we traveled for an entire day across the Nepali countryside, bound for the small village of Sauraha. As the sun settled into the horizon, we approached the Sapana Village Lodge, located right on the edge of Chitwan National Park.

After a good night's rest, we woke early for breakfast in the beautiful riverfront oasis. Our first activity of the day was an elephant ride to the outer zone of the park. We were expecting to drive to the park entrance, but suddenly our meal was interrupted by the sound of elephants chanting to one another. We quickly finished eating and ran to the front of the lodge, where our four-legged transportation awaited. We caravanned through the village with smiling local children running behind us.

As soon as we entered the park, we came across a family of rhinos. Being on the backs of elephants allowed us to get within just a few feet of them. Our morning of wildlife viewing also included crossing a river where a sunbathing crocodile sat stalking its next meal. Once our herd of elephants returned us to the park entrance, we thanked the *mahouts* (the elephants' keepers) with a small tip and showed our gratitude to our elephants with some green bananas that we purchased from the locals.

With this part of the adventure over, two friends and I opted to walk back to the lodge via the village. We were amazed as every villager greeted us with a smile and warm "*namaste.*" It was only 11 a.m. and this was already the best day of our trip—and there was still more to come! When we returned, the owner of the lodge asked if we'd like to help wash the elephants. We promptly changed into our swimsuits.

Hopping onto an elephant's bare back, we headed down to the river. Then, out of nowhere, the elephant was given the command to sit back, and we went flying off into the river. Don't ask me how, but I just knew the elephant thought it was hilarious. Waterlogged, I scrubbed the animal's coarse hair as it sprayed water at me through its trunk. Ten minutes later it was time to finish up. My elephant was apparently not too happy about this, as he immediately started playing with dirt.

After a warm shower (another great feature of the lodge), we headed off for the final excursion of the day: the elephant breeding center. A brief jeep ride through the village took us to the center, where we saw elephants ranging from a few months old to adolescents. The young elephants were allowed to roam freely. Some stuck close to their mothers while the more adventurous ones made new friends with visitors. We were able to witness amazing moments, like a mother nursing her young and a pair of twin elephants learning how to eat on their own.

Back at the lodge once again, the day came to a perfect end: playing with the house dog and cat, engaging in a game of badminton, and enjoying happy hour on the riverfront patio. After the chaos of India, I would always remember this day—the peace of our surroundings, the kindness of the locals, and of course, the camaraderie of the elephants at work and play.

### *Sapana Village Lodge*

Sauraha Village

www.sapanalodge.com

### *Getting to Sauraha*

If taking a private car to the lodge's front door isn't your style, you can hop on a daily tourist bus from Kathmandu or Pokhara to the Chitwan bus station or fly into the Bharatpur Airport. If you give advance notice, a representative from the lodge will meet you at the bus station or airport.

### *Giving back*

The Sapana Village Lodge is part of a Dutch development project that aims to relieve poverty in the area by producing jobs and revenue. All of the decor in the rooms is made by the locals, and most is available for purchase in the small onsite gift shop. You can also walk across the street to a building where local women make handicrafts and textiles for the lodge. Kristina had a purse custom-made for her here in just a few hours.

### *Keeping busy*

You can easily spend a few days at the lodge, as it offers an extensive list of activities. For adventurous types, there are multiday treks and canoeing. And if you'd like to immerse yourself in the local culture, you can take a cooking class or learn traditional Tharu stick dancing.

### *With this ring*

Looking for a unique way to get married or renew your vows? You and your partner can participate in a daylong Tharu wedding ceremony complete with traditional garments and jewelry as well as henna tattoos for the bride. For your wedding night, stay in the lodge's multilevel jungle watchtower.

## Dhulikhel

*Rex Turgano reaches the last resort on the way to Tibet*

As I headed out for a weekend getaway at The Last Resort, three hours from Kathmandu, rafting was initially on the radar of the volunteer group I was traveling with. The resort is on top of a river gorge on the way to the Tibetan border, making it ideal for water activities. But seeing that this was the height of the monsoon season, we decided to forego our original plan, as the rapids were extremely high and rough—even our Nepalese guides seemed reluctant to go. Instead, some of us went canyoning and a few indulged at the spa, while the majority of us did the high ropes activity.

The eight-station high ropes course, although not as thrilling as rafting when you first look at it, definitely came through with its what-the-heck moments. It was probably the most mentally and physically challenging thing that I have ever done. In a nutshell, each station—perched on a tree that was at least four stories high—had different rope apparatuses set up in order to get to the next.

For most of us, the hardest station was the initial ladder climb, as it required some arm strength, and for me, my own patented offline, swinging-foot/mounting technique. The skateboard station demanded a lot of balance because the rolling skateboard-on-the-ropes contraption was moving in every direction, making it difficult to get over the "heights" factor. I almost flipped out on the high-wire-walk-on-poles station. And the high-wire-hanging-ropes station was profoundly psychedelic. Really!

Although these various stations served as personal challenges, each of us who undertook them was not alone. We did the rope activities in partners, thus allowing us to coach one another through the motions. As our Nepalese guide said, "Four eyes are better than two." Of course, we had harnesses and were given safety ropes/carabineer attachment training—very useful, since you don't really want to accidently detach *both* your carabineers and your partner's.

Overall, despite the adrenaline-rush moments, this trip was relaxing. I learned a lot about myself. I can jump from tree to tree using ropes. I suck at charades. And I'm eager to return to do that rafting I missed out on. As for the bungee jumping, who knows, maybe I'll even give that a try, too.

### *The Last Resort*

The buffet food here was excellent, the service great, and the tents and beds very comfortable. The well-timed heaviest rainfall of the year during the night was a nice touch. Bought the T-shirt, too!

www.thelastresort.com.np

*High ropes tips*

I highly recommend wearing closed shoes and perhaps pants and or long shorts, since it's easy to get scratched or even cut up during the activities. Also, if you go during the monsoon season, look out for leeches.

## Langtang Region

*Brian Smith seeks the past on the Tamang Heritage Trail*

When I tell people that I am going trekking in Nepal, most instinctively think of the big hikes like Everest Base Camp and the Annapurna Circuit, or maybe even the Langtang Valley. Few know about the Tamang Heritage Trail. My wife Kim and I had heard that because it was new and had relatively few trekkers, many of the villages it passed through were reminiscent of what the Langtang region looked like before it was developed. The idea of hitting one of these trails before they became major tourist routes was appealing, so we decided to give it a go.

We took a very long and uncomfortable bus ride to Syaphru Besi, the gateway to the Langtang Valley. However, we were not heading into the valley like the other trekkers on the bus. Instead, we set off to the east, up and over Rongga Bhanjyang Pass to the day's destination of Gatlang. This traditional Tamang village has hardly been visited by tourists, and ethnic clothing mixed with Western imports was common. Most of the women also wore ornate, traditional earrings, and some were even adorned with large nose rings. There is only one guesthouse and the community lodge, where we stayed and were treated with exceptional hospitality by Mr. Dawa Nurpa Lama, who runs the lodge.

The Tamang are a Tibetan people that came south into these valleys of Northern Nepal. Buddhist *chortens*, shrines, and *mani* walls line the trail, all attesting to Buddhism being the major religious influence among the Tamang. This is not to say that the trail was only highlighted by its cultural backdrop. Almost as soon as we headed up toward Rongga Bhanjyang, we were greeted with views of Langtang Lirung, a peak that was perfectly framed by the valley from our vantage point at the community lodge.

As we started down the sloping trail toward the Bamdang Khola (River) the next day, we passed women winding yarn as they walked, men plowing their fields with pairs of yoked cows, and children who would yell "*namaste*!" as we passed and then ask for a photo. For lunch we stopped in the small village of Gongoling, a good ways up into the climb toward that day's destination of Tatopani. The guesthouse owner was delighted to see people on the trail and arranged two large plates of *dal bhat* to be brought to us before sneaking off and leaving us in the capable hands of his wife. While we were dining, some women came into town singing and dancing, accompanied by our host, who had a great big grin on his face.

We continued on to Tatopani, which translates as "hot water"—an apt name for hot springs. After asking if it was okay, we soaked our tired bodies in the warm rust-colored pool. We sat and talked with some of the locals through gestures and broken English and emerged from the waters feeling relaxed and rested.

The following morning we climbed through a rhododendron forest that occasionally broke to reveal awesome views of the Ganesh Himal. While gazing at the mountains I noticed a large troop of gray langur monkeys moving through the forest just ahead of us. We took some photos before continuing on to the picturesque town of Brimdang, which we fell in love with.

Offering excellent views of the Himalayas, Brimdang sits on the side of the mountain in green fields, with a small Buddhist monastery suspended above it on a rocky crag. Not much higher up is Nagthali Ghyang, the highest point of the trek (3,165 meters). Approaching this were some steep drops off the side of the trail, and I often felt like I was at the edge of the world. At the top was an almost 360-degree view of all the surrounding mountains, from Langtang and its adjacent peaks in the east to the Ganesh Himal in the west. At the north side was a small Buddhist monastery and a few guesthouses. As it was late February, snow here obscured the trail. Seeing our confusion, a pair of Buddhist monks assisted us in finding our way and guided us down toward the village of Thuman, where we spent the next night.

The monastery at Thuman was still performing rituals for Losar (Tibetan New Year) and occasionally the sound of horns and chanting emanated from it. Meanwhile the village was full of people performing their daily chores of pounding rice and weaving yarn. Animals gazed out from barnlike areas at the base of the homes, and the people above stared at us curiously from intricately carved wooden windows. From here we worked our way back down to the river valley and up near the Chinese border at Timure. It was a short walk to the Chinese border crossing at Rasuwagadhi, but the fort that once stood there is an uninspiring pile of rocks now, and there was little else to see.

On our last day we walked on a mix of new "road" and old hiking paths that took us back to Syaphru Besi. Walking past the prayer-flag-draped village of Lingling, we could hear the dynamite of Chinese road crews below in the valley by the river. The road from China hopes to bring trade through Nepal and into India. While I certainly can't blame people for wanting roads and other modern conveniences, it was a reminder that the world is always changing and what we see in the hills of Nepal today will not always be there to experience.

Between worrying about just how far the drop was off the edge of the road, I had time to think about this on the bus ride back to Kathmandu. The Tamang Heritage Trail was an excellent getaway from the normal tourist treks, and although all things inevitably change, it is for now an experience that still gives travelers a look at Nepal untouched by the passage of time.

### *Tamang Heritage Trail*

Brian recommends guides only when necessary, and in his opinion, this loop trek (which took five days) is best enjoyed independently. The most useful resource for this trek is an excellent map put out by Nepa Maps called "Langtang: Tamang Heritage Trail." The best time of year to do the trek is early March to early May and late September to early November.

### *Getting to Syaphru Besi*

From Kathmandu the bus ride is a brutal nine to eleven hours—for just 120 kilometers! The bus leaves around seven each morning from the street just northwest of Gongabu bus station, though tickets can be purchased at the station. Alternatively, you can hire a 4WD to take you, but it will set you back about $250, while the bus costs only $3.

### *Where to stay*

The community lodge is a little hard to find, being at the far end of the village, but it is much nicer than the village guesthouse. Mr. Dawa Nurpa Lama, who runs the lodge, went out of his way to make Brian and his wife feel at home—more so than anyone else they have encountered while trekking, and that's saying a lot!

## Jomsom Trail/ Annapurna

*Laurie Weed praises Girl Power on the Jomsom Trail*

After forty-eight hours of spinning through Kathmandu's Thamel District, I was tired and no longer certain I wanted to try the next planned phase of my trip: trekking. But on a tip from a friend, I hopped a flight to Pokhara and went straight to 3 Sisters, a women-owned company that trains female guides and porters to trek with other women. There, the calm and professional Nicky Chhetri listened carefully to my vague notions of what I wanted to do and came up with exactly the right plan for me. I spent the night at the 3 Sisters' cozy guesthouse, and the next morning I was off into the Himalayas to "go walking" with a twenty-year-old female porter named Batuli.

The first time I saw my new travel companion, I had a few concerns. I'm generally not the Outward Bound type, and I knew I would have to rely heavily on this petite, shy young woman. But once we started walking, Batuli's strength, skill, and confidence won me over. Although she was only a trainee, she set the perfect pace, kept an eye on me at all times, and knew before I did when I needed to rest or wasn't drinking enough water. As we ascended slowly through the diverse Annapurna mountain range, she taught me about the local flora, fauna, geology, and villages.

What fascinated me even more were her stories about her previous life in a small farming village in Jamu. After two of her schoolmates were "recruited" by Maoist guerrillas, never to be heard from again, her terrified parents took her out of school at age fourteen and kept her home on the farm. Two years later, when her province became increasingly unstable, she found herself boarding an airplane for the first time in her life and flying to the comparative metropolis of Pokhara, far away from everything and everyone that was familiar.

There, the Chhetri sisters educated and motivated her. Once she finished her mountaineering apprenticeship and learned basic English, she started working as a porter on group treks. Soon, she was sharing a small apartment in Pokhara with two friends from the program, earning a good wage, and continuing toward her goal of becoming a mountain guide.

"I love to be in the mountains," she told me, her eyes shining. "I am so happy I can learn to do this. I love this job because I learn so much."

For eleven days and nights, Batuli was my shadow—and when the walking was hard, she was my inspiration. If she can do it, I would chide myself several times a day, you can do it. She never stopped smiling, or watching out for me, or cheering me on. One morning, we ran into another 3 Sisters' group coming around the mountain the other way, through the famously difficult Thorong La Pass. All seven of the women looked trail weary but ecstatic. Over lunch, the other Westerners and I traded the usual trekkers' yarns: how high, how hard, how harrowing, but overwhelmingly, the stories we told reflected our gratitude for the unique privilege of experiencing Annapurna with these young Nepalese women.

Like everyone who has walked in the Himalayas, I'll always remember gazing up in reverence at the jagged, looming peaks. I'll keep the images of the stacked-stone houses scattered against the mountainside, and the beatific smiles of the Nepalese and Tibetan people I met along the way.

I might even retain the rhythm of my hiking boots thumping against ancient stone—all day, every day, up and up and up along the mountain's timeworn trails. If I close my eyes, I can still smell wood smoke and hear the jangling, snorting commotion of mule trains passing by; the low chanting of monks; the glacial rush of the Kali Gandaki; and the shrieks of runny-nosed children who bounded up the steep trails after me, demanding rupees and pens. I'll remember sweating up the "4,000 Steps" and then wobbling down the other side, calves sprung, and hauling myself up Poon Hill in the dark to watch the sun rise over the rooftop of the world.

But most of all, I will cherish the memories of walking with Batuli—my guide, my cheerleader and confidant, my little Nepalese sister from whom I learned so much. If I am ever lucky enough to return to the mountain, I can't think of anyone I'd rather go walking with.

### *3 Sisters Adventure Trekking*

The Chhetri sisters organize and customize treks for individual women travelers or any size group of women, from "teahouse" trekking in the environmentally and culturally rich Annapurna region to camping and mountaineering trips on the more challenging routes around Langtang, Upper Mustang, and Everest. All treks are designed to be environmentally and socially conscious.

www.3sistersadventure.com

### *About the sisters*

Entrepreneurs Lucky, Dicky, and Nicky Chhetri have been blazing trails in the trekking industry since 1994, hiring women from all over Nepal (often from poor minority villages) and turning them into professional guides and porters for women trekkers. Through empowering, educating, and supporting women in a traditionally male-dominated field, the Chhetris have built a wildly successful business and the award-winning nonprofit Empowering Women of Nepal Project.

## Annapurna Region

## *Renee Robertson kids around on the Annapurna Circuit*

Never in our wildest dreams did my husband and I think we'd find ourselves trekking through the Himalayan mountains, and certainly not with two little girls in tow. Would Rylee (eight) and Raegan (seven) be able to handle five, six, seven, even eight hours of trekking a day? Having arrived in Kathmandu, we'd soon find out.

After a good night's rest and a hearty hotel breakfast, we caught a

Yeti Airlines "puddle jumper" flight to Pokhara. At the dinky Pokhara airport, we collected our bags and went outside to look for our guide, Dambar Raj. He spotted us first, and welcomed us each with a silky yellow scarf. He also gave us two large duffel bags—all the space we were allowed for our personal belongings. Silly me, I brought a hair dryer. Needless to say, that was left behind.

It was a couple hours' drive to the Annapurna Circuit trailhead. Because we had the two children with us, we had not only our guide but also a pair of porters, Marni and Dhaka. They loaded our bags on their backs and off we went ... for about ten minutes. Suddenly, Raegan's nose began to bleed profusely. Already the altitude was taking effect. It was quite a scene as curious local children gathered around while I was wishing I'd brought more wet wipes. Just minutes into our trek, and already we'd used an entire package stopping the river of blood.

Back on the trail, as we made our way toward Tikhedhunga, the scenery was spectacular—stony paths, Nepalese women in brightly colored saris working in the fields, and stunning terraced hillsides. The kids were doing great, and they were tickled to discover small "snack shops" here and there where they could get a Snickers or even a Twix. But about two hours from our stopping point, our luck ran out as it started to rain. At first just a little, but then it progressed into a full-on downpour.

We broke out the rain ponchos and plastic bags to cover our backpacks. We could handle the rain fine, but suddenly found ourselves in a tricky situation. A small river separated us at point A from point B. Our trusty guide tiptoed his way across, giving each stepping stone a "test jiggle" before proceeding. Our porters followed after him, secured our bags on the other side of the river, and crossed back over to fetch Rylee and Raegan. Our girls looked at us with wide-eyed trepidation when they realized they too were going to be piggy-backed over the slippery rocks across the river. Of course they made it across safe and sound, and most importantly, *dry*. That's more than I can say for Rick and me and our sloshing wet shoes and socks.

Five hours after our departure from the trailhead, we arrived at Indra Guesthouse in Tikhedhunga, where we woke the next morning to a beautiful blue sky, bright sunshine, and our most challenging day of the trek. We started off with an Indiana Jones-style suspension bridge that Rick and the girls thought was "cool." I, on the other hand, discovered my fear of heights—or maybe just a fear of suspension bridges. We safely scampered across what I would later find out was the first of many such bridges along the way.

About six hours into the trek, having ascended more than four thousand feet in elevation to nearly ten thousand feet, we turned the corner to find the biggest, most vibrantly colored rhododendrons we'd ever seen.

Being from the Pacific Northwest of the United States, we were used to nearly everyone having rhododendron shrubs in their yards. These were not shrubs! Bright red, dark pink, and deep purple rhododendron trees filled the small forest. This was surely the day's highlight, we thought, little knowing what was to come.

As we crossed over a wooden footbridge, the girls screeched to a halt when they realized that the bridge, the trees, the plants, and the ground all around us were covered in ladybugs. A little girl's delight! Rylee and Raegan had red and black ladybugs crawling all over them and could literally scoop up handfuls of the sweet little insects.

Finally, it was time to move on, and soon the sky began to darken. Sure enough, the rain began to fall. We were nearly an hour from the guesthouse and hoped we could make it without a drenching, but the raindrops turned into enormous balls of hail, pelting us with such force that they stung even through our thick rain gear. The girls were getting upset, as thunder began to rumble and the hail pounded down harder. Thankfully it didn't last long, and we finally walked up the path to the Sunny Hotel in Ghorepani—as the sun came out, and with it a gorgeous rainbow. Our reward for enduring an hour of hail.

Hot showers, a roaring fire, spaghetti, enchiladas, and Twix rounded out the night, which ended too soon, as Rick and I had chosen to make the 4 a.m. trek up neighboring Poon Hill for the sunrise. When we returned, we found that the girls had just woken up and were playing a game of UNO with Dhaka. While the previous day was an uphill day, day 3 would be a downhill day, and at the end of it, at the Hotel Grand View in Tatopani, we came to the conclusion that we preferred going up over going down. Rylee and Raegan spent the evening teaching two French boys their age how to play UNO, and before long they had a few others joining in. And we thought our kids would go crazy without TV.

Back on the trail, day 4 provided a combination of up and downhill, as well as copious amounts of butterflies in a kaleidoscope of colors for the girls to chase. We made our way into Ghandruk in just under six hours and spent the last night of our mountain journey at the Trekkers Inn. We were most impressed with this guesthouse. We actually had an attached bathroom—with a Western toilet of our own that worked!

The final day of our trek dawned with glorious blue sky and a view of Annapurna's stunning south peaks. Because things had been going so well with the kids, we questioned our decision to take a five-day trek versus a seven-day trek. But it turned out we'd made the right choice. We were about two hours out from the end of the trail when Rylee started to look a little punchy. We didn't have a thermometer with us, but my mother's intuition told me she was running a fever. She had taken so much pride in the fact that she had walked every step of our journey, and although her spirit was still strong, her body was weak, and she gave in and let Marni hoist her up on his shoulders. Raegan too began to tire, so up she went on Dambar's shoulders. Poor Dhaka got stuck carrying our two enormous bags.

We knew how much the girls wanted to finish our trek on foot, and when the trail end came into sight, we had them get down and walk the rest of the way out. We did it! Five days trekking through the Himalayas with two little girls. We were thrilled to be done and looked forward to a nice hotel, hot showers, and working toilets. But we would miss the glory of the mountains—not just the beautiful scenery that surrounded us, but the beautiful people we met along the way. When we reached the van for our ride back to Pokhara, we celebrated with a group "high five." Needless to say, at the Fish Tail Lodge on Phewa Lake, we all slept like logs that night.

### *A helping hand*

Renee adds: Rick and I wondered if the girls would soon tire of the daylong treks, and we were so thankful for Dambar. He would take one or sometimes both of them and lead the way. They would often be half an hour ahead of us, and we'd catch up to find them sitting at a trailside snack stand sharing a Coke. Once, Raegan needed a break so Dambar added his pack to Marni's already loaded back and gave her a piggyback up one of the tougher points of elevation. While we don't know if other guides and porters are as helpful when it comes to children, ours were most impressive. Dambar Raj Adhikari can be contacted through Lineup Travels & Trekking in Pokhara.

adhikaridamber@hotmail.com
www.lineupnepal.com

### *Creature comforts*

When Renee's family approached the first guesthouse on their trek, Raegan, the youngest, said, "We're staying here? It's so small!" Having never been trekking before, the girls had no idea what a guesthouse would be like. They'd been spoiled by five-star hotels and resorts and were taken by surprise. Especially when they discovered that everyone would not be all together in one room because each room had only two small mattresses on a handmade bed frame consisting of a piece of plywood and some two-by-fours. Later, at the Indra Guesthouse, they were able to share a room, where they huddled together since the walls weren't exactly airtight. Crisp, cold air poured in through the slits and cracks around the windows and doors. It was here that Renee was particularly happy to have brought her own sheets—a recommendation from a friend prior to the trip. Although the guesthouses appeared to be clean and tidy, she says it definitely felt good crawling into bed with her own sheets and pillowcase.

### *Shopping on the go*

Being a bit of a shopaholic, Renee loved the fact that she could shop along the trail. As they passed through little villages, she found an array of trinkets and knickknacks, wool hats and socks, and even some jewelry for sale. Shopping at ten thousand feet. Now that's what she calls a "high" high!

### *Fish Tail Lodge*

Pokhara

www.fishtail-lodge.com

### *According to Rylee*

Nepal was one of my most favorite trips ever. I loved everything about it, especially when it started hailing on us, even though I started to cry. I cried because it hurt. I also liked seeing snow since we were living in a hot country (Sri Lanka). I really liked that there were lots of ladybugs. I liked it a lot when we stopped for a candy bar to get more energy. One day a lady from Nepal dressed me up in the native clothes. It was kind of embarrassing but it was fun too. I thought trekking was going to be really hard and boring and then it turned out to be really fun! I would love to trek in Nepal again someday.

## *Sherry Ott finds her rhythm in the Annapurna Sanctuary*

Get up at six thirty. Pack everything by seven. Eat breakfast. Hike from seven thirty to four or five. Unpack and change out of sweaty clothes. Choose dinner from the same menu as the night before—even though we're at a different teahouse in a different village. Drink a big thermos of tea. Put on all of the warm clothes I have with me and go to bed at nine.

Routine formed within days on the Annapurna Circuit hiking trail, but other things were in constant states of change. My dad and I were making our way to Manang (via Chame and Pisang), the rest spot on the twenty-one-day trek up the mountains. As we trekked upward, our bodies tried to adjust and adapt, and the initial signs of thrusting ourselves into this high-altitude climate were beginning to show. I slept restlessly, tossing and turning. This was accompanied by crazy, vivid dreams that woke me in a cold sweat. All symptoms of existing with not enough oxygen. I wondered if I would ever sleep soundly again.

The environment was also ever changing. We hiked through terraced rice fields to windy valleys filled with pine trees. We entered a world of snow-capped peaks. If I closed my eyes and sucked in a big nose of air, I was transported to the American northeast, with its smell of pine and crisp fall air. Colors exploded in red, yellow, and burnt orange on the mountainsides. The comforting aroma of wood fires wafted throughout the villages.

The temperature was shifting too. Every day I would begin with yet another layer of clothing, and each night I would sleep with more on. I tried not to use all of my clothes too early on, since then I'd have nothing left to layer with when it was really cold. Teahouse lodging never had any heat (and rarely electricity), and by day 6 I was sleeping in long underwear, a wool sweater, a wool hat, wool socks, and a scarf—all of this tucked into a sleep sheet and a down sleeping bag. I was the size of the abominable snowman!

Along with this, my muscles were undergoing transformation. They screamed out in pain each night and morning thanks to overuse and undertraining. This is where the Tiger Balm came in. We'd get out our little container and put it in one of our pockets for about an hour to warm it up. Then my dad and I would take turns putting the balm on all of our aches and pains—and there were many. After a few days even my sleeping bag smelled like Tiger Balm.

Because of everything our bodies were going through, we started reading up on AMS (acute mountain sickness). We were now at over twenty-seven hundred meters. This is when your body starts to say, "What the hell are you doing? Retreat to where I can breathe!" Since I'd actually had severe altitude sickness before when I failed to summit Kilimanjaro, I was concerned about getting it again. The memories flooded back—delirious sleep, asthmalike breathing, headaches, puking.

I intended to do everything possible to make it over Thorong La Pass, and I didn't want a little thing like lack of oxygen stopping me. But our breath was heavy and slow already, and even though the hiking was flat and relatively easy, my legs were tired, my bag seemed heavier, and blisters were forming on my heels. What should have been easy seemed hard, so we took our time and tried to make lots of stops. Still there were more than enough moments that made it all worthwhile. As we trekked toward Manang we had a long walk through a winding valley where we began to see beautiful, high snowy peaks. Despite our physical agony, there was something amazing about standing on solid ground at three thousand meters and peering at peaks that are seventy-five hundred meters high.

As we continued through the valley we were exposed to the daily life of the Nepalese. We came across locals out harvesting, carrying large bundles of hay for their animals. The basic rule was, if you were old enough to walk, you were old enough to haul hay. Yaks started to appear, and so did the signs for yak cheese. People cut up lumber, thrashed millet, and plowed fields. Everyone was working hard on these cold fall days, following the rhythms of the season, just as my dad and I were finally hitting our own rhythm on the Annapurna trail.

### *Finding your rhythm*

Sherry adds: When it comes to finding your rhythm on the trail, like anything else related to traveling in a developing country, you just have to be patient and let everything around you sink in. It took me about three or four days to get used to trekking and establish a bit of a routine.

## *Alessandra Kim avoids avalanches in Annapurna*

Like me, my husband is an avid traveler. When we met we compared our travel wish lists and happily found Nepal at the top of both. So it was fitting that we took our first trip to Nepal together. Our objective was to get up close and personal with the great Himalayas, and we decided to trek through the famous Annapurna Sanctuary.

The sanctuary is one of the most popular treks in Nepal because it is uniquely surrounded by ten mountains. All ten peaks, including the great Machhapuchhare—called the "Fish Tail" because of the shape of its peak—soar to more than six thousand meters above sea level. The sanctuary is also considered a sacred Hindu site, shrouded in myth and much revered by the local Gurung people. Unfamiliar with this culture and never having done any serious trekking, we anticipated a true adventure.

We knew, as most trekkers do, that the cool dry season of late autumn is prime trekking time—the monsoons are over, and the skies are clear. But we chose to go a bit later, at the end of December, in order to avoid the crowds. That decision greatly affected our journey.

Our twelve-day trip started off in Pokhara, the popular, dusty resort town on Phewa Lake. From Pokhara we climbed dirt trails, navigated stone paths, and crossed shaky bridges through towns with names like Landrung, Dhampus, Deuralim, and Ghandrung. Along the way, we encountered friendly villagers, beautiful children, deep gorges, ancient houses, weathered prayer flags, water buffalo, many donkeys, and of course, stunning views of the great peaks.

It seemed that some paths went right through private property, but instead of being disturbed, villagers were always gracious, often inviting us into their homes for tea or just to warm up in front of their stoves. On narrow trails, many locals stood aside to let us pass, even when they were carrying heavy loads. And everywhere we were greeted with a friendly "*namaste.*" The Nepalese do not address each other by name, but by terms that describe their relationships with one another. For example, a woman might be called *didi* (older sister) or *bahini* (little sister), depending on her relationship with the speaker. This tradition includes foreigners and instantly made us feel welcome and part of the community.

It takes about four days to hike from Pokhara to the entrance of the Annapurna Sanctuary. When we were less than two days away from our goal, we began to run into locals and Sherpas returning from the area. Each person we met along the trail advised us to turn back. There had been heavy snowfall in the months preceding our trek. This meant the high possibility of avalanches. Our guide agreed with the advice, and we set out the next morning on a detour.

In the late afternoon, we reached Gurjung, a small village southwest of the sanctuary. By the time we arrived, the porters who walked ahead had set up our tents on the grounds of the local teahouse, and the cooks worked their magic with the portable stove. Still, we were all in somber moods. But the locals were not. By nightfall word of our arrival had spread throughout the village, and dozens of residents made their way to the teahouse. As we sat and socialized, an impromptu show was performed. Garlands of marigolds were bestowed upon us, and everyone sang and danced well into the night. Just a few hours earlier we were begrudging the snowfall and our detour. Now, I was grateful, for it had given me my favorite memory of Nepal.

*Staying in Gurjung*

Should you find yourself in Gurjung, the teahouse where Alessandra stayed is easy to find ... it's the only one in town!

## *Sherry Ott faces her fears in the Annapurna Sanctuary*

What is it about growing older that changes us? Not only do our feet get bigger, but we tend to develop irrational fears. I've been aware of it for some time now—my growing fear of heights. As each year goes by I become more like Jimmy Stewart in *Vertigo* ... high up, I freeze, the world seems to spin around me, and I have to talk myself through the panic. So why on earth did I think that a trekking trip in the Himalayas would be a good idea?

After hiking for a day, my dad and I reached the main Annapurna trail. This tourist route had little villages peppered along it offering an endless supply of drinks, fruit, food, people watching, and lodging. The downside was that it was like a superhighway. On day 1 we were surrounded by locals, and from there on out we were surrounded by tourists. We had chosen to hike the trail at the best time of the year (October/November), since the weather was perfect—no more monsoon, and the freezing cold had yet to come. No wonder everyone else was there at the same time.

As we took off and crested the hill from Bahundanda, we dipped down into a stunning green valley of rice terraces. The green grass met the blue sky. The landscape seemed to explode. It didn't take long for trekkers and porters to start passing us. They had walking poles—klink, klink, klink on the rocks as they came up behind us. As groups walked briskly past us, I wondered, *Why are they in such a hurry*? We were in beautiful scenery nestled among the Himalayas, and we had all traveled presumably long distances to get there, but I seldom saw any of the people look up from the trail. They just maintained their pace, all so they could get to the next village and ... wait for the next day to begin? Granted, I might dawdle too much and take too many pictures, but I subscribe to slow travel I guess. I want to soak it all in.

Every time we seemed to gain some elevation on the trail, we promptly turned around and lost it. Up and down, up-up and down, up-up-up and down. We also ran into some trail issues—rock slides. They would force us to use alternate routes, often sending us way up a steep mountainside with loose rocks or down to a bridge to cross over the river.

One of the bridges looked as if it were made of toothpicks that had been slapped together a few hours before we arrived. I watched others cross over it slowly. It looked easy enough, and I waited my turn. I walked gingerly onto the bamboo poles, which creaked and flexed with each step. All I could hear was the water rushing below me as I tried to balance on the three poles. I rejoiced silently when I stepped on solid ground again, little realizing the greater challenges to my fear of heights that lay ahead.

If it wasn't rock slides slowing us up, it was road construction. Yes, sadly, a road was being built on the Annapurna Circuit. When I first read about it, I was quite concerned about what it would do to the trail. However, once I got there and saw it in person, I realized that the road would progress even slower than U.S. universal health care legislation. You may wonder how a road is built in a third world country, high up in the mountains through solid rock on a cliff face. Wonder no more: five men, a sledge hammer, and a shovel. Yup, that road won't be finished in my lifetime.

The road construction led to some entertaining photography and videos, but it also led to obstacles that sent my adrenaline through the roof. As I stopped to get footage of this slow, laborious project, my dad and our guide, Bishnu, went on ahead. They had long since grown tired of waiting for me and my camera. I got the footage, joked with the locals, and left with a smile. But when I rounded the corner the smile quickly disappeared, and my heart pounded in my chest.

The blasting for the birth of the road left rock slides and a narrow little loose dirt trail that danced along the edge of the cliff face. I don't mind climbing; I don't mind descending;

I don't mind carrying heavy packs. But I hate narrow trails near ledges that could send me plummeting to my death. This new trail was about a meter wide, but in my terrified mind it looked like so much less. As I took a few steps, I felt as if I were hanging off the side of a mountain. I slowed down and took each step as if it were my first ... and sorta my last.

My brain raced with thoughts of everything that could go wrong. I tried to tune out the sound of the rushing river seven hundred feet below me. I was acutely aware of the big pack on my back and how it could throw off my center of balance and leave me nowhere to step to recover. Time slowed down, and I slowly took each step, concentrating so hard I began to talk to myself.

I was thrilled to catch up with my dad and Bishnu, as we entered the village of Dharapani. I wanted to make sure they safely made it through that section of the trail. Needless to say, the only thing that would have made that narrow passage worse would have been to watch my seventy-three-year-old dad cross it. Then I really would have been a basket case, rather than just a crazy acrophobic hiking the highest mountains in the world.

### *Facing your fears*

Sherry adds: Coping with a fear of heights is different for everyone. For me, I honestly do talk to myself—taking on the role of my own coach. I remind myself that I know how to walk, and that a trail is no different than a sidewalk. It also helps to focus on the trail about two meters in front of me. Not sure why this works, but it does!

## Solukhumbu District

### *Lone Mørch practices patience in the Solukhumbu District*

Trekking easily becomes an obsession in Nepal. No matter where you look, a beautiful peak will tempt you with its grandeur, its challenge, and its promising panorama. As will the stories of the legendary climbers such as Hillary and Mallory, who forged the first paths up the highest mountain of the world.

Over years of hiking in various regions and climbing a few nontechnical peaks, I, like so many before me, succumbed to the desire of becoming a real mountaineer. The fact that of the thousands who've climbed Mt. Everest, more than a hundred are still up there frozen eternally didn't dampen my dreams. That said, for my first "real mountain" I decided to start with Imja Tse. A popular trekking peak of 6,189 meters, it is also called Island Peak because it floats among the Lhotse, Makalu, and Ama Dablam mountains.

Climbing a trekking peak doesn't require extensive preparation, so with my brother and boyfriend of the time in tow, we met our guide and two Sherpas, whom we hired in Kathmandu, at the foot of Imja Tse. Our guides led us, fed us, and provided safety ropes on the steep parts up the mountainside, and after many arduous hours of "one step at a time," we finally reached the top. The peak was indeed an island, floating in a sea of white—white snow, white ice, white sky. We tasted what heaven might be like during those ten minutes of pure white silence. And thus began my love affair with Solukhumbu.

The Solukhumbu District, where Imja Tse resides, is for connoisseur walkers, amateur climbers, mountaineers, and extremists alike. Despite the Everest hype and crowded trails, I've returned to that region because I like the freedom it offers. You don't need a guide, you don't need a tent, you don't even need to carry food. The trails are so self-evident it would take some effort to get lost, and there are plenty of villages with teahouses for overnight stays along the way, complete with cooks serving sturdy meals. Around the tables, or even better, fireplaces, I met people I still know today. I drank *raksi* with tired porters and played cards and shared life stories with travelers from all thinkable backgrounds. I talked and walked with just plain crazy people, and I even encountered mountaineers whose lives ended only six weeks later on Everest.

The first three days of trekking Solukhumbu are always painful: my muscles hurt, and the load on my back feels unfamiliar and awkward. On the fourth day, though, the straps that dig into my shoulders and hips become part of me, and I find my stride. The pendular movement of my arms and legs settles into a natural rhythm. My body and mind align with the surroundings. It's what I love so much about hiking—walking, wandering, wondering to the sound of the wind swooshing down the corridors of the valleys and brushing up against the mountainsides, and the occasional "clok, clok" of the bells dangling around the donkeys' necks.

The trails absorb everything. In high altitude, which often makes its presence known in the form of headache, dizziness, slight nausea, and lack of appetite, there seems to be little or no energy for engaging in any significant discussion. It's as if I become pure body, yet my mind is constantly coaxing me forward, upward. I've often compared two weeks of trekking to a Vipassana meditation retreat. I return to the world empty, light, and as added bonus, with a much firmer behind.

You can of course experience this on any extended trail, but to me, the Solukhumbu District is especially unique. Within ten days I can move through several geographical zones, from a temperate to an alpine landscape, still wearing shorts on good days, and find myself amid the tallest mountains in the world, so close I can almost touch them. Just being there—heart pounding, heaving for air, feeling the chill from the calving glaciers, and pondering the massive cathedrals of ice and rock that come before me—is worth the effort. I don't have to climb the peaks, not even the simple ones like Gokyo, Chukhung, or Kala Patthar, to feel a sense of achievement. Patiently, persistently, I just have to get myself to Solukhumbu.

*Getting to Solukhumbu*

Lone flew by helicopter to Lukla and hiked in to the Solukhumbu trails. Both airplane and helicopter flights can be booked through any tour agency in Kathmandu. If you want to hike in and out of Lukla from Kathmandu, add at least another ten days to your trip.

*Everest news*

Lone suggests checking out the following website for comprehensive news and information about Mt. Everest.

www.everestnews.com

## Namche Bazaar

*Jacqueline Sonderling takes a break in Namche Bazaar*

I was in Namche Bazaar on my way to Tengboche.

Doesn't that sound just so ... exotic? And adventurous?

For the uninitiated, Namche Bazaar is the main trading center in the Solukhumbu District. It's nestled in thick forests, surrounded by majestic snow-capped Himalayas. It's a tough climb to get there—but worth the effort. You climb a little, crossing rickety bridges. And then you start to really climb. And climb. And climb. And it is steep. Very steep.

Although the trail is hard, the surroundings make the work worthwhile. At one point, across a small tree-filled gully, we stared out at a stark, sharp mountain. Down its angular face were what in warmer weather would be waterfalls. They were frozen by the December cold. It was breathtaking. That is, it took away whatever breath I had left.

Up the switchbacked hillside of the Sherpa homeland we climbed, keeping pace with what seemed like dozens of porters, loaded down with goods. One of the main attractions of Namche is the Saturday market, and these people were all on their way.

The porters' packs were amazing, even to Kalu, our trek *sirdar* (leader), who had made this trip forty or fifty times over the years. The bulk of the weight of their loads rises above them, towers of goods that are often piled as high as the porters are tall. The whole load is braced against the forehead with a strap. In addition to what's in the soaring baskets on their backs, they carry cases of beer and Coke, gallon cans of soybean oil, boxes of noodles, and such stacked on top. I counted up to eight cases of Carlsberg beer on a single porter. Another had four of the soybean oil cans, plus a couple of boxes of noodles. And, of course, there was the occasional animal carcass, the meat dried and preserved.

The porters also carried walking sticks with thick, slightly curved handles. At first I thought that was odd. The porters I'd seen on my last trip carried heavy loads but no walking sticks. Then I saw these guys lean on the sticks when they took a few minutes' break. They braced their butts against the curved handles, able to take a rest without putting down their loads.

In early afternoon, we arrived at the "city limits" of Namche, with another half hour's steep climb ahead of us to get to our lodge. The walk through town was fascinating. We passed a *konditorei* (a German-style bakery)—just about the last thing I expected to find on the side of a mountain in Nepal! I made a mental note to come back later.

The following morning, Kalu got us going at about eight. The famed Saturday market was starting. The shopping paradise I had envisioned for the last seven thousand feet was waiting, with the treasures I would find and later display nonchalantly to my friends. "Oh, this?" I would casually say, "I picked it up on the side of a hill in Nepal."

Unfortunately, the market mostly consisted of basic household goods for the Sherpas, which, of course, made perfect sense. It was the cooking oil, beer, and other items we had seen coming up the hill on the porters' backs. There was also fruit, lentils, and clothing. We bought some bananas, took the obligatory pictures—and left.

Rather than go back to our lodge for breakfast, a couple of us returned to the row of shops in the center of town where I'd seen the bakery the day before. Hermann Helmer's turned out to be a top-notch place started by a German entrepreneur. In the dining room of this sunny café, we selected delicacies from a European-style glass case. The choices seemed endless: sticky buns, bread, cookies, doughnuts, chocolate or cheese-filled pastries, chocolate cake, and pizza, to name just a few. Then we sat down with our treats over cups of coffee and espresso.

Not one for giving up on shopping, I hooked up with Kalu and one of our guides, Kul. They were on their way to the Khumba campground to shop. I tagged along, looking forward to a lesson in how the locals do it.

Almost every Khumba we met tried to sell us necklaces made with a strange-looking stone. Later, I found out these black-and-white beads are called *dzi* and are considered precious. They have a design that looks like eyes, and the more eyes the stone has, the more expensive and auspicious it is. After shopping for rugs and jewelry, I had just one last bit of business to attend to before heading back to our lodge: a trip to the Namche post office.

I followed the signs to a long, two-story stone building with a small door at the very far end—so small I had to duck to get through it. Once inside, I was in some kind of storage space filled with firewood. There were no lights, so at first I couldn't see the wooden stairs off to the side, leading to the second floor. At the top of the stairs, a small room was partitioned off with plywood. The post office.

A young Sherpa postmistress sat behind an old metal desk, carefully checking the mail set in front of her. She took my single postcard, examined it closely to make sure it had enough postage, and off it went on its journey to Los Angeles, which seemed a universe away as I headed back through town, gearing up for the next stage of my trek.

### *Getting to Namche*

Go to page 65.

### *Organized trekking*

For her trip, Jacqueline used Peter Owens Asian Treks. She says that it was reasonably priced and excellent. Peter works in conjunction with Crystal Mountain Treks.

www.crystalmountaintreks.com

### *Where to stay in Namche*

The wood-and-stone Sona Lodge is somewhat deluxe and exclusive, relatively speaking. There are only five rooms, plus a larger "dorm" room that the trekking staff can share. According to Jacqueline, the hands-down best thing about the lodge (even better than the TV and VCR!) was the shower. One hundred rupees bought about ten minutes of steaming hot water pounding down in a good, strong spray from the outdoor shower. The lodge is located at the top of Namche. It's a bit far from the center of town for traipsing up and down in the dark (the stone steps are steep), but it's also away from the noise and will provide a restful atmosphere with great views of the surrounding mountains. And in case you've forgotten anything, the lodge also sells woolen socks, caps, shawls, sweaters, and so on.

### *In-house dining*

The restaurant at the Sona Lodge is quite good, offering a wide selection of dishes, from Tibetan *momos* to yak steak. You can also get drinks as mild as ginger tea or as potent as the locally brewed liquor, *raksi.*

## Everest Base Camp

*Linzi Barber shares Everest Base Camp pros and cons*

"Ten minutes to landing," came the call, as the seatbelt sign was illuminated and I stared out the window. Hypnotized by the snow-covered Himalayas stretching beyond the Kathmandu Valley, I contemplated the enormity of my plan. I'd come to Nepal to trek to Everest Base Camp.

An hour after reaching baggage claim, our luggage still hadn't arrived. Despite our silence, I knew we were sharing thoughts of the walking boots that we'd spent the past six months breaking in. Finally, we spotted our battered rucksacks, and with a sigh of relief followed the heat and noise to the chaotic exit.

After less than two days in Kathmandu—seeing the sights, catching up on our sleep, meeting our guide and fellow trekkers, stocking up on candy, and, more importantly, toilet roll for the journey—we were back at the airport. With our walking boots on, day packs full, and mineral water in bottles with purification tablets, we boarded a fourteen-seat Twin Otter. As we left the haze of the city behind, cabin service on our thirty-minute flight consisted of cotton wool and a sweet. The plane swooped like a bird, so close to the Himalayas that I felt I could reach out and touch them.

We veered onto the runway at Lukla, narrowly avoiding the wall at the end. We stepped from the plane into a sea of porters, and I gulped the mountain air, refreshing after the smog of Kathmandu. We were at just twenty-eight hundred meters, and I had religiously taken my altitude sickness medicine—still, I felt apprehensive about the unknown challenges that lay ahead.

The following six days I experienced everything from sunburn to a sleepless night during which ice fell off the window inside the teahouse and soaked my sleeping bag. But by Lobuje and a 5 a.m. wake-up call to watch the sunrise over Mt. Everest, such discomforts were forgotten. As were the vast amounts of bland noodle soup we ate, supplemented with tinned tuna and SPAM. It was the hospitality of the Nepalese people that stayed with me, consistent at every restaurant, food stall, and teahouse, as they welcomed us like family with their cries of "*namaste.*" We frequently left small villages like the Pied Piper, with children of various ages trailing behind us.

The day before our final push to base camp, we were offered the chance to summit Kala Patthar, billed as the best place to photograph the peak that I'd come all this way to see. The going was tough, the snow swirling all around us, but despite blizzard conditions, we made it and were rewarded by the clouds parting like curtains as I struggled to sit upright in the wind and take the photo that I would so proudly show my friends and family on my return. Hand in hand with my guide, I literally ran back to Gorak Shep. With the snow still pounding down, it was getting dark, but suddenly the next day's goal of base camp, at 5,365 meters, now seemed achievable.

To our surprise, trekking from Gorak Shep to base camp turned out to be the least interesting day in terms of scenery. Despite the 360-degree view of glistening mountains all around us, we were walking through a channel of rocks. There was none of the lush greenery we had enjoyed so far, and morale was mixed. But this last stretch was why we had come all this way, and we cheered when we reached a sign proclaiming, "Base Camp this way." We stopped for photos, to prove we'd made it this far.

The final going was tough. Two nights of sleeping at over five thousand meters was taking its toll, and the eerie silence around us was broken only by the thud of boots pounding the baked ground and the occasional crack of a distant avalanche.

"Stop here," our guide commanded. Tents of Korean and U.S. teams preparing for an ascent came into view at almost the same moment as the peak of Mt. Everest rose beyond the Khumbu Icefall, totally clear from the clouds. Finally, we had arrived at base camp, and I have to be honest—uninspiring doesn't even come close to describing it. While I felt fantastic, we were standing in what was basically a pile of rubble with no area flat enough to pitch a tent on. We even struggled to find somewhere to sit for our impromptu picnic of pomegranates, cheese, and crackers.

After we toasted each other with bitter purified water, it was time to turn back. Although we'd achieved our goal, no one could even crack a smile at the thought of the walk we still had ahead of us. The cold was fierce, the wind burned my face, and walking through the rocks required my total concentration. Nobody was talking, and I willed Gorak Shep to come into view. Finally, at around four, with darkness falling fast, we stumbled into the Snowland Inn. Several cups of tea and Mars bars later, the realization of what we had accomplished hit us, and our spirits soared, reaching their highest point.

Exhausted, I was hoping for a decent night's sleep, but my sun-blistered and wind-burned face put paid to that. The following morning as we set out for our four-day downward trek back to Lukla, I relished my accomplishment but was already setting new goals: a toilet I could sit on, a hot shower, and clean clothes.

### *Getting to Everest Base Camp*

From Kathmandu, flights are available to Lukla Airport (Tenzing-Hillary Airport) every day. Sita Air, Tara Air, and Agni Air are among the most reliable for this twenty-five-minute flight. Expect delays in the rainy season. When you book a trek with a tour company, the company will generally book your flight for you. Once inside Sagarmatha National Park you will need to show your passport and pay the 1,000 Nepali rupee entry fee. This fee is generally not covered by the guide companies. For more information on getting to Everest Base Camp, go to page 33.

*Snowland Inn*

www.snowlandhighestinn.com

## Singalila Ridge

*Cameron Burns sees the light on the Singalila Ridge*

I stumble over the sleeping bags strewn across the floor, accidentally kicking a few snoring souls as I make my way to the door of the hostel, faint light guiding my way. The air is smoky and heavy with the odor of *chapatis* and tea. My fellow traveler, a Brit named Steve, follows close behind, his hand resting lightly against my back in the darkness. I reach the door and gently tug it open.

Cool air rushes in, carrying with it the scent of hydrangeas and the sound of faraway voices. Then we see it, an enormous white pyramid, taller than everything around us, including the trees—Kanchenjunga, the world's third-highest mountain.

We're at a place called Sandakphu, a tiny outpost halfway along a roughly hundred-mile trek that joins the tiny settlements of Manebhanjan, Tonglu, and Phalut. The trek takes in parts of the Singalila Ridge, which also forms the India-Nepal border here. The Ganges watershed is on the west side, the Brahmaputra's is to the east.

Steve and I scramble up to the top of a small hill and soak in the entire panorama. The 8,000-meter peaks of Everest, Lhotse, and Malekhu are off to the left, and a peak in Bhutan, the 7,315-meter Jomolhari, is off to the right. Straight ahead, almost in our faces, is the massive south side of Kanchenjunga.

There's a funny thing about the light here, which, as veteran mountaineers and photographers, both Steve and I have noticed. Although it's the same crystal-clear light we've experienced in other high alpine regions such as Colorado, Switzerland, and Peru, here it's especially intense, as if we're looking at everything on a high-definition television screen. Objects seem to explode with color—the deepest reds, the brightest oranges—as if they are all hooked up to some massive electricity source. Every traveler knows it's the smells, good and bad, that sharpen the South Asia experience and latch to the memory files, but here, on the Singalila Ridge, there's a much stronger case for optics.

Steve and I had been invited on this trip, the Mt. Everest Challenge Marathon, by the creator of the race, Mr. C. S. Pandey. But during a quick organizational meeting several days earlier in Mirik, West Bengal, we'd learned that the several dozen runners were all writing about the experience for various magazines. None of them had a photographer, and Steve and I, seeing an opportunity (and the chance to make a little cash), volunteered to fill the void. After all, it was going to be the photos that made their articles, regardless of what they wrote. Hell, words weren't going to do this "story" justice.

Our silent vigil before the peaks was interrupted by a jeep roaring along the rough road that the race followed. We flagged it down and climbed aboard, diesel fumes choking us and the runners who followed behind. We bounced along the road and barked at the driver when a particularly appealing composition of the race route, Mt. Everest, and a docile gaur came into view. We hustled to set up our gear, and as the first runner—a wildly successful novelist by the name of Michael Collins—came around the corner, we started clicking away. (One of my images of Michael would later make it into the London *Times*.)

After the herd of runners had passed, Steve and I started walking along the road, which was sporadically dotted with small buildings inhabited by shepherds. These were similar to establishments I'd encountered in Europe, where the farmers have set up restaurants in old farmhouses to serve wandering tourists. Steve and I stopped at the first and drank several cups of tea. Satisfied, we walked a few more miles and found another farmhouse-cum-café. Another cup of tea. Another walk. Copy, paste, repeat. Many times. Toward the end of the day, a jeep came by, picking up stragglers. We climbed aboard and were taken to the next overnight stop, another rough hostel.

There, runners sat in the rooms, sipping tea solemnly, sharing hushed war stories, and honestly, seeming generally miserable. One fellow, a man from Iran, had tripped and broken his nose. He would have looked almost comical if he weren't so gloomy. A woman from Eastern Europe had a slicing wound on her leg. No one was smiling.

"Did you see those Nepalese guys carrying the sacks using their foreheads?" I asked one runner.

"No, I saw the mountains, but that was about it," came the response.

"Did you see the gaur around that small lake?" I asked another.

"No, where was that?" he replied.

The runners were obviously pushing themselves to the extreme. As climbers, Steve and I have had our share of difficult challenges in beautiful places, but we had to wonder about this particular journey. Most climbers see walking, hiking, jogging, running, and every other form of foot travel as a method for getting to the climbing, not as an end in itself. The more we saw what the race was all about, the happier we were with our decision to pursue photography instead. We followed a daily regimen of walking, chatting, shooting, drinking tea, and cheering on runners.

Then, we descended from the Nepal-India border into West Bengal and were hit with another reminder of what *really* makes a trip to Asia. As the runners sprinted through tiny mountain villages, dashing past peasant women drying corn on terraces and small grubby children running up to greet us, we realized the racers weren't experiencing any of this: the warm shouts of hello, the ear-to-ear grins, the invitations to visit, the eager children's hands out for *mithai* (sweets). The entire scene must've been a blur.

After the race, Mr. Pandey held a sort of awards banquet, where he gave trophies to the fastest runners. The mood in the hall was somber. At the end of the ceremony, an argument broke out. A South African man and his wife, who had run well but not won anything, were angry about the rules and the support (water, food, etc.) along the racecourse, as well as the money they'd paid to take part. Harsh words flew between the couple and Mr. Pandey's staff, and the South Africans stormed out, never to be seen again.

"Steve, want to go get a beer?" I whispered to my like-minded friend. "There was a funky little café back on the main road."

"Yeah, let's get out of here."

Separately, we each made our way to the back of the hall, then slipped out into the cool Himalayan evening, where the scent of fried *papadums* and the sounds of playing children rode on the air. We wandered down the road, greeted a few people, and took up seats at the café, which was more or less in the street. Yellow incandescent light, tinted red by gaudy plastic shades, made the dirt road a calming brown color. We started chatting with the locals while a smart waiter brought a round of drinks and several plastic baskets of strange-tasting delicacies.

Certainly, we'd hardly achieved anything tangible. We hadn't even really pushed ourselves, while our respect for the runners (Michael Collins had set a new course record) was undeniable. Yet somehow, after all we'd witnessed—all we'd tasted, smelled, and touched along the way—we knew we were the real winners.

### *Trekking the Singalila Ridge*

To get to the start of the trek, take a bus or taxi the 26 kilometers from Darjeeling (access from India is about the only access there is) to Manebhanjan (altitude: 2,150 meters). Wander northwest on the main street and just out of the village, and look for a very steep jeep road. Go left. This climb is the toughest part of the trek, as you gain nearly 1,000 meters in elevation. After 11 kilometers, you will reach Tonglu (altitude: 3,070 meters), where you can stay in a trekkers' hut.

For the next few days the trek follows the Singalila Ridge proper (which is also the Nepal-India border). The second night is typically spent at Sandakphu (altitude: 3,636 meters), the highest point in West Bengal. The third day entails a twenty-one-kilometer trek along the ridge to Phalut. The mountains will be with you the entire way, as well as the occasional local yaks and their herders.

There is one must-do activity at Phalut: sitting outside and watching the sunset on Everest, Makalu, and Kanchenjunga—and then, of course, the sunrise. From Phalut, the trail descends through forests of rhododendrons and magnolias (a fellow trekker happened to mention that there are red pandas in these forests, so naturally Cameron was looking in the trees and not at the trail) and soon emerges in cultivated fields. The last night is spent at Raman, with a final day's trek to Rimbik, a quaint village perched on the side of a steep, deep valley.

From here, you can arrange transportation back to Darjeeling. The trek can also be shortened considerably by cutting off the Phalut portion of the walk. Two kilometers before reaching Sandakphu, there's a settlement called Bikhay Bhanjang. From here, you can drop straight down to Rimbik in just a few hours.

## *To hire or not to hire*

This trek can be undertaken independently or with a tour operator. If you are doing it independently, you'll need (at least) a sleeping bag, food, sturdy hiking boots, a water bottle (or two), and everything else you'd take on a fairly high mountain trek. There are trekkers' huts along the way, but camping is also an option.

Numerous U.K.-based firms offer Singalila Ridge treks, including The Mountain Company, Classic Journeys, and Mountain Kingdoms. In India, Rimo Expeditions and Ladakh Adventure & Trekking Tours also organize Singalila Ridge treks.

www.themountaincompany.co.uk
www.classicjourneys.co.uk
www.himalayankingdoms.com
www.rimoexpeditions.com
www.ladakhtrekking.com

## *When to go*

The area sees stable, pleasant weather between mid-March and the first week of June, as well as from late September through early December.

# General Nepal

## *Roberta Sotonoff relishes the diversity of Nepal*

After spending a few days getting acclimated to life in Nepal, my husband and I embarked on a multisport adventure called Mountains, River, Jungle. According to the itinerary, which began in the mountains, "The trek starts with a short climb ..."

### Mountains

The so-called "short climb" was more than three hundred meters on a local path, in the presence of some of the world's greatest mountains. As we began our ascent, villagers hauled huge loads in *dokos* (baskets) anchored to their foreheads with rope belts. Most wore only flip-flops, but they left me and my high-tech hiking boots in their dust. As for our eight Sherpas, as they prepared lunch, they looked rested despite having carried our tents, cooking gear, shower, portable potty, and everything else we needed for the first four days of our journey on their backs.

Our "easy" trek continued with more uphill climbs (and a few downward slopes). As we made our way to our campsite near the village of Bhumdi, the not-so-easy easy parts became well worth it when we saw that where we would stay the night was surrounded by the soaring, snow-covered mountains of Annapurna II, III, IV, and South; Lamjung Himal; Hiunchuli; and the sacred fishtail mountain, Machhapuchhare. We stared in amazement as the giant white massifs reached for the sky, disappearing into a haze while clouds floated below.

After a dinner of chicken, soup, and my favorite, yak cheese, we were treated to entertainment by our Sherpas. Though they hauled our gear and then cooked dinner and set up the camp, they still found time to sing and dance. But it had been a long day, and by eight we were exhausted. Under a shower of stars, my husband and I made our way back to the tent.

Tea and warm water for washing came with the 6 a.m. wake-up knock. Day 2 of the trek was spent figuring out just how to fit my foot on each tiny, angled stone in the path. "This is much harder than the last time I did it. The rocks were smoother," said our guide, Raj, as the path snaked up, around, and down in a misty rainforest of ferns, berries, moss, slippery rocks, roots, and rot. "There was a landslide," added Namgyal, the head Sherpa, who quietly trekked alongside us.

We were greeted on day 3 with a morning shrouded in fog. "Today we take a few steps up," Raj told us. He meant 350 giant steps up. At the top,

Buddhist prayer flags billowed, each of the five colored flags representing earth, water, fire, air, or sky. This was followed by a lunch stop in the charming Gurung village of Bhangjang, about three hundred meters below. Standing beside stone and thatched-roofed houses, villagers eagerly posed for pictures before we moved on, passing boys on a ledge playing chess, surrounded by chickens and water buffalo. Our trek continued with more roots, mud, water, buffalo droppings, and stairs, but we were rewarded with a cake the Sherpas had managed to bake for us. "Hope you had a nice trek, *Namaste*," the icing read.

The last trekking day was a "down day," figuratively and literally. As we descended through villages and around cows, water buffalo, and roosters, there was a flurry of activity—children running off to school, and people working in their fields, tending their livestock, and even building a house. After walking lightly for four days, my very last step was into a giant water buffalo chip. Namgyal, in his gentle way, bent down, removed my shoe, and cleaned it, reminding me that the best part of the journey so far was the people who had accompanied us along the way.

### River

With our legs still sore from trekking, we prepared to rack our upper bodies with a two-day rafting trip down the Madi, Kosi, and Seti rivers. Our trekking guides delivered us to the Madi River near Pokhara. Shouting paddle commands—"Forward please, forward, stawp!"—Bhim, our new guide, directed the raft through riffles and Class III rapids that brought screams and icy-water-soaked clothes. As the sun started to sink, we stopped at a lonely beach where two bulls were fighting on the sand. This was the local convenience store.

"We need some eggs," said Bhim, sending his assistant ashore. The assistant disappeared into the wilderness. A while later, he returned with a dozen eggs stuffed between two pieces of lumpy cardboard. They were placed atop the gear. Given the task of keeping the eggs from breaking, I surrendered my paddle. It turned out to be a daunting task as we hit three sizable rapids on the way to camp. I'm proud to say the eggs, though wet, were intact when we docked on a remote beach.

The foggy, chilly night made our snug down sleeping bags enticing. The sound of flowing water brought sleep easily, and we stayed put until dawn and breakfast followed by another day of "forward please, forward, stawp" down the rapids. Early on our raft hit a rock and Raj made an unscheduled exit. He crawled back into boat without a word, and we were all glad that the rest of the trip was an easy downriver paddle.

### Jungle

Chitwan National Park is a scrubby place filled with tall elephant grasses and Asian rhinos. Located in the southern, subtropical Terai region, the large flatland is teeming with animals. One of the best ways to see its monkeys, rhinos, antelopes, crocodiles, boars, and abundant bird life is from atop an elephant—so we boarded a beast and lumbered through the park. Our jungle guide, Pradip, spotted wild boar, bark deer, monkeys, and crocs, while the seventy resident leopards and hundred Bengal tigers eluded us.

We began day 2 atop the elephant again and plodded our way to the river, where we took a short jaunt in a dugout canoe. Among the river wildlife, the birds were especially fantastic—egrets, kingfishers, storks, peacocks, and mallards—and crocodiles were everywhere. In the afternoon we took a jungle walk, again in search of wildlife. The walk, however, was the least successful.

From feet to beat-up jeep, we then began our bumpy journey down the pockmarked road to a Tharu village. Small houses made of clay and cow dung were decorated with pictures of animals. The Tharu marry young, lead simple farming lives, and do not read or write. On the return trip, children stood on the road waving and yelling. Their only English word, *bye-bye*, was a reminder that it was time to return home, leaving behind the mountains, rivers, and jungles of Nepal for a land where yak cheese and water buffalo chips would become the stuff of happy memories.

## *Exploring the diversity of Nepal*

Roberta's Mountain, River, Jungle journey was offered by Snow Lion Expeditions, which has become Asia 360. She was impressed by how well the company took care of its clients—very important in a country where a popular tourist souvenir is amebic dysentery!

www.asia360travel.com

## *Tips on tipping*

Before departing Kathmandu, find out how much money you will need to tip the various guides and Sherpas on your trip. You want to be sure that you have enough to pay them fairly, especially since these people are often so much more than just "staff"—friendships form, particularly in the mountains where you will find yourself relying greatly on these climbing experts. They are also your intimate window onto the country. Roberta fondly remembers how during the trekking part of her adventure, Raj kept a running commentary about Hinduism, movies, and music, with corny jokes thrown in. And gentle Namgyal's laughter and made-up ditties, such as "one, two, three, bumblebee," eased the difficulty of hours-long trekking.

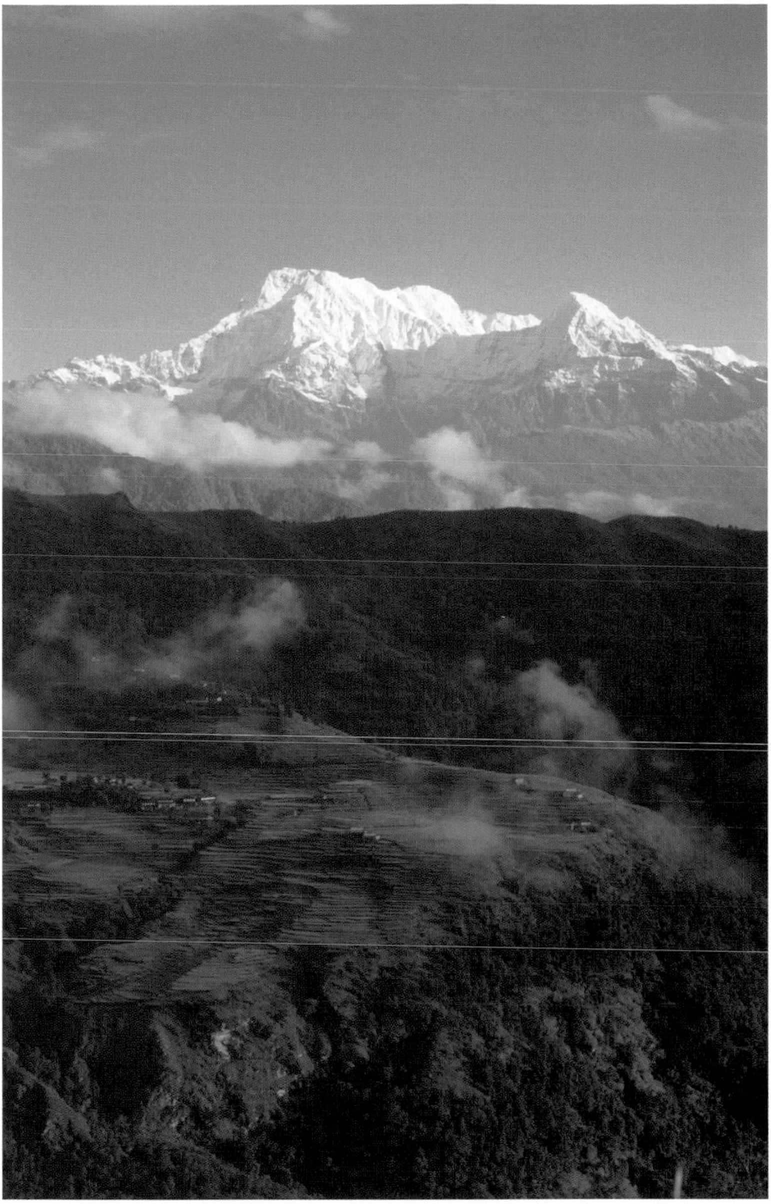

*Mountain range & rice terraces in the Annapurna Region*

# When in Rome

*Lessons on living local and making yourself at home*

People make a place unforgettable. Immersion gives a journey substance. Because of this, "When in Rome" has always been a favorite chapter for contributors to the To Asia With Love guidebooks. It is the opportunity for them to share the experiences that plunged them fully into the culture, resulting in a deeper understanding not only of a country, but also of themselves.

Each such transformative moment is as individual and unique as the person it happens to. For Scott Berry, it's the funeral ceremony of an old friend (the first foreigner ever cremated at the Bijeshwari temple) in Kathmandu. For Sherry Ott, it's a self-imposed attitude adjustment on the Annapurna trail. And for Tariq al Kashef, it's participating with gusto in a festival tradition, which transforms him (at least for a short while) into a "local" in the traveler-infested Thamel District.

Observing tradition is a guaranteed way to get closer to a country, whether it be a touristy rite with a local monk in Manang or a full-blown citywide celebration in Bhaktapur. Often, it's done by being open to the unexpected, as Karen Coates is when she stumbles upon an exorcism on the Indian border.

Most notable are the encounters that inspire friendship, even if that relationship lasts only a day. As Elizabeth Sharpe, Kevin Curry, and Gerry Kataoka are welcomed into homes around the country, they learn that while our differences are intriguing, it is our similarities that cement bonds, from a shared fascination with Cher in *People* magazine to a mutual desire to make the world a better place.

*Tourist district in Kathmandu*

# KATHMANDU

## *Scott Berry bids farewell to an old friend in Kathmandu*

One sunny February morning, an aging multinational crowd—Italian, British, American, French, Japanese, Tibetan, and Nepalese—gathered on the banks of the Vishnumati River, across from the Bijeshwari temple in a city that was barely recognizable as the Kathmandu that had first attracted us nearly forty years before. Air pollution, traffic, and strikes had eroded much of the charm that I remembered. Amid the political tumult, we had come to bid farewell to a little bit of the old Kathmandu and an old friend.

Some of the Westerners, starting out as penniless drifters in the '60s, now had worldwide reputations, their books and translations standard reading for historians and Dharma practitioners. Others had immersed themselves in Himalayan art or music, or started small businesses that had benefited both themselves and Nepal. The common bond was their acquaintance with the deceased, who was yet to arrive. Proceedings were scheduled to begin at 11 a.m., and we lightened the mood with reminiscences.

"I met him in Benares in 1970," remarked a tall Italian, who like our late friend sported a long, gray ponytail. "I remember he was always impeccably dressed. Don't know how he managed."

"I've known him since 1968," said an American with a walrus mustache. "Our first 'business' was selling Tibetan wood block prints to hippies on Freak Street."

"He was a terrible businessman, but a great artist," someone else chimed in. "Never had any money. I think he'd have felt he was prostituting himself if he had actually earned anything."

The odd man out, having known our late friend for only five years, I speculated aloud on whether, since he was always late for everything, he would actually manage to be late for his own funeral. We had a laugh, and wouldn't you know it, he showed up on time, wrapped in orange and laid out in the back of a van.

In spite of the years we had all spent here, none of us had been so closely involved in a Newari Buddhist cremation before. The guest of honor's oldest friend, one of the few Westerners to speak fluent Newari, stood in as next-of-kin, with a Vajracharya priest to guide him through the rituals. He had arranged everything, and this was to be the first time a foreigner would be cremated at the Bijeshwari temple.

Once the earthly remains were deposited on the bier, his friends started covering him with garlands and Tibetan sutras, only to be told that this was done later, so everything had to be taken off again. It didn't matter, or even mark us as inexperienced outsiders. While in life our friend would have laughed at such a sentimental notion, there was little doubt that this was the funeral he would have wanted.

Until a year or two before, when he began to have such trouble getting around, he had walked up the filthy banks of the Vishnumati to Bijeshwari every morning to do *puja*, his daily worship. He told long and convoluted tales of the Newari artist Siddhi Muni Shakya and the cleaning and repainting of the images of the deity Tara inside.

One could even imagine him laughing as his friends uncertainly took off their shoes and socks (for a barefooted walk through Kathmandu's insalubrious streets is not for the fainthearted), picked up his bier, and under priestly direction began to make circuits one way and another, nearly falling over as their natural anarchical tendencies made it difficult for them to keep in step. But at any rate, our old friend had begun the final leg of his journey that had started so many years ago in Argentina and Italy.

Across the river at the ghat, a pyre had been constructed by Newar of the Pode caste. They are a jolly crowd. Death is their living, an everyday affair that they can take casually. Unlike the dour funeral directors of the West with their professionally grief-stricken faces, they make no pretense. Having built the pyre, they sat around snacking, drinking tea or *raksi*, laughing, and chatting amiably. Behind them a crowd of Tibetan monks began chanting.

The years of illicit substances and missed meals had taken their toll, and the emaciated body was quickly consumed. Up in smoke with it went a lifetime of knowledge. There went the monologues lasting for hours about characters—foreign and Nepalese—he had known in the old days, about life in prison in Kathmandu and Bangkok, about a Tibetan girlfriend who turned out to be married to a murderous butcher with a long knife, about obscure mother-goddesses, and about the medieval history of his adopted country.

As the smoke rose and we gathered near the pyre, someone remarked that now that the way had been paved for us, we knew where we would all end up. And somehow the thought made us all feel better. The funeral began to seem more like a beginning than an end, and we remembered how much Kathmandu had enriched our lives and how lucky we were to have been in touch with such an extraordinary personality.

### *Bijeshwari temple*

The temple is located above the west bank of the Vishnumati River on the way from Thamel to Swayambhunath.

## *Tariq al Kashef discovers local color in Kathmandu*

Kathmandu is one of the most colorful places in the world. Deep blue skies contrast with purple, snow-capped mountains. Rainbow-colored prayer flags blow in the noisy, dusty streets, where beautiful Nepalese women walk to and fro, wearing magenta and turquoise dress. As if this isn't vivid enough, every year at the beginning of spring, the city is given a vibrant touch-up in a religious festival that could easily be described as the world's largest game of paintball.

The evening before the Holi festival began, I was warned to buy a few bags of powder paint, which I duly did. I wasn't quite sure what to expect, but when I got up midmorning, as usual, I could already tell just by peering down from my balcony that this day was a little bit different.

Below me the streets of Thamel were quieter than usual, and the few people who were out looked around cautiously as they walked along. Many already bore the telltale signs of a Holi ambush—the ubiquitous red splodge of paint.

Around the corner to my left, a group of young Nepalese men and women were huddled mischievously. Every now and then they darted out to attack passersby with homemade paint bombs. Some of the victims returned fire, but most just ran. For locals, the assaults were expected. For tourists, they were a novelty. As I observed, I quickly realized that being a foreigner did not gain someone immunity. The game seemed almost compulsory, and no one escaped unmarked. The less paint a person had on him, the more he became a target.

My Nepalese pal, Arjan, a Holi festival veteran, encouraged me to wear my worst clothes in preparation. Now, suitably attired, we looked down from our lofty vantage point and launched our paint bombing campaign on the group that had been hiding in the corner and terrorizing people all morning.

For about an hour we enjoyed complete aerial domination and received supportive cheers from the shops and restaurants below.

Reaching for the last paint bomb, Arjan said, "Go and get the rest of the paint."

"Err ... we've run out," I replied.

"That's all you bought, man?" he asked, horrified.

It seems I had vastly underestimated the amount of paint required for a full day of Holi festivities.

After some debate, and the universally recognized system for making any decision (rock, paper, scissors), I was elected to go down into the street while it remained relatively quiet and purchase fresh supplies from the store around the corner.

Holi is good business for any shop, and most convenience stores will be fully stocked with powder paint, water pistols, and credit-card-sized plastic bags from which to make the hugely popular paint bomb. Armed to the teeth with my colorful weapons, I headed back to base camp.

But less than half a block from the front door, I looked up at the balcony to see Arjan waving and pointing frantically. As the first makeshift paint warhead made a direct hit with my chest, I realized why.

I was completely surrounded. I ducked into the nearest restaurant, but my attackers were in hot pursuit, and I ended up covered head to toe in red, green, and blue paint—along with every waiter and customer in the restaurant. But they were laughing, clapping, and cheering jubilantly with all the fervor usually devoted to a religious celebration.

And then I remembered: oh, that's right, that's exactly what this is!

### *Legend of Holi*

Holi is one of the oldest and most important festivals on the Hindu calendar, believed to date back several hundred years before Christ. The festival takes its name from Holika, the evil sister of Hiranyakashipu, a demon king who believed himself to be so powerful, he enforced a law that everyone should worship only him. His own son, Prahlada, a devoted follower of Vishnu, disobeyed, and as one version of the legend goes, Hiranyakashipu recruited Holika to punish Prahlada by walking him into an inferno. Apparently, she had the ability to withstand fire, but she perished in the flames, since her ability turned out to rely on her being alone. Meanwhile, Lord Vishnu saved the child as reward for his faith.

### *The Holi festival*

Holi takes place over two days in late February or early March. On the first day, bonfires are lit to celebrate the burning of Holika. On the second day, the Dhulandi (paint fight) occurs. Holi corresponds with the arrival of spring, when the change in weather is believed to bring illness, and the throwing of colored paint is thought to have medicinal value.

www.holifestival.org

## PASHUPATINATH

### *Robert Tompkins confronts life and death at Pashupatinath*

Located at the crossroads of ancient trading and pilgrimage routes, Kathmandu is a place associated with the exotic. My wife and I had anticipated mystery, enchantment, and mysticism from this city founded in 723 AD. We certainly were not expecting a corpse.

"Oh, good, we are in luck. There *is* a body."

Diwakar, our guide, beamed at this good fortune.

We were at Pashupatinath, one of the largest temples dedicated to Shiva in the world, and the holiest site in Nepal for followers of Shiva. Although a Hindu shrine of some kind is said to have existed as far back as the fifth century, we were told that the present temple was constructed in 1687 and had undergone many additions and alterations since. Because non-Hindus are not allowed inside the temple, we had climbed the terraced hill on the opposite side of the river and were looking down on the temple complex.

"The feet of the body are in the water so that the soul can be released into the Bagmati River, which is a tributary of the sacred Ganges," explained Diwakar, seemingly unaware of our uneasiness. "After the cremation, the ashes will also be swept into the river."

The body was being attended to by three people who were washing the corpse—with difficulty, since it was wrapped in a pink sarong. "One must be cleansed before entering a different plane," Diwakar commented.

Nothing in his tone reflected how surreal my wife and I found this scene. Near the body, milk from cows kept in the temple flowed down the embankment. Tourists, their cameras on tripods in order to focus on the stack of wood on the cremation ghat, awaited the flames. Monkeys jumped from rock to rock begging for food, while scores of dogs either slept in the sun or tore at garbage. A girl of about twelve, selling a necklace with a mandala charm, harangued relentlessly.

Finally, realizing our discomfort and leading us away, Diwakar philosophized, "It's a matter of conditioning."

Never a truer statement had been made, I thought as I looked down the river, where women washed clothes as they had been doing every day for centuries, whacking blouses and pants against rocks. A water buffalo wandered along the muddy banks. Monkeys splashed. Dogs drank. And meanwhile, in the midst of it all, a soul was being prepared to take its leave of the earth.

### *Pashupatinath*

The UNESCO World Heritage Site of Pashupatinath is located along the Bagmati River, about four kilometers east of Kathmandu's city center. Robert visited with a guide from Yeti Travels.

www.yetitravelsonline.com

## Boudha

### *Elizabeth Sharpe loses her mind outside Kathmandu*

Not far from crowds, cars, buses, tuk-tuks, and too much diesel in the air, I found sanctuary. Kopan monastery rises atop a hill, overlooking the rice-terraced fields of the Kathmandu Valley. About 360 monks—most from India, Nepal, and Tibet—live and study at Kopan, and not far away, nearly 400 nuns inhabit a convent of their own.

I wasn't looking to turn in my blue jeans for a set of monastic robes, but I did hope that discovering more about the spiritual side of Nepal would bring me closer to a balanced life. Kopan Monastery offered a weeklong introduction to Buddhism course, allowing me to learn from the monks and nuns who epitomized the peace I sought.

As I walked through the monastery gates, I saw the distinctive Tibetan influence in the architecture of the buildings. But what captured my attention were the monks in saffron robes flying kites. They couldn't have been older than twelve. Like boys around the world, they joked and teased each other, laughing and smiling as the kites caught in the wind and sailed high above their heads. The scene was so contrary to the image I had in my mind of the quiet, serious monastic experience, and I was intrigued.

The next morning the day began at 6 a.m. with a cup of tea and the first meditation—visualizing the Buddha and reciting the mantra "*Tayata om muni muni maha muniye soha,*" which roughly translates to "Give me great control and wisdom." I was in a hall full of Westerners, and along with the rest of the students, I sat cross-legged on a flat pillow on the floor. My hands rested on my knees facing up, with the forefinger and the thumb lightly touching. We learned the mantra together, reciting it in a monotone, and from the moment we woke until lunchtime, this was the only sound we uttered, since we had pledged to be silent, mindful, and not distracted by conversation.

Before we started the meditation, our teacher, Ani Karin Valham, a Buddhist nun originally from Sweden, had instructed us to let our thoughts go by "untrapped." I imagined mine like a string of Tibetan prayer flags unfurling behind my closed eyes. One by one they danced past in the wind, but every once in a while, my mind's eye caught one, and I found myself studying it, the way I might examine the curls of Tibetan script or a Wind Horse on the real panels of colorful cloth that hang throughout the region. Consciously releasing the thought, I focused on letting it slip away.

With each new day of meditation—and each thought I let go by unexamined—I felt more of the peace that I saw in the relaxed demeanor of the monks and nuns. My life outside the monastery gates seemed to belong to someone else: filled with to-do lists and the stress that comes with always thinking about more. I wondered if it was possible for me to reinvent that self. Carve out some of my go-go-go tendencies and replace them with the calm I felt when my mind was able to drift right past its string of Tibetan prayer flags.

Now that I'm back in the "real world," I realize that the path to enlightenment is only as true as I am to my intentions. To that end I often turn to a book I bought by Ani Karin, to make sure I don't forget the mantras—those prayers that take me back along the lighted path to a place where my thoughts are as free as the young monks' kites dancing and tossing in the wind.

### *Meditation courses*

Kopan Monastery offers three to four seven-day ($80) or ten-day ($110) introductory courses a year. There is also a well-attended one-month retreat ($420) in the fall; if you're interested, book early, as it fills up quickly. Course dates change from year to year, so check the monastery website for the current schedule. Rates include dormitory accommodation, all meals, and course material. Accommodation other than a dorm or tent can be had for an extra charge. Payment must be made with Nepali rupees, with the exception of the monthlong class, which can be paid for by credit card online.

www.kopan-monastery.com

### *Short-term study*

If you're short on time, the monastery offers a meditation and discussion group led by Ani Karin every morning in the Chenrezig *gompa*. On Sundays, a Dharma video replaces the discussion group. Price per day, including breakfast, is less than $10, depending on accommodation—dorm, private room, shared bathroom, etc. Additional meals (lunch, afternoon tea, and dinner) are available. Meals are vegetarian, and they are so popular that the monastery offers a cookbook for sale in its bookshop.

### *What to bring*

Bedding is not included in rooms with shared facilities, so a warm sleeping bag is recommended in the winter months, since nights in Kathmandu get very cold and there is no heat in the rooms. In the fall, a light sleeping bag is best, as the nights are still chilly. In the summer, the days are hot, but Elizabeth used her sleeping bag as padding, since the beds don't have very thick mattresses.

Bring a flashlight (or better yet, a headlamp) if you are in shared facilities. Toilet paper is available at the monastery, but it never hurts to have a small stash of your own. Also bring hand sanitizer.

Use a water filter or iodine tablets to treat the water you drink and even the water you use to rinse your toothbrush. Bottled water is also available for sale at the monastery.

While closed walking shoes are a must in Nepal, you'll also want shoes that slip off easily for the monastery, where you will remove often before entering sacred places such as the *gompa* and temple.

## Bhaktapur

### *Caroline Martin meets the ghosts of honor in Bhaktapur*

Crossing the border from India northward to Nepal, I felt that I'd moved both forward and backward in time. Forward, because Nepali standard time jumps precisely fifteen minutes ahead of Indian. Backward, because a glance at the calendar on the immigration office wall showed it was no longer 2010, but 1130 Nepal Sambat. The date was not August 29, but 13 Bhadra.

Official Nepal may call itself a newly secularized nation, but popular Nepal still lives by traditional Hindu and Newari timelines. An ancient cycle of holy days still rules; the year runs to the rhythms of agriculture and a lunar calendar. Each seasonal gradation brings prescribed rites and observances.

It was one such gradation, in late August, that caused me to hop a bus from Kathmandu's dusty Bagh Bazar to Bhaktapur, in search of false cows and dead relatives.

The Gai Jatra ("Cow Pilgrimage") festival is a sort of Nepali version of the Mexican Dia de los Muertos (Day of the Dead). Families who have lost a member during the previous year guide the soul to its final destination, and in this predominantly Hindu country, a cow must be used to lead the spirits into the next land. The best place to witness this uniquely Nepali holy day, I'd heard, was Bhaktapur.

Nowhere is Nepal's time-warp quality more evident than the "City of Devotees." The former kingdom's dim alleys, sunlit squares, and traditional architecture are protected under UNESCO World Heritage status. The city gates once stayed armies of rival kings; they are now manned by guards who extract the requisite 700 Nepali rupees ($10) admission from foreign visitors.

Forking over the fee, I stepped into a world of medieval pageantry. Everywhere were movement, sound, and color, distinctly ordered by the tempos of tradition. Bands of Newari musicians beat hypnotic rhythms down the brick lanes, overlaid with shrill fifes and clashing cymbals. Men in masks danced myth into life, bringing demigods and demons to meet the deceased. Children faced off in a double-line dance, clacking sticks together, then whirling to change place. And overhead were the guests and ghosts of honor—Bhaktapur's recently passed, staring down from above.

Bereaved families had been at work all week, constructing their *thaha macha*, or "false cow," a towering scaffold of bamboo branches. Each loomed overhead like a swaying radio transmitter. Covering the bamboo spires were garments of the deceased—black for women, white for males. Bright paper and tinsel decor, a comical hand-painted cow face, the straw "horns" of the cow, yak-tail tassels, and large portraits of the late relatives completed the *thaha macha.* As I looked up, I could see protective parasols perched atop the towers, a sign of respect in a land that's alternately sun-baked and monsoon-drenched.

Family members (usually males, but increasingly women as well) carted these contraptions through the narrow streets on their shoulders. The process was impressive, since it took at least four people to maneuver the *thaha macha*, and the modern intrusion of electrical wires required special finesse.

From time to time, the groups would pause at a particularly crowded intersection, or for a cross-current in the parade to pass. I was moved by the sight of young marchers making small adjustments to the pictures and clothing. One young man straightened his grandmother's crooked portrait, and for a moment they were face-to-face, as she stared at him from the other side, her features reflected in those of her grandson.

Along with this family ritual, political satire, playful stick-dancing (*ghintang kisi)* in the streets, general goofiness, masking, and even transvestitism are important parts of Gai Jatra. While Gai Jatra has been celebrated since ancient times, these customs stem from a queen, wife of seventeenth-century monarch Pratap Malla, who lost her favorite son. She was inconsolable in her grief, unable to speak or smile. Finally, the king offered a reward to anyone who could make the queen laugh. The festival's conclusion in satire and comedy finally brought a smile to the queen's face, and thus a new tradition was born.

Today, street theater tableaux lampoon the current Nepali political situation (which admittedly supplies the actors with ample material). I saw children dressed in the mismatched combo of Western suits and topis, mocking the Maoist prime minister. Some were draped in twisting green vines, referring to the rebels' claim of coming "out of the jungles." Not unlike our April Fools' Day, "mad" comics and satirical newspaper spoofs are printed. For kids, Gai Jatra has turned into a sort of Halloween. I observed many plastic masks;

Spider-Man is especially popular with both little boys and girls.

Whether or not a person has lost a loved one recently, every local resident has a role to play in Gai Jatra. Each Newari community has its own funeral society, which support one another in collecting the materials required for death rituals. Elder men carry brass jugs of water, suspended from either end of a pole, to distribute to thirsty marchers. Senior women, clad in their elegant black and red *haku patasi* saris, stand at corners offering specially prepared ritual food on plates made of dried leaves.

All the guidebooks describe Gai Jatra as a one-day event. In Bhaktapur, however, it's the beginning of a weeklong festival. Each day hosts different processions, with various street dances and costumes, till the final day of Sri Krishna Janmashtami (Lord Krishna's birthday).

Late in the afternoon, having circled the town one last time, marchers convened at the ancient Durbar Square. Beneath the five-tiered Nyatapola temple, the towering cows gathered in a moving circle, a macabre May Day dance. The final round was led by what looked like a lofty haystack. This straw effigy represented Lord Bhairav, who presides over the dead. Flutes, drum, and cymbals chimed as Bhaktapur's dead performed their final dance.

With darkness falling, I followed the false cows, which were led to the banks of the Hanumante River and hacked apart with hand axes. As the day came to an end, all disposable parts—bamboo, paper cow-face decor, tinsel, and straw—were received by the waiting water, rippling silver in the moonlight.

### *Getting to Bhaktapur*

Go to page 23.

### *Timing your trip*

Bhaktapur seems to host a festival every week, but Gai Jatra occurs in late August or early September, according to the lunar calendar. The proprietors of Bhadgaon Guest House keep an accurate calendar of the city's festival dates.

### *Where to stay*

Bhaktapur is an absorbing city with many layers, and Caroline recommends staying at least one night. Bhadgaon Guest House is an elegant choice and has superb views of Nyatapola temple. Also highly recommended are the simpler but friendly Sunny Guest House and its neighbor, Pahan Chhen Guest House, with similar facilities and views.

www.bhadgaon.com.np

## Manang/Annapurna

### *Zhou Zhang receives a hundred-rupee blessing in Manang*

Whenever my husband Kevin and I weren't trekking or eating, I spent my time lying fully cocooned in my sleeping bag—usually asleep. If you do the math, this means I spent about sixteen hours a day sleeping. This is only a slight exaggeration.

But on our "rest day" in Manang, I dragged myself out of my cozy sleeping bag so we could take a side trip to aid our acclimatization. Our choice: climbing another five hundred meters to meet a famous ninety-three-year-old Buddhist monk, known as the "100-rupee monk," who lives on the mountainside. This monk blesses all the trekkers who come to see him, and in my own distorted high-altitude version of reality, this would mean that if we were blessed by him, we would make it over the Thorong La Pass successfully.

After hiking for an hour and a half, we took off our shoes and went inside the ... well, I'm not sure what to call the place. It was a small room, about fifty square feet, carved right into the mountain. The 100-rupee monk sat cross-legged on the ground behind a small table. There were pictures everywhere, including a few of the monk himself and one of a *Time* magazine cover with the Dalai Lama on it. Tapestries covered the wall behind him. The only furniture was a small desk, which the monk sat behind, and a bench on the side of the room. There were also lots of little trinkets that previous trekkers had left, including a clock shaped like Australia. I felt as if I were in a tiny dorm room—inhabited by a monk!

We knelt down in front of the monk and bowed our heads, waiting to receive his blessing. It was at this very solemn and spiritual moment that he looked at us and said questioningly, "Camera?"

Camera. Of course. Silly me. I got up, took out the camera, and went to the bench, where I took a video of Kevin receiving his blessing. He did the same for me a few minutes later.

For the blessing I ate some questionable-looking little black seed things and drank some questionable yellow liquid that the monk poured into my palm from a small gold jar decorated with peacock leaves. Then he started to say a prayer as he tied a small rope necklace around my neck. I could hardly understand a word, but as I looked at him and saw his serious and kind eyes looking back at me, I couldn't help but feel that he knew exactly how I felt—that I had never been so mentally or physically exhausted as I had been in the week prior, and that I needed his encouragement and strength to go on.

It's strange, but this little old man—whom I had never met before and couldn't even understand—managed to bring tears to my eyes through his blessing. Even though the whole ritual took less than ten minutes, it's one of the experiences I remember most vividly from our trip.

As we left the monk's little dorm and headed back down to Manang, I felt better about the upcoming trek than I had for days. I lingered over the few words of the blessing I had been able to understand. *Good luck. Thorong La Pass. Me ninety-three—you good luck ninety-three.* He had wished us good luck until we were ninety-three, just like him, and if that didn't get us over the pass, then I didn't know what would.

### *Visiting the 100-rupee monk*

On the main road through Manang toward the end of town, there is a signboard with all of the area day hikes. Follow the one called Praken Gompa. It's one of the shorter hikes listed; it took Zhou and her husband about an hour and a half to reach the monk and just another forty-five minutes to get back to Manang.

Though gifts are not expected by Lama Deshi (the 100-rupee monk), it is a nice gesture to bring something from home, such as a postcard or other small souvenir.

Zhou adds: The trail to visit Lama Deshi's abode starts off on the north side of the road running through Manang. Once you find the start of the trail (we got lost and used the view of a stupa above to finally find it), it is pretty well marked and offers a nice view of Gangapurna Lake, which is also worth visiting (just a thirty-minute walk from Manang). You can also see the prayer flags marking the monk's abode from the bottom of the trail.

## Annapurna Region

### *Kevin Curry makes himself at home in the Himalayas*

We'd been hiking the Himalayas in the pitch-black night for more than forty-five minutes. The town lights that had been guiding our way were now hidden somewhere out of view. If I were with some larger person who could take care of me, I probably would have broken down in tears. But I was with my five-foot-two wife. I had to stay strong.

My mind raced through every possible scenario of how this night might end, including (a) falling asleep under a tree and being eaten by vicious snow leopards, (b) being attacked by spiders similar to ones we had seen earlier on the trek, and (c) falling off the side of the mountain and *then* being devoured by spiders and/or snow leopards.

Then a light flickered in the distance ...

This trip to Nepal had started out simply enough: my girlfriend and I decided we would quit our jobs, get married, and take a yearlong honeymoon around the world. One of our main goals was to step outside our comfort zone, so why not make our first trekking experience the approximately 240-meter long Annapurna Circuit?

By the time we found ourselves hiking through the dark, it was our fourteenth day of trekking. We were exhausted. Fatigue had set in during the day's five-hundred-meter climb, prompting my wife to declare that we were staying at the next lodge we saw, "No matter what!" Soon thereafter we spotted a guesthouse sitting invitingly on the edge of a beautiful cliff. It was the place for us. Or so we thought.

I'll spare readers the details on why we decided to leave. Suffice it to say that after meeting the creepy drug addict cousin of the lodge owner, we happily discovered that the next village was only fifteen minutes away. We could see the lights ahead on the mountainside. Even though the sun had set long ago, I decided that with our trusty headlamps, the walk to a safer lodge would be no problem.

Half an hour later, not only were we still stumbling over jagged rocks in the darkness, but we had also lost sight of the village lights. At one point, we lost the trail completely but were luckily able to retrace our steps. Another fifteen minutes passed, and there was still no sign of human life.

Just as I finished apologizing to my wife for the tenth time for making the mistake of leaving the last guesthouse, a headlamp flashed in our direction. The welcoming young man behind it made me feel as if I'd just won the showcase on *The Price Is Right*. I would have done a dance if I hadn't used up all of my energy thinking about doomsday scenarios. Instead, I just hunched my shoulders in relief, and we accepted the boy's offer of a room for the night.

The boy and his family went to work preparing our bed, and it soon became clear that they were giving us one of their own rooms. Obviously it was going to be expensive. But the dad waved off our attempt to pay and almost appeared embarrassed that we even asked. "Oh," he said, "no money for the room."

We had shown up in the dark, clearly willing to hand over whatever they charged for a place to sleep. We couldn't see if there were any other lodges nearby, so we had no leverage. But the parents of this family of seven gave up their own room for us and didn't want anything in return. To top it off, the father repeatedly made sure we had our own sleeping bags before sheepishly asking if he could use his own blanket to keep himself warm.

After settling in, we were invited to join the family by the fire in the next room. For the next couple of hours, we all chatted over roasted soybeans and popcorn. We didn't fully understand each other, but it didn't matter. Though my wife and I had traveled thousands of miles, that night we felt like we were at home.

Around the world, we learned how to be very aware of our surroundings. Foreigners are often viewed as easy income to locals, especially in poorer regions. Money is hard to come by in this area of the Himalayas, but this family did not want any. They gave us their room, shared their food, and asked for nothing in return. What started out as the worst night on our trip ended up as the best and most memorable. Even so, my wife insists that we'll never go trekking in the dark again.

### *Excellent View Guest House and Restaurant*

On their way to Ghara on the Poon Hill Trek (and after fleeing the Santosh Top Hill Lodge & Restaurant), Kevin and his wife had the good fortune to find Excellent View. They did not realize it at the time, but Excellent View was one of the very first lodgings in Ghara. If they had kept walking, they would have found many others.

### *Guesthouse standards*

Kevin adds: As for guesthouses in general on the Annapurna Circuit, we discovered that lodging and food prices are usually set by the Annapurna Conservation Area Project (ACAP). Venues not approved by ACAP set their own prices. Although travelers should not negotiate prices, most lodge owners immediately offer a price lower than that set by ACAP, knowing that if you stay at the lodge, you will probably eat meals there as well. We never negotiated a price but often got good deals.

www.ntnc.org.np

### *Chez Nisa*

Located in Marpha, this restaurant and lodge made an impression on Kevin and his wife Zhou. When the owner noticed that Zhou's makeshift walking sticks were too big, she immediately took them away and gave Zhou a pair of real walking sticks—usually, these sticks are sold to trekkers.

### *Getting an education*

At one point, two of the kids at Excellent View brought out their homework assignments for Kevin and Zhou to look at. One was learning English prepositions, while the other was working on trigonometry. The majority of the residents in the Annapurna region might never even travel as far as Kathmandu in their lifetime—they'll most likely become farmers or yak herders or restaurant chefs in the towns they grew up in—but high in the mountains, they have the opportunity to learn trigonometry. As Kevin notes, it boggles the mind.

## *Sherry Ott ponders positivity in the Annapurnas*

After ten days of decreasing temperatures and increasing wind, my body is rebelling. My lips have become as parched as the Gobi Desert, and my hands are so dry they look like they belong to a sixty-year-old. My dad and I hiked slowly from Gunsang to Ledar today. We saw ice for the first time on the trail. We saw no trees. We breathed harder than we had the day before. Now we're holed up in the one of three guesthouses in the encampment of Ledar—waiting for our bodies to acclimate a little more.

During one of our trekking breaks today our guide Bishnu said, "Ohhhhh, I'm smelling like a donkey! I can't wait for a shower." Not only did the donkey reference make me laugh, but it also made me realize that I've been wearing the same pants for ten days, the same shirt for nine days, the same jog bra for nine days, and the same socks for four days. This is beyond donkey filth! On top of it, everything smells like Tiger Balm. I do wonder at times if these clothes will ever be clean again, or should I burn them for warmth at high camp? I guess the good news is that everyone smells equally bad. Like a pack of donkeys.

Even more troubling than my odor is my mental rebellion. After ten days I'm annoyed. The sunroom in our guesthouse is buzzing with various conversations I find hard to ignore. I don't understand why trekkers only like to share bad stories about people who have disappeared, or were robbed, or died from acute mountain sickness. Why isn't anyone telling any heartwarming stories—the ones about people making it? Or is it that people don't ever make it ... no ... that's just my mind playing stupid tricks on me. Right?

All of this negative talk is making me feel ill, but that's not all there is to it. Of all times, I got my period today. Not only am I exhausted, cold, and sore—I have cramps. Even though this is a subject that my dad and I have never once discussed in my lifetime, I decide what the hell, I'm an adult and we're trekking partners. I mention why I'm not feeling well. His reply: "Well, at least you're not pregnant."

Wait a minute ... is this my dad? My dad making a very funny joke about a subject that we've never talked about before? I'm in shock. I feel as if I have entered the *Father Knows Best* twilight zone. This is why I love traveling with my dad. I get these glimpses of him that I never had exposure to before. Previously I only saw the "father figure," not the man.

That afternoon as I sit and try to journal, doing my best not to listen to the horror stories around me, I look over at my dad. He is just fine. In fact, he is great. He doesn't seem worried or annoyed like me. Instead he seems really happy. I start to think about how far we've come. In all of that distance, I haven't seen anyone near his age attempting what he is attempting. I'm sure plenty of people more than seventy-three years old have made it over Thorong La Pass, but they're not my dad, and that's who I care about now.

We're a good father-daughter team. We lean on each other and provide encouragement when we need to. I realize this is the longest time we've ever spent together alone. In fact, this is the longest time he's been away from my mom in their fifty years of marriage. I think the best thing about growing older is that your relationship with your parents changes from unequal to equal—and I suppose that will shift again eventually. It's made me understand that instead of being annoyed with everything, I need to enjoy this. Sure, I'll still worry about our ability to get over the pass as a team, but I will also appreciate every moment of our teamwork.

That teamwork is never appreciated more than when we go back to our cold, dark room to sleep. I enter with my headlamp providing a narrow beam of light cutting through the darkness. I go to put my journal on my bed, and that's when I see it—two beady eyes staring back at me. A little mouse is scurrying around on my bed as if it's his. I scare the crap out of it; it scares the crap out of me. I turn around to my dad, who is closing the door, and announce, "There's a mouse on my bed." With a precision team effort and two headlamps we chase the outnumbered mouse off my bed and out the door. I slam it shut ... whew!

In reality, I know the mouse has mentally scarred me. This will be a worse than usual night of sleep at altitude. After all, that mouse got in our room when the door was shut. We are in *its* house. I pull my sleeping bag string tighter, attempting to shut out any possible entrance for the pesky rodent. One good thing, though, about my excessive anxiety about the little creature: it keeps me from worrying about whether or not my dad and I are going to make it over Thorong La Pass!

### *What to pack*

Sherry adds: Annapurna is a difficult trail to pack for as you are in a really hot, strenuous climate in the beginning and end, but in a very cold, snowy climate while going over the pass—and the guesthouses aren't heated. Therefore, the best thing to do is pack layers of clothes and socks. She also recommends quick-dry (sports) fabrics. It's hard for things to dry overnight, which means you have to put wet clothes back on in the cold mornings, and who likes to do that! Along with hiking boots, bring one comfortable pair of shoes to change into once you get to the guesthouses. As for what she wishes she'd brought, the main thing would be clothespins to hang up wet, sweaty clothes.

Each guesthouse has little clothing lines strung up for trekkers to dry out their clothes, but it's usually windy, and if you don't want to lose your socks, then you need clothespins.

## Khumjung

*Elizabeth Sharpe takes the road less traveled to Khumjung*

Pem Futi stood next to a large, black, wood-burning stove. She had just replenished an enormous Chinese thermos with more sweet, milky tea. My cup was still full, and I insisted for the third time that I honestly couldn't drink any more.

My friend Kim and I had arrived just that afternoon in the village of Khumjung. Although we had carefully planned our three-week trek in Sagarmatha National Park to view Mt. Everest, at the last minute we decided to deviate from the more popular route via Tengboche. Our final destination was still Gokyo Ri (just as high as Everest Base Camp but more beautiful because from Gokyo Ri we would be able to see the top of Mt. Everest from across the valley), but on the way we had taken an impromptu detour, which delivered us to Pem Futi, the wife of the owner of the Himalayan Guest House.

When we first reached the lodge, clothes sopping wet from the rain, Pem Futi pulled us into her cramped kitchen. "Come sit by the fire. Sit, sit," she said firmly, settling us on a bench and pressing the hot ceramic mugs of tea into our hands.

To be in a family kitchen was unusual. Trekkers usually sat at tables in the dining room. But I liked this better, and I could see Kim felt the same way as she wrapped her hands around the mug, steaming in the chilly air.

"What would you like for dinner?" Pem Futi asked.

A small girl was huddled near the doorway, watching us shyly. Kim and I were the only guests that night, and I saw a rare chance for us to spend time talking with a Sherpa family. I said, "Whatever you're having."

Pem Futi shook her head in disbelief. She recited all the Western dishes she could prepare—pizza, spaghetti, etc.

"Please," Kim added, "don't go to any trouble for us."

As Pem Futi turned back to the stove, Kim opened one of the copies of *People* magazine she had stuffed into her backpack. Leafing through it, she was stopped on every page.

"Beautiful," said the little girl, edging closer and pointing to the picture of Keanu Reeves in a suit and tie.

"Yeah, beautiful," I said and laughed.

The next page revealed Cher in a sequined gown. The girl, now standing behind us, reached out to point at the rock icon's dark black hair. "Beautiful," she said again and smiled up at Kim.

"I think I know what to do with this magazine," Kim said.

"That's for sure." I looked at the girl, who was grinning up at me, knowing nothing of what Kim and I were saying because she spoke no English, other than a few words that included *beautiful*.

By this time Pem Futi was done cooking, and she handed us each a plate of potatoes, accompanied by a dollop of creamy yak cheese that had been mixed with freshly made chili-paste chutney. She gave her son and daughter potatoes before taking one for herself. Her hands were small, her fingers thick and callused, and I watched as she peeled the skin from the potato, which she ate, as we did, with just the condiments. So simple. So delicious.

After eating our fill and drinking yet more tea, Kim and I stood up to retire to our room. But Pem Futi's daughter was eager for us to stay, and she asked if we wanted to listen to some Hindi disco music.

Kim was up for it, but I was exhausted, beginning to feel the altitude. So I went outside to rinse my face in the tap. Then I looked up at the night sky. With so few lights in the village, it yawned open wide, and specks of stars filled every inch of it. It was so much brighter up above than down below where I stood. I was shivering, but I couldn't make myself step back inside, mesmerized as I was by the faintest outline of the peaks rising in every direction around the lodge.

The sound of music made me turn to look in the window. There in the dining room, Kim was holding the little girl's hand, twirling around and dancing. The music and laughter were contagious, and Pem Futi had joined in. As I stood there in the cold, I knew that the sight of my foreign friend disco dancing with a generous Nepalese family in a village high in the Everest region was one that I would cherish for a very long time.

### *The road less traveled*

After acclimating for a night or two in Namche Bazaar, many trekkers heading to Gokyo Ri opt for the route straight toward Tengboche, where a famous Buddhist monastery is located. But for those wanting fewer crowds, the path via Khumjung is the better option. Even at the height of trekking season in October, Elizabeth encountered few other trekkers in Khumjung, a picturesque village on a plateau high in the mountains.

### *Getting to Khumjung*

To reach this village, follow the steep trail up and out of Namche Bazaar. Head toward and past Syangboche, with its now-defunct airport. The trail rises steeply, then descends, and soon becomes paved with wide flat stones that lead straight to Khumjung. On the outskirts of town, the path opens up into a wide field. To the right of the trail stands a well-constructed school founded by Sir Edmund Hillary's Himalayan Trust. On this path you will encounter many Nepalese laden with supplies. Most likely they live in Khumjung or another nearby village. Don't hesitate to strike up a conversation. They know the trail well and can steer a traveler in the right direction. Elizabeth and Kim ended up at the Himalayan Guest House because they met a relative of Pem Futi's on the trail who gave them directions to the lodge.

### *Himalayan Guest House*

Along with sleeping quarters, this guesthouse has a dining area where both Western and Nepali food are served. Precaution should be taken with cold water, even if the lodge owner insists it has been filtered. Use your own filter or iodine tablets before drinking. Boiled water, such as in tea or coffee, is considered safe.

### *Altitude sickness*

The Everest region is sometimes called "Death Valley" because of the trekkers who climb too far, too fast, and succumb to altitude sickness. Signs of altitude sickness include severe headache and nausea. If the symptoms worsen to vomiting or staggering, for example, descent with a healthy companion is essential. Even the healthiest, fittest person can get altitude sickness. Never climb more than three hundred meters in a day, which in the Everest region may mean trekking for several hours. Some people take Diamox as a precaution when trekking in high altitudes, but watch out for its side effects. Elizabeth's was a bursting bladder—quite troublesome when the only bathrooms are outhouses! As an alternative, Nepalese Sherpas swear by ginger tea as a remedy for nausea; this is in ready supply at most lodges.

# Kaiyankata

*Karen Coates crashes an exorcism on the Indian border*

It's a cold, crisp morning on the second day of our trek along the India-Nepal border. Wind slaps against the lodge where we slept the previous night, and icicles cling to the rocks outside. But the sun shines brightly, and the trail zigzags upward along a steep switchback course.

In time, my body warms, and I begin to sweat. When I reach the top of a tree-lined hill, I pause for a few moments among green leaves covered in tiny berries. Rhododendrons bloom all around me.

Not much farther on sits a tea stop and rest area called Kaiyankata. The trail here is lined with fluttering flags, denoting the international border: the road is India, the tea shop Nepal. I stand precisely on the border line, jotting notes. I am everywhere and nowhere on that line.

The air way up here is so blue, so clear; the breathing is clean and easy. It's amazing how much air can exist in a place with so little of it.

In addition to serving tea to trekkers, the villagers near Kaiyankata keep fields of green peas, and they make rock-hard cheese and butter—commodities sold in Darjeeling, a day's hike away. Occasionally on the trail, we pass villagers heading to the city with yaks and backs saddled with heavy goods.

We sit in the sun, sipping sweet tea and appreciating the silence for a while. Then, just as we prepare to hit the trail again, we watch an old man scurrying back and forth with greens in his hand. Our guide explains: a woman in a nearby house is afflicted by an unhealthy spirit, and the villagers have called for an exorcist to perform a ritual to make her well.

Really? Can we see?

Our guide consults with villagers, and they welcome us warmly. We are led into a kitchen where three men sit beside a bright blue wooden table. A fire burns in an earthen stove, and eight-inch lengths of hard cheese hang from the rafters. Beyond the kitchen is another room, visible through two tiny glass windows. The kitchen is dark, but the other room is bright with sunshine beaming through a skylight of plastic sheeting. The ailing woman sits inside that room.

We watch intently. We have no idea what to expect. We have never seen an exorcism before.

And thus, the ritual begins. The exorcist, a thirty-year-old man named Tirtha Bahadur, sits in the center of the kitchen. He places a dried flower into a tiny bamboo basket shaped like a cone. He sticks the basket into the wooden floor beside an array of items: a small fire burner, a tray of raw rice with a piece of ginger, a vase of green leaves, and a plate of incense shavings. The woman enters the kitchen and sits beside Tirtha.

He sprinkles vermilion over the flower, then lifts a few pieces of dried incense and hums a scripture. Three times he sprinkles incense onto the glowing embers of his hot little burner. After each sprinkling, he clasps his hands in prayer. Then he grabs a few grains of rice and sprinkles those onto the flower. The room fills with the perfume of incense.

Tirtha raises the green leaves over the flower, then lifts rice in his right hand and ginger in his left. The rice grains spill onto the flower. He lifts the greens again and sprinkles water from their stems onto the flower. Then more rice onto the flower. Then rice raised to the woman's head. Two more handfuls of incense are tossed into the embers. Flowery, spicy smoke sails upward; the room smells of cedar now. Throughout all of this, Tirtha chants. He swings his right arm around the woman, circling her with a handful of rice.

This continues for about ten minutes as Tirtha whispers soft prayers between quickly moving lips. He raises his hand to the woman, gives her a few grains of rice, and holds the bamboo cone for her to spit into. She fingers the rice, eats a few grains, and places the rest in a scrap of paper. She returns to her little sunlit room.

With that, the ritual ends. "He has called all of the deities he knows," our guide explains. "He has been trained. And he has asked the deities to cure the lady."

I talk to Tirtha for a few moments. His name means "to go on a religious tour," he tells me. "I have been doing this for eighteen years. I was born this way. My parents knew—when I touched someone, he was cured." He travels far and wide to perform these rituals; he requires food and a little money as payment.

I enter the small room and talk to the woman, who is named Daki. She is unable to move her arm, which looks out of place and oddly bent at the elbow. "I didn't fall down or anything," she says. It just stopped working one day. "The medicine man came six months ago. My arm got better. It comes and goes." She says she must eat seven grains of raw rice for the next three nights before she goes to sleep. She is certain she will get better.

## General Nepal

### *Gerry Kataoka cherishes bonds with a Nepalese family*

We flew over Mt. Everest on Buddha Air. We ate at the famous Rum Doodle. We shopped in Thamel. But we learned the most about Nepal, and the humble, generous people who inhabit it, when our tour guide Raj invited us to his home for lunch and to meet his family.

Each morning during our trip, Raj and Angela, his nine-year-old daughter, came to pick us up at our hotel. We often invited them in to the Hyatt's dining room for some breakfast. After a few days, we discovered that we had a bond. Not surprising, perhaps, given that we were spending so much time together, sharing stories about our homes and families.

Raj told us of his work with clinics in the countryside, and that he had recently returned home to build a water tank for his village. He was kind and patient with us throughout our trip—our first to Nepal. He taught us much about local customs and the ways of life there. So we were honored when he extended the lunch invitation.

Raj lives near the airport in a small, dark, one-room dwelling with his wife, daughter, and elderly mother. The room has a cement floor, space for two small beds, and dark plastic sheets that look like garbage bags covering the ceiling. There is no running water, and because there is no electricity, he uses gas to power a small three-burner stove. As we entered, he placed newspaper on the beds and asked us to sit on one of them. His mom sat quietly on the other.

It was a true lesson in the life and culture of a Nepalese family, and my family was grateful to see it. We chatted as Raj's wife prepped our meal on the floor. When she served us lunch on large silver plates, these were also placed on the floor. Despite the meagerness of the surroundings, the food was exceptional, and we knew what a treat we were being given as we ate rice, potatoes, greens, pickles, and chicken. We tried our best to eat in the style of the Nepalese—no forks or chopsticks, just our right hands. We were especially fascinated to see that Raj's wife had her lunch only after we were finished.

Although the meal was easily the highlight of our trip, we did not take any photos. We did not want to embarrass Raj or his family. After all, it was a gift to be able to share a meal with such kind people. The fact that he opened his home and his heart to us, giving us an up-close look at daily life, was overwhelmingly thoughtful.

My wife had tears in her eyes as we said goodbye to Raj at the airport the next day. Our lunch with his family had been a fitting climax to an interesting and educational experience in a different culture. We will never forget it. We still keep in touch with Raj via email, so we know that he continues working as a tour guide in Kathmandu and leading treks on the Annapurna Circuit. Inspired by his generosity, we plan to return and help him build a school or clinic in his hometown just as soon as we can.

### *Raj Kapali*

Gerry adds: We left feeling blessed that we had found Raj. So many Nepalese, like Raj, leave their homes in the countryside to brave the hectic life of Kathmandu so they can educate their children and make extra money for schools and clinics back home. For those who would like to hire Raj for tour services, he can be reached at the following email.

kapali77@hotmail.com

### *Rum Doodle*

www.therumdoodle.com

# Paying it Forward

*Suggestions for giving back while you're on the road*

While Nepal is rich in hospitality, spirituality, and natural beauty, it is also a place of great poverty. The reasons for this are vast, from the isolation of communities in remote regions to the internal displacement of more than a hundred thousand people during the civil war, which ended in 2006. As a visitor, your presence has the potential to make a great impact, and even a few hours of your time or a few dollars (or yen, or pounds) from your wallet can go a long way.

The essays in this chapter merely touch on the many opportunities for contributing as you explore Nepal. Your investment in the country's welfare might simply be to buy a sticky bun and coffee at a bakery that employs deaf waitstaff, as Joe Bindloss suggests in Patan. Or if you're looking to invest in a good cause, you might follow Rex Turgano's advice and provide a small-scale loan to help an individual start a business.

Those with time to spare (and share) will find that teachers are desperately needed throughout the country. Searching for a way to give a little something back before he returned home from his trip, Tariq al Kashef wound up teaching English to Tibetan refugees at a non-government-funded school in Boudha ... for six months! Monasteries are also a good place to look if you're interested in teaching, since they often provide the only education for the many underprivileged Tibetans who have made their home in Nepal. As Patrick Moran and Erin and Dan Cassar discover at a monastery school in Parphing, this kind of volunteering is particularly rewarding, as math, reading, and even basketball skills are exchanged for a deeper understanding of Nepali culture.

Every person who donates to Nepal's well-being also donates to its self-sustenance. A perfect example of this is Global Institute Press, founded by Cristi Hegranes, the coeditor of this book. By teaching the women of Nepal how to tell their own stories to the world (an experience recounted in this chapter by Kalpana Bhusal), this organization does what all volunteers and charitable groups should strive to do: empower from the inside out.

*Tibetan women making a carpet in the Kathmandu Valley*

## KATHMANDU

### *Conor Grennan witnesses wide-eyed joy in Kathmandu*

It is in every traveler's nature to study guidebooks before arriving in a new country. We know what the Taj Mahal will look like before we walk through the gates, and we're pretty sure the culinary specialty of Ecuador, fried guinea pig, will approximate the taste of rabbit. But while you can knowingly anticipate Nepal's ancient stupas, colorful monasteries, unique mix of Hindu and Buddhist cultures, and even the majestic Himalayan mountain range, there is nothing in any guide that will prepare you for Machhapuchre House, run by the Umbrella Foundation in central Kathmandu.

On the picturesque postcards that you will mail home—and your family will love and put on the refrigerator—Machhapuchre House will not be depicted. The building is not a UNESCO landmark. It's not included on a Lonely Planet walking tour, although if you're here, you'll be mere steps away from the magnificent Swayambhunath temple, where monkeys leap across the rooftops and steal bananas from local vendors.

Unlike the many tourists that sightsee unawares near Machhapuchre House, the kids who live there took a different path to Kathmandu. As one of the city's largest children's homes, Machhapuchre is inhabited by about forty children taken from remote villages by child traffickers and abandoned in destitute orphanages. They are considered lucky to have been rescued and brought here.

This is why it's so surprising, when you arrive at Machhapuchre House, to find groups of children playing, laughing, and wrestling outside. They will shout and run to greet you. As they begin to climb on you—which they invariably will—you will quickly sense the most miraculous thing about them: they live wide-eyed, without a whiff of self-consciousness or self-pity.

For the duration of your visit or time volunteering at Machhapuchre, you will have children stuck to you like magnets. You will also find that they will fill you with joy and break your heart in the same instant.
They don't need games or toys. The products of their imaginations are far better than anything that comes in a box. Instead, they need what every child needs: love, attention, and the knowledge that there are people who care that they are fed, clothed, and educated. Who care that they even exist in the quiet back streets of Kathmandu. They are beautiful, these kids. Hidden away, they are the heart of Nepal.

### *Machhapuchre House*

For the protection of the children, we cannot publish directions to Machhapuchre House or the other affiliated children's homes of the Umbrella Foundation, but the neighborhood they are in is an easy taxi ride from the Thamel District and is located in one of the most beautiful and peaceful areas in Kathmandu. If you are interested in volunteering or visiting one of the homes, please visit the website of the nonprofit Umbrella Foundation organization.

www.umbrellanepal.org

## *Tariq al Kashef shares his accent in Boudha*

My most treasured memory of Kathmandu is standing in front of some thirty cross-legged, saffron-robed Buddhist monks, holding up a laminated card with the letter *A* printed on it, and saying, "Repeat after me. *A* is for apple."

That moment took place in a small school in Boudha, the city's Tibetan district, just a short walk from the enormous Buddhist stupa of the same name.

I hadn't planned to end up there. In fact, I had arrived in Kathmandu at the tail end of a round-the-world trip, low on funds and intending to head home to London. But the place quickly endeared itself to me, and I was soon to discover that there was an abundance of young Westerners in the city, many of them working as volunteers, teaching English classes or assisting other needy institutions. I loved the idea of giving back to a country that had shown me such hospitality, while simultaneously doing something productive at the conclusion of what had basically been a pretty hedonistic journey.

I did some research and was appalled to find that most of the volunteers I met had paid thousands of dollars to an agency in their respective home countries to find them their placement. Being the proud owner of a depleted bank account, this was out of the question for me, and as no agency I called was prepared to help me without the required fee, I resigned myself to the fact that I would indeed be heading home as planned.

Fortunately, one lady I spoke to at an agency in the U.K. was kind enough to offer me some useful advice. "Although I can't give you the names of any of the schools we use," she said, "I can tell you that Nepal is crying out for volunteers, and whether you have one hour or one month free to help out, there are hundreds of places that will gladly accept your help. Just look around."

As it turned out, she was right. That same day I found a worn sign on a café notice board asking for volunteers to help the English teacher at a non-government-funded school in Boudha. The school was for refugees from five to seventy-five years old. Many had never had formal schooling, and most were Tibetan monks. I went there with the intention of practicing conversation with the students for a few short afternoons. I stayed six months, devoting myself to the school and the wonderful, lovable, and unfailingly enthusiastic students that studied there.

Volunteering is not a purely altruistic pastime, and we all get some sort of personal reward from our experience, whether it's the satisfaction of helping others, the opportunity to live and work abroad, or simply the work experience itself. For me it was in part all of these things, but mainly it was standing in front of room full of monks and hearing them repeat my every word in complete unison ... and in time, hearing them do it with a distinctly London accent.

### *Volunteer agencies*

Following are reputable agencies that arrange volunteer placement in Nepal:

**i-to-i**
www.i-to-i.com

**INFO Nepal**
www.infonepal.org

**Lattitude**
www.lattitude.org.uk

**Projects Abroad**
www.teaching-abroad.co.uk

### *For a small fee*

In hindsight, Tariq can see why agencies charge a fee. You're paying for volunteer placement, as well as the support you receive for the duration of your contract. Relocating to a new continent to live or work can be a pretty daunting endeavor, and it's good to know that there's someone out there to organize the details and be only a phone call away should things not work out as planned.

## Patan

### *Joe Bindloss eats sticky buns for a cause in Patan*

Backpackers eat in Thamel. Well-heeled tour groups dine in the showy hotel restaurants around Lazimpat. But when Kathmandu expats want to get their culinary kicks, they head south of the Bagmati River to the nearby city of Patan. In the streets around the Jawalakhel neighborhood, an astounding variety of international cuisines are represented. There are pizza parlors, steak restaurants, tandoori houses, and even a passable Malaysian *nasi ayam* place, but for sticky buns and coffee, as well as beer and sizzling platters, you can't beat The Bakery Café just up from the stadium at Jawalakhel Chowk.

Founded by the phenomenally successful Kakshapati brothers in 1991, The Bakery Café chain fast become the Nepali Starbucks, with branches across the Kathmandu Valley. But this is Starbucks with a heart: most of the staff, from the bakers to the waiters, are deaf. You might think this would prove a hindrance in a busy restaurant, but diners write down orders on pieces of paper, which are translated into sign language or passed by hand to the kitchen, and orders arrive in double-quick time.

I first discovered The Bakery Café while staying with friends in Jawalakhel. After a steep cycle ride uphill from the National Stadium in Tripureshwor, fighting for a place on the road with weaving taxis and daredevil minibus drivers, I needed somewhere to catch my breath. The café seemed to offer a haven of calm and quiet. It was only after feasting on a huge plate of steamed *momos* and a giant mug of coffee that I realized why it was so calm and quiet, and I delved deeper into the history of the chain.

The Bakery Café has generated quite a buzz amongst the Kathmandu middle classes as the first restaurant chain run by and for Nepalese. The restaurant also serves an important social role. There is no safety net for the disabled in Nepal, and the alternative to working at The Bakery Café could easily be a lifetime of begging or depending on handouts from Western charities. All in all, this makes it a far worthier place to spend your pennies than the collection box on the counter at McDonald's.

### *The Bakery Café*

www.nanglo.com.np/foodchain.html

### *Getting to Jawalakhel*

You can reach Jawalakhel by taxi or local minibus on the main road between Kathmandu and Patan. Alternatively, rent a motorcycle or pushbike in Thamel.

### *Shopping in Jawalakhel*

While in the neighborhood, drop into the excellent fair-trade handicrafts shops around the Kupondole area. Run by local NGOs, these charitable emporiums sell carpets, clothes, pashmina shawls, bags, shoes, and woodcarvings made by Tibetan refugees and other disadvantaged groups. The Jawalakhel Handicraft Center specializes in Tibetan carpets made by refugees, and you can tour the workshops to see the carpet weavers in action. Other top recommendations include Dhukuti and Mahaguthi.

www.jhcnepal.com
www.acp.org.np
www.mahaguthi.org

## Dhading District

### *Rex Turgano pursues possibilities outside Kathmandu*

Last April, I attended a daylong Room to Read site visit in the Dhading District, which is about an hour from Kathmandu. I had no idea what to expect in the classrooms, beyond the simple tables and chairs neatly organized into rows and all facing a giant blackboard, and I certainly wasn't prepared for the dim lighting, dusty floors, and grim, concrete walls.

This surprised me not only because the school was fairly new (about five years old), but because it was the most popular among the villagers—all of the parents wanted to send their children to a Room to Read educational institution. It wasn't until I visited the library and computer classroom that I realized why the school was such a big hit.

The library was filled with books, toys, visual aids, and posters of animals, the solar system, and places around the world. Compared with the rest of the building, it was vibrant and engaging. I learned that the three teachers who maintained the library often had to keep a waiting list and schedule children to use it. It was clearly *the* most popular place in the school.

Still, the library was not what impressed me the most. Next, I visited the computer lab. It was *really* nice—this, coming from a computer techie. Each computer was fairly new and loaded with popular software and productivity applications. It was uplifting to see, considering that the cost of the computer lab was certainly more than the combined wealth of the entire village. Even more inspiring, I was told that children came to use the computers on weekends, and that the favored application was Microsoft's "Encarta kids." I even met a young student who came during his own school holiday just to use the facilities. What kid does that back home?

Most often, children in Nepal are taught to simply grow up, get married at a certain age, and work on the family farm. But with a Room to Read library and computer lab, kids have the chance to dream about *and* learn how to pursue many other possibilities with their lives.

*Room to Read*

If you would like to visit a Room to Read project in Nepal, check the "site visit" section on the organization's website.

www.roomtoread.org

## Pharping

### *Erin and Dan Cassar settle in at a Pharping monastery*

When the Chinese claimed Tibet in 1950, Nepal expanded its border to include a region of the Himalayas that was formerly a part of that country. These days, ethnically Tibetan students come from remote villages in that area, sometimes walking for six days to get to the road that will take them to study at the Manjushri monastery in Pharping. The boys live at the school for ten months out of the year, and visit their families for two months.

Through a volunteer organization, my husband Dan and I decided to spend a month teaching at the Manjushri school. Dan taught a computer class to the older boys, covering topics such as basic hardware and Microsoft Windows, but it turned out their favorite thing to do was learn how to use creative software, including Photoshop. They were all eager and completely filled his break times asking for extra help, although sometimes they would get diverted and end up discussing Buddhist philosophy or politics in Tibet.

I taught English. My students ranged from age six to seventeen, and naturally there was quite a variety of levels in my classes. After a completely botched attempt to teach "I'm a Little Teapot," with me desperately acting out a teapot pouring tea to blank five-year-old stares, I decided I needed backup. The other language volunteer and I decided to split the classes. With an elementary school teacher for a mother, Lara had come prepared with materials. So after the first week, she took the younger ones, and I took the older ones.

With the lower classes, I read picture books and taught letter-writing skills and haiku; the older students were excited to read excerpts from *Harry Potter and the Sorcerer's Stone*, learn essay skills, and even analyze a Shakespearean sonnet. The monastery actually does have a full-time English teacher, so students receive basic grammar instruction, but the volunteers supplement these lessons with fun activities. Most importantly, the students get to converse with native speakers from all over the world.

The older classes had only four students each, while the youngest of my classes included about ten. I relished teaching such small groups who were so well behaved. The children stood up when I entered, and said, "Thank you, miss!" in chorus as I left. They tried to do every task I set for them and participated enthusiastically. What a different experience than the one I had teaching in New York City!

We ate lunch every day with the local teachers, some of whom spoke English well. One had even lived in the States for a while. The meals were always enjoyable, since the monastery grows most of its own fruit and vegetables in its massive garden and has a cow from which it gets fresh milk each day. The masala *chai* was absolutely the best tea we'd ever had. And we never got sick of the *dal bhat* (rice and lentils, the quintessential Nepali meal).

We also spent some time visiting the surrounding monasteries. There are eighteen in town, including one built around the Padmasambhava cave, where the lama who brought Buddhism to Tibet was said to have achieved enlightenment. People flock to the tiny cave to meditate. It was also at this monastery where we sat in on several Buddhism classes taught by Lama Oser, former attendant to the Dalai Lama. His presence was inspiring, so at peace, so kind as he gave us his blessing and invited us to tea.

Dan and I were having such a great time that we decided to forgo a trip to Pokhara and the Annapurna District in favor of spending more time teaching at the monastery. We were a bit disappointed not to visit the great mountain region, but we had happily settled into our nice daily routine. In fact, we were astonished when our month was up. We hadn't been able to visit Tibet when we were in China earlier, since the border was closed, and this was the next best thing. In fact, probably better, since the Chinese demand that tourists visit on an organized tour, and only for three days. We felt that we got a real slice of Tibetan life at the monastery, and were very sad to leave our new friends.

### *Getting to Pharping*

Pharping is located in the corrugated rice fields of the southwestern Kathmandu Valley, twenty-five kilometers from the city. Buses run between Kathmandu and Pharping daily, but they are overcrowded and unsafe, with people sitting on the roof. Through their volunteer organization, Erin and Dan arranged to travel by car, a trip that took only forty-five minutes. Additionally, a taxi can be hired for around 400 rupees. Give yourself as much extra travel time as possible, due to the habitually broken-down buses stuck in the road. While the drive shouldn't take more than an hour, heavy traffic can triple the time.

### *Manjushri Di-Chen Buddhist Learning Center*

By volunteering to teach at a monastery in Nepal, you can make a significant difference in a child's life. Many villages in the remote Tibetan border region do not even have schools, so monasteries such as this one are the only option for a free education. Traditionally, each Tibetan family sends one son to a monastery, and monasteries are the main institutions in Tibetan life. If you are interested in volunteering at Manjushri, you will find the monastery at the top of the main road in Pharping, a ten-minute walk from the city bus stop, adjacent to the looming six-story Tara temple. It is always open to visitors, whether you're making a day trip or seeking a long-term volunteer engagement. Speak to one of the older students, and he will arrange a tour or translator. And don't mind the guard dogs. Although their bark may sound ferocious, they couldn't be more loving. A small donation is always welcome.

www.drubthobrinpochenp.org
whitelotushere@yahoo.com

## *Where to stay*

Erin and Dan did not have a good experience at the Family Guest House, but since they had already paid for their lodging and meals for their monthlong program, they were stuck—especially since it was the only guesthouse in town. Their room was dirty and smelled like smoke, and the bathroom was one of the filthiest Erin had ever seen. The power went out daily at erratic intervals, and because there were no laundry facilities in the whole town, once a week they washed their clothes with a bucket and soap.

Then there were the three days without any water at all, and when the water did finally return, a weeklong festival arrived with it. For seven days, from 6 a.m. to 9 p.m., an assortment of accordion players, singers, speakers who laughed at their own jokes, a single song on repeat for hours at a time, and other intriguing sounds came blasting into their window from the PA system in the tent down the street—even when their power was out!

Later, Erin and Dan found out that they could have stayed at one of the nearby monasteries, in cleaner rooms, for half the price that Family Guest House charged ($4 per night instead of $8). They didn't need to go through the program at all, in fact, as their monastery also houses volunteers. If you decide to volunteer at the monastery, it's best to skip the third-party organization and contact a monastery directly at the website/email above.

## *Dining options*

Meals were included in the program fee. Breakfast consisted of toast and tea; a good lunch was provided; and a meager dinner alternated between dal bhat and "fried rice" (a plate of rice fried in butter with a few carrots), noodles (again, fried in butter with some carrots), or soup (butter, sparse vegetables, and toast). Often, Erin and Dan ate their evening meal at a tasty Tibetan-run restaurant called Himalayan Café down the street.

### Repelling mosquitoes

Although there was no malaria in the area, Erin says that mosquitoes were a constant problem. Luckily, a teacher at the monastery suggested a product called Good Night, which cost less than $2. A plug-in mosquito repellant, it worked great.

## Patrick Moran shoots hoops with monks in Pharping

The sun is barely over the horizon. Through the cracked window pane I can already hear the morning chant, which just happens to take place right outside my room. Out of all the alarm clocks in the world, there isn't one quite as wonderful as the students of the Manjushri Di-Chen Buddhist Learning Center in Pharping. Every morning at 5:30 a.m., fifty-five young monks gather in their respective classes and sing the prayers of the coming day. Although my body screams at the notion of such an early wake-up call, it is hard to ask for a better start each morning.

With my classes spread throughout the day, I spend my time planning lessons, reading on top of the volunteer quarters, and (my personal favorite) teaching basketball. A few years ago a group of American volunteers built a basketball hoop in the recreation area, giving the football- and cricket-obsessed monks a brand-new game to conquer. At first they had little interest, but their overall love of sports soon lured them in.

Between teaching English conversation to first and second graders, I break up the monks into teams for short games of ball. Practicing the English from their classes, they use the time as both a study period and an adventure. Eventually, though, the game culminates into a madhouse of "Everyone versus Teacher Pat!" in which I am chased around the court by screaming monks.

Without any electricity, the night comes quickly. Darkness envelops the valley like a blanket. After the last game is played, we gather in the meeting hall to laugh about the day. Nyima, one of my students, passes out our evening meal of *dal bhat* and *thukpa*. As he turns to leave, he grips the bowl like a basketball, smiles, and whispers, "Swish!"—his new favorite word.

Is he fluent in his new language? No. But it doesn't matter. The translation is universal.

### Volunteering in Pharping

Go to the fact file in the previous essay for travel information and more about volunteering at Manjushri.

## ANNAPURNA REGION

### *David Hammerbeck does his part for the Annapurnas*

Having trekked both the Annapurna Sanctuary and Annapurna Circuit routes, I can attest to the region's astounding natural beauty and cultural diversity. From the lush foothills in the south of the Annapurna Himal to the dry, Tibet-like landscapes in the north, this area offers towering peaks, pine forests, sites of historical and religious importance, tumbling mountain rivers, and villages peopled with the many faces of the central Nepali Himalayas, including the Thakali, Gurung, Khampa, Tibetan, and Chhetri.

While the Circuit and Sanctuary treks are justifiably popular, it's not hard to find side trails that can get you off the beaten path: the area also connects with restricted treks around Manaslu and Dhaulagiri and into Upper Mustang. And it offers the opportunity to walk through the world's deepest canyon, the Kali Gandaki, as it passes between the twin eight-thousand-meter peaks of Annapurna and Dhaulagiri.

This entire 7,629-square-kilometer Annapurna region is encompassed by the Annapurna Conservation Area Project (ACAP). Founded in 1986 as part of the King Mahendra Trust for Nature Conservation (now the National Trust for Nature Conservation), the ACAP also contains within it, besides spectacular scenery, hundreds of villages and more than a hundred thousand residents.

The ACAP came about as an attempt to provide a comprehensive environmental plan for the area that included input from these inhabitants. Park personnel work closely with village participants in formulating workable, ecologically sound decisions regarding community-based land usage, land rights, livestock grazing, and resource management. The ACAP has also educated lodge and teashop owners on sustainable tourism, heritage conservation, environmental issues, and conservation procedures, in particular regarding sanitation and deforestation. The latter includes a ban on wood-burning stoves higher up on the treks in order to preserve forest resources.

This project has greatly benefited trekkers, beginning with the formulation of set prices for lodging, food, and porters' wages, thereby eliminating problems such as price gouging or the undercutting of competitors. For example, rates for food are set by determining the cost of transportation. You will notice that a cup of Nepali tea at Thorung Phedi or Annapurna Base Camp is more expensive than lower down at Jagat or

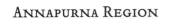

Chomrong. Room prices are regulated as well, which gives all lodge owners a fair shot at gaining your business.

Trekkers are asked to do their part to keep these consistencies in place by not haggling down the set prices. Rates are already low by Western standards, and if lodge owners were to start negotiating for food and rooms, it would upset the area's well-balanced economic framework. For the system to work, you need to respect not only the mountains and people who call this beautiful area home, but also the rules that have been thoughtfully established. In return, you will earn mutual respect, as well as the knowledge that you have contributed to the survival of the Annapurna's richly diverse culture and ecology.

### *Annapurna Conservation Area Project*

By following the guidelines set by the ACAP when trekking in Annapurna, you are contributing to the livelihoods of those who live in this mountain region. Your participation begins with the purchase of your permit before you start your trek. Annapurna trails have checkpoints along the way, where you will be asked to show your permit. If you do not have one, you will be fined. You can find out more about permits, as well as what else you can do to help the project, at the official website.

www.kmtnc.org.np

## General Nepal

## *Rex Turgano loans out advice on small-scale lending*

A few years ago, I heard about Kiva, a U.S.-based nonprofit organization that facilitates microlending from people all over the world to individuals in need. The concept sounded intriguing and dead simple—lend money, and the borrower pays it back.

I was skeptical at first because of the obvious accountability issues, and I was reminded of the email scams from people in impoverished places requesting funds. However, after reading through Kiva's operational model, I decided to sign up to learn more and perhaps test it out. Soon thereafter, I found out that it was not accepting any more lenders and thus I was put on a waiting list. I didn't think about Kiva again until I came to Nepal.

One of the organizations I volunteered for, General Welfare Pratisthan (GWP), has a microlending component that helps empower marginalized communities in Nepal as part of their peace building through self-employment program. Specifically, this program focuses on supporting women who are greatly susceptible to trafficking and who are likely to be forced to enter the sex trade. Along with microloans, GWP also provides peer support counseling and various work skills workshops.

As a volunteer, I read (and proofread) many reports and success stories about how people benefited from this type of self-empowering support program. Examples from GWP include accounts of women and families starting their own sheep and goat farms, farming vegetable crops, creating and selling recycled paper products, making candles, opening grocery stores, and even starting a beauty salon. All beneficiaries said that the microloans system immensely improved their lives for the better, as it not only provided the needed start-up funds, but it also enhanced their self-esteem and made them more accountable and self-sufficient in the end.

I was able to see this for myself when I traveled to GWP's field office in Hetauda. There I met two staff members, both teenage girls who had recently started working for GWP. One came from a family of goat farmers, and the other from a family that made and sold candles. They were a little shy to tell me about their families' businesses at first, but after a while, as we got to know each other over *dal bhat* and milk tea, I could tell they were proud and grateful for their livelihoods, as they supported them through school and continued to provide food on the table for their extended families. It wasn't until much later, after I returned to Kathmandu, that I found out GWP sponsored these girls' families by giving them microloans to help jump-start their businesses.

After hearing so many stories and meeting the people who had benefited from microloans, I again thought of Kiva. I began to think about the bigger "development" picture, and although certain safeguards and checks have to be in place, I can see that microfinance is one of the most powerful tools to address global poverty, and it does so in a way that builds confidence in the individual and independence in the institution providing the financial services. Better yet, it often works in synergy with other development organizations, such as those that promote health, nutrition, HIV/AIDS awareness, migrant workers' rights, democracy, and education.

*Kiva*
www.kiva.org

*General Welfare Pratisthan*
www.gwpnepal.org

## *Kalpana Bhusal changes her country one story at a time*

I come from the small village of Kritipur, where I was a student. I had always wanted to be a journalist, but lack of opportunity deprived me of living my dream. Global Press Institute (GPI) gave me a chance to make my dream a reality, and I can now proudly say that I'm a senior reporter for GPI. Through the stories I write, I have the chance to change the conservative attitude of my society and country. I have gained financial independence and am able to support my family, which makes my parents, especially my father, proud.

Having worked for GPI since 2007, I have seen many positive changes as a result of my association with the organization. I love all of the stories I have written, but my favorite is "Transgender People Press for Equality in Nepal." Basically, this issue is important because transgender people don't have citizenship rights and must fight for their own identity. When my story was published in support of transgender/third gender rights, I felt honored to receive the gratitude of the country's transgender society and specifically Sunil Babu Pant, the transgender representative for and member of the Constituent Assembly of Nepal.

Overall, GPI is a unique media organization that trains and employs women across the developing world to be ethical investigative journalists. GPI provides this opportunity not only for journalists, but for others, such as housewives, as well. GPI uses journalism as a development tool to educate, employ, and empower women, who in turn use their new skills to increase access to information and ignite social change. In Nepal, GPI is one of the most popular online media outlets.

Through GPI, the voiceless now have a platform from which to tell their side of the story. In the form of my articles, GPI has provided me with the opportunity to bring to light the issues of communities in remote and isolated areas of Nepal. Most importantly, it has helped bring a better understanding of our country to people around the world and has made a positive impact on our society.

### *Global Press Institute*

Founded by this book's coeditor, Cristi Hegranes, the nonprofit Global Press Institute gives voice to women around the world by training them as journalists. To learn more about the institute, as well as read Kalpana's story about transgender issues, go to the organization's website.

http://globalpressinstitute.org

*Nepali boy in Harkapur*

# Resources for the Road

*Practical advice to help you prepare for your travels*

The goal of *To Nepal With Love* is to inspire and also (hopefully) entertain. It is not intended to be a comprehensive guide for planning your trip. For that you will need tried-and-true guidebooks and expert guides—as well as the recommendations in this chapter. Like the rest of the essays throughout this book, the offerings here are eclectic and subjective. But put together they can help you build a foundation for your trip to Nepal.

We have not included a listing of websites, because for the most part they change and grow outdated so quickly. We do, though, suggest that you keep an eye on the *Nepali Times* online, not only for news, but also for current information on art exhibits, music performances, and more. While most of the movies our contributors write about are documentaries, covering subjects as diverse as street kids and extreme skiing, a Bollywood-style film has been included, to give a taste of modern culture. Equally democratic are the classical and pop music selections, which showcase the country's growing diversity.

Overall, the focus of this chapter is on books, from volumes about Buddhism, social structures, and the civil war to tomes covering food, trekking, and language learning. Then come the tips on where to find all of these books when you're in the country. Even if you've already done your shopping beforehand, we recommend you visit Kathmandu's bookstores, anyway. They serve as gathering places for local and expatriate literati and academics, and so provide the kind of insight that can only come from one-on-one encounters, which are, in our opinion, the best possible resources for hitting the road.

*Sunset on Phewa Tal in Pokhara*

# Book Recommendations

*Editor's Choice: Books*

**Bringing Progress to Paradise: What I Got from Giving to a Mountain Village in Nepal**
by Jeff Rasley

As author Jeff Rasley recounts his conversion from tourist to activist, he explores essential questions about the impact of installing schools, electricity, roads, and running water in a place virtually untouched by modern society. In his efforts to help one small village in the Himalayas, he encounters the difficulties of introducing essential "progress" (such as antibiotics) without also opening the door to consumerism and other less savory aspects of Western society. This book is a good primer for travelers considering volunteerism, as well as those interested in a firsthand account of the effects of modernization on ancient culture.

**Customs & Etiquette of Nepal**
by Sunil Kumar Jha

Reading a guidebook and memorizing a few keys words and phrases is a good start for every traveler. But taking a few extra steps to understand the culture before you arrive in Nepal will be greatly appreciated. This basic book explains issues such as common courtesies and taboos. As well, it puts customs and etiquette in context with historical information, such as the country's absence of a colonial past and lack of major Western influences. From Hinduism and Buddhism to flora and fauna, this little book—though a bit unfocused—is filled with welcome insights.

**Kidnapped in Kathmandu**
by Esther Lum

Ripped from the headlines, this novella tells the story of two little Nepalese girls kidnapped on a holiday in Kathmandu and lost to human trafficking and the international sex trade in the red light district of Mumbai. Lum paints a colorful tapestry of vivid and mesmerizing scenes set against the stark reality of the sex trade. For more information on this issue, read the article "An Open Secret: Sex Trafficking in Nepal" at Global Press Institute.

http://kidnappedinkathmandu.com
http://globalpressinstitute.org

**New Nepal: The Fault Lines**
by Nishchal N. Pandey

Although Nepal's armed conflict ended in 2006, questions about identity, ethnicity, language, religion, and culture remain. These "fault lines" of a new Nepal are explored by Pandey, as the country is restructured. Security, stability, policy, and democracy all play a role in this book, which also takes on Nepal's evolving relationship with neighboring India and China. While this is a hefty read in regard to its subject matter, it is concisely written, making it ideal for those interested in the future of Nepal.

*Brian Smith studies the history and culture of Nepal*

**Blood Against the Snows: The Tragic Story of Nepal's Royal Dynasty**
by Jonathan Gregson

On my second trip to Nepal, during the height of the Maoist insurgency, I wanted to get a better understanding of the nation's past and what had caused the civil war that was at the time raging throughout the country I had fallen in love with. Nothing I read explained it better than *Blood Against the Snows.* This book covers the Nepalese royals from the eighteenth century to the royal massacre that occurred in the summer of 2001. Outlining a saga that read like a Shakespearian tragedy, the book gave me insight into a country whose institutions and practices were alien from my own experiences and understanding of history.

**Forget Kathmandu: An Elegy for Democracy**
by Manjushree Thapa

Published just after the dissolution of the world's last Hindu monarchy, Manjushree Thapa's excellent first-person account reveals an educated Nepalese trying to piece together her own country's past and figure out where its future is headed. The book covers in detail the lead-up to and aftermath of the 2001 royal massacre and its effect on the psychology of the people of Nepal. Most importantly, it is brutally honest and gives a better understanding of the mind-set of the people of Kathmandu than any other book I have read about this region. It is indispensable to anyone who wants to understand the cultural undercurrents that flow through the political and social processes of modern Nepal.

**Into Thin Air: A Personal Account of the Mt. Everest Disaster**
by Jon Krakauer

Jon Krakauer's account of the fatal 1996 expedition to the top of Mt. Everest is a modern mountaineering classic. It is also the most common book to be seen in the rucksack of a trekker on the trails of Nepal. Along with offering a great introduction to what goes into large mountaineering expeditions, and exploring the cultural impact and often humorous mix of East meeting West, Krakauer tells a truly riveting story. He conveys with skill the personality and spirit of the people involved in the expedition, and when the true dangers are brought forcefully to light, you can't help but be saddened at their inevitable loss. As I read this on my way up to Everest Base Camp, I found myself looking at the locations mentioned in the book with different eyes.

## *Charis Boke explores the struggle between old and new*

Samrat Upadhyay's short story collection, *Arresting God in Kathmandu*, brings readers into lives that are at odds. Kathmandu—as the anchoring point for these well-crafted tales—is revealed as an increasingly complex, changing world, rife with all the contradictions that come hand in hand with the concept of "globalization." Traditions clash with new ideas in this exploration of relationships, in which parents and children are in opposition, and men and women struggle to identify and articulate desires and needs. Called a "Buddhist Chekhov" by the *San Francisco Chronicle*, Upadhyay moves away from romanticizing culture and religious practices, as well as glorifying any particular lifestyle, and instead offers a nitty-gritty view of contemporary life in the city.

### *Further reading*

Charis also recommends *Tutor of History* (a novel set in a small town in central Nepal before a set of local and national elections) and *Tilled Earth: Stories*, by Manjushree Thapa, author of *Forget Kathmandu*.

## *Caroline Martin samples Nepal through the written word*

**The Cult of Kumari: Virgin Worship in Nepal**
by Michael R. Allen

In my opinion, this is the best study of Nepal's syncretic Hindu-Buddhist-Tantric tradition of choosing young girls to be worshipped as living goddesses. Combined with the film *Living Goddess* (see page 185), it offers a well-rounded look at not only this unique practice, but also the larger issues of gender roles and socioreligious life in Nepal.

**The Power Places of Kathmandu: Hindu and Buddhist Holy Sites in the Sacred Valley of Nepal**
by Keith Dowman and Kevin Bubriski

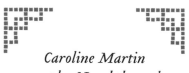

For travelers interested in the spiritual side of Nepal, this coffee-table tome provides a panoramic introduction to the many mysterious temples and shrines of the Kathmandu Valley. Through photographs and text, it explores the ancient traditions of goddess worship, animism, and shamanism, and their centuries-old coexistence with Buddhist and Hinduism.

www.keithdowman.net
www.kevinbubriski.com

**Travelers' Tales Nepal: True Stories of Life on the Road**
edited by Rajendra S. Khadka

This eclectic book features a range of stories, including at least one harrowing near-death experience in the former kingdom of Nepal. From trekkers to Peace Corps volunteers, the writers offer a good mix of mysticism and grit. Among the well-known contributors: Peter Matthiessen, Jeff Greenwald, and Jan Morris.

**Trekking in the Everest Region**
by Jamie McGuinness

With sixty detailed route maps, this is the definitive guide for travelers exploring Everest. McGuinness is one of the country's most active and authoritative tour operators, and his expertise is invaluable.

**The Waiting Land: A Spell in Nepal**
by Dervla Murphy

In her inimitable voice, the indefatigable Irish travel writer Dervla Murphy tells tales of a Nepal new to tourism. (The book was published in 1967.) Though she clearly feels affection for the country, her refusal to exoticize Nepal and its people is refreshing.

www.dervlamurphy.com

## *Elizabeth Mathews edits her way through Nepal*

It's strange that much of my freelance editing work comprises books set in places far from my home in California, because traveling makes me miserable. When I travel, I wallow in the anxiety of unfamiliarity and the seaminess of my surroundings at least as much as I delight in novelty and surprising human connection. And in the moments when I'm not overcome by the terror and delight of newness, I am inevitably drawn to venture inward, to contemplate my life from a distance. I remember neglected friends and rue old patterns and delve into my stash of troubles that aren't easily solved.

The travel books I most respond to embrace the murky complications of physical place and human ties while celebrating the richness of life. Jeff Greenwald's *Snake Lake* exemplifies why I love this kind of writing, as well as why I love my job. I did more than police its grammar and query its inconsistencies. I welcomed it into my life as it resonated with the very things that spur me to keep reluctantly setting out into the unknown.

*Snake Lake* plunges into life's difficult passages with honesty, beauty, and humor. Greenwald, who has been visiting Nepal for years and feels more at home there than anywhere else, witnesses the stirrings and aftermath of the People's Movement of 1990. The tumult in Kathmandu converges for him with a new love and a family crisis. Greenwald intertwines the stories of his visits to Nepal with his romance with a freakishly unlucky photojournalist and the emotional and spiritual journey he undertakes because of his desperately alienated brother back in the States. He balances keen political and cultural awareness with vivid dialogue, sensuous descriptions, insightful meditations, and a gripping plot. Life and death coexist in every chapter: holidays and violent demonstrations, lovemaking and cremation pyres, inappropriate jokes and Buddhist wisdom.

As I edited my way through *Snake Lake*, I found myself relishing not just the way that Greenwald's narrative navigates a time in Nepal's history when horror intermingled with exhilarating possibility, but also how he marries it to a deeply personal story of agony and redemption without losing sight of the details and dailiness that underpin life's dramas.

## *Rex Turgano cooks up a book recommendation for foodies*

From the archives of VSO Nepal volunteers past, my colleagues and I found a really good cookbook for people living and working in Nepal. *Himalayan Gourmet: A Guide to Cooking in Nepal* is a hundred-page booklet written by Peace Corps volunteers. We always baked from the desserts section—especially the lemon sauce, which was our favorite since we could get lemons easily and the sauce could be paired with almost anything.

Along with its collection of recipes, the booklet provides useful tips, such as ingredient substitutions and methods for building MacGyver-type ovens. Creating our own "miracle oven" was a challenge, and it certainly made baking a chocolate cake an adventure ... sometimes it would work, sometimes it wouldn't. This booklet also serves as a historical artifact, since the Peace Corps pulled out of Nepal during the Maoist insurgencies in 2004, and it is uncertain if/when the organization will return.

### *Himalayan Gourmet*

This book is hard to come by, since it was not officially published and distributed. Fortunately, a PDF can be found in the "documents" section of Peace Corps volunteer Scott Allan Wallick's website.

http://peace-corps.scottwallick.com

### *VSO Nepal*

To learn more about volunteering with VSO, go to the following website.

www.vso.org.uk

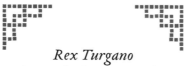

## Bookshops

*Scott Berry runs into familiar faces in Kathmandu*

*I think I recognize you. Can it be? Are you ...?*

It was, and I hadn't seen him in twenty-five years. He had been a lecturer at the university where I was a student.

*Is your name ...? I thought so. We last met in Putney in 1989.*

Conversations like this are not unusual at Kathmandu's Vajra Book Shop. Back in the days before so many people started coming to Nepal on package tours, when travelers had time on their hands to browse and read, Kathmandu's English-language bookstores were one of its main attractions. To some of us, they still are.

"The remarkable thing about this place," someone said to me recently in Vajra, "is that if you buy a book here, you are likely to meet the author, as well." (This is perhaps only a slight exaggeration.)

Compared to other local bookshops, Vajra is relatively new. It was opened by Bidur Dangol, a founder of Mandala Book Point. Mandala is one of the most popular bookstores and publishers in Kathmandu, and serves as an evening gathering place for Nepalese scholars and intellectuals. Smaller and more specialized, Vajra concentrates on Nepal and the Himalayas with a Buddhist slant. Its associated publishing house, Vajra Publications, has also produced a remarkable number of titles.

Like Mandala, Vajra has become an evening gathering place. Nepalese journalists and scholars are among the regulars. As for the foreigners who drop by, I have met development experts, historians, anthropologists, doctoral candidates, and scholars of Buddhism.

Of course, Mandala and Vajra are not the only places to buy books in Kathmandu. A book lover can easily spend days here exploring the city's countless shelves. So if you're one of *those* people who can't pass a bookstore without walking in, make sure to save time in your itinerary for discovering some of the best shops in Asia. You never know who you might meet.

### *Mandala Book Point*

This shop is located on the busy Kantipath just north of Rani Pokhari.

www.mandalabookpoint.com

### *Vajra Book Shop*

Vajra has locations on Jyatha Road across the street from one another, next to the Hotel Blue Diamond and Hotel Utse. Vajra Book Shop caters mainly to tourists (fiction, mountaineering), while Vajra Books focuses on academia and Buddhism, and has a showroom where academic presentations take place. Vajra Books publishes more than a hundred titles on Nepal, Tibet, and the Himalayas, including Scott's *From*

*Goddess to Mortal*, which is in its third printing. The shop maintains an excellent website.

www.vajrabooks.com.np

## *Rex Turgano becomes a loyal customer in Kathmandu*

When it comes to reading about Nepal, there's no end to great books about customs, culture, and more. Volunteers are told they *must* read the "oldie but goodie" *Fatalism and Development: Nepal's Struggle for Modernization* (Dor Bahadur Bista), as well as *Forget Kathmandu: An Elegy for Democracy* (Manjushree Thapa). On the fiction front, the novels *Arresting God in Kathmandu* (Samrat Upadhyay) and *Palpasa Café* (Narayan Wagle) are top critical choices.

Among my personal favorites, *Leaving Microsoft to Change the World* (John Wood) touched home. I started reading it after living in Nepal for a few months, and when I finished the first chapter, I chuckled to myself and thought, "I felt exactly the same way." This book is a great introduction to Nepal and how visiting the country can change a person's perspectives.

In reading about Nepal, it can be hard to know which books to choose, but I always know where go in search of something to satisfy me. Travelers will inevitably encounter Mandala and stumble upon Pilgrim's, but the underdog United Books is my favorite in Kathmandu. This small store is packed with "not your average" tourist shop books. You can definitely spend a couple of hours digging around here.

One day I asked owner Lars M. Braaten if he had all three of volumes of "A People War" trilogy, edited by Kunda Dixit. These heavy-hearted coffee table books capture Nepal's civil war (1996-2006), focusing on the victims through photographs, letters, and personal accounts from people around the country. He had only the third, *People After War*, and he immediately scrambled on the phone to find the other two: *A People War* and *Never Again*.

Unfortunately, I didn't have time to wait around. I had to pack, since I was leaving Nepal for good the next day. I apologized for taking up so much of Braaten's time and wrote down his email address. Two months later I contacted him, and he remembered me. He quoted me a fair price (easily paid through PayPal) to ship the books to my address in Canada.

In the end, I appreciated the personal attention and the fact that United's prices were not overly marked up, as in other bookshops around town. Simple stuff, but enough to make me a loyal customer, even after I left the country.

### *United Books*

United Books has outlets throughout Kathmandu, including its main one in Thamel on J.P. School Road.

### *A People War*

www.apeoplewar.com

# Movie Recommendations

## *Editor's Choice: Movies*

**Children of God**
Directed by Yi Seung-Jun

This documentary chronicles the lives of the impoverished children who live near Pashupatinath along the banks of the Bagmati River in Kathmandu, a sacred Hindu cremation ground where the dead are burned daily. Through the eyes of twelve-year-old Alesh Poudel, the film follows a group of young people and captures their efforts to survive, as they search corpses for food and dive for coins tossed into the river as funeral offerings. The contrast between the care lavished on the dead and the disinterest shown to the children is particularly moving.

**Living Goddess**
Entering the lives of three young girls who have been removed from their homes in order to serve as living goddesses, this documentary shows the clash between past and present as their world of tradition is juxtaposed against the struggle for power that defined Nepal's 1996-2006 civil war. While ordinary people take to the streets to demand freedom from the monarchy, ancient rituals persist behind temple walls. Exploring the reasons for and against maintaining the practice of living goddesses, this film sheds light on the complexity of life in modern-day Nepal.

For more on Nepal's living goddesses, go to page 40.

www.livinggoddessmovie.com

**The People's Nepal**
Presenting the "untold story" of Nepal's 2006 revolution, this documentary is narrated by actor Peter Coyote. Of the handful of films made about the revolution, this film truly captures the realities of the conflict as it explores political, cultural, and social issues, including those leading up to the overthrow of the monarchy. Archival photographs of the country's royal history combine with personal accounts of extreme poverty (particularly in rural villages), revealing the inequities of a caste system and its role in the country's ten-year civil war, which resulted in the establishment of the People's Republic.

www.thepeoplesnepal.com

**A School of Their Own**
Located in a remote region of Nepal, The Riverside School educates poor, homeless, and tribal children. The idea behind the school is to create an environment free from the caste system and gender prejudice, where all children can flourish. This documentary follows the school's struggle to survive during the civil war, as children are either accused by the king's government of being Maoist

rebels or being recruited by the Maoists (as early as age twelve) into their army.

http://ihcenter.org/projects/riversideprojectnepal

**Skiing Everest**

Adventure junkies (and those of us who like to live vicariously) *must* see this documentary. Directed by Mike Marolt, son of Olympic ski racer Max Marolt, it follows an elite group of high-altitude skiers (including Mike's twin and the brothers' friends) as they ski a region of Mt. Everest known as the "Death Zone." This is thrill-seeking at its best, as the group climbs alpine-style without supplementary oxygen, carrying their skis without the help of Sherpas or guides, in order to ski terrain that includes ten-thousand-foot sheer faces. Including the history of high-altitude skiing and interviews with Hans Kammerlander, the first person to ski from the summit of Everest, this movie complements the 1975 Academy Award-winning documentary, *The Man Who Skied Down Everest*, about Japanese alpinist Yuichiro Miura, who skied Everest in 1970.

*Charis Boke explores life in modern-day Nepal*

**RETURNED: Child Soldiers of Nepal's Maoist Army**

In this documentary, filmmaker Robert Koenig and his crew effectively capture the complexities of the conflict that the Nepalese people found themselves in from 1996 to 2006, caught between the strong arm of the Maoists and the hard hand of the Royal Nepalese Army. Though wrenching to watch at times, *RETURNED* offers relevant and essential background for any traveler who is considering going to Nepal, whether for a ten-day trek or a six-month volunteer stint. The movie also provides a compelling start to addressing the challenges that are still being faced by people both urban and rural in the aftermath of the civil war. Answers that seem so easy from afar become more complicated up close. If anything, that's what I took away from this film—an acknowledgment that there are no simple choices in the face of civil conflict, and no quick ways to heal in the aftermath.

http://nepaldocumentary.com

**Kagbeni**

An epic story anchored by the gifting of a talismanic, wish-fulfilling monkey's paw, this feature-length film was funded, written, and directed by Nepalese. In some respects, it follows the conceits of other South Asian film genres, mixing action/adventure in with suspense, mystery, romance, and a greatly expanded time frame. In other ways, though, it deviates from the traditional Bollywood style. I'd recommend watching at least part of it (it's very long!), especially if you're interested in the aesthetics that are popular in parts of urban Nepal and the kinds of films that are being made in the country today.

## *Rex Turgano admires the female trailblazers of Nepal*

Shot in the beautiful Annapurna region of the Himalayas, the documentary *Trailblazing* profiles the fledgling few women working as trekking guides in the country's heavily male-dominated adventure tourism sector. Through the telling of their stories, gender barriers are revealed—not only in the trekking business, but also in the larger context of Nepali culture.

The film opens with the story of a trio of determined sisters who operate the first and only female-owned trekking agency in Nepal's highly competitive adventure tourism industry. The agency 3 Sisters Adventure Trekking caters mainly to women travelers who want to use female guides and porters. The Chhetri sisters saw a niche in the market when women tourists returning from treks told of incidents of inappropriate behavior from their male guides.

To meet the high demand for female guides, the sisters have developed a training program for women wanting to enter the industry. They are experienced guides themselves and train approximately twenty to twenty-five young women twice a year. Another first: 3 Sisters is a "social enterprise," using 5 percent of the annual income generated through its trekking company and guesthouse for a training organization for female guides and porters.

*Trailblazing* captures the pioneering spirit and determination of the sisters as they continue to break down gender barriers and stereotypes. It also shows how their entry into a nontraditional field for women challenged the social order of the marketplace. By including several of the program's young trainees, it gives a good overall sense of the social conditions and limited expectations for young Nepalese women within the country's conservative mountain culture.

### *Trailblazing*

Funded in part by the Canadian International Development Agency, this twenty-four-minute film is in English (no subtitles) with a small portion in Nepali (English subtitles).

http://trailblazing.ca/

### *3 Sisters Adventure Trekking*

To read more about this organization, go to page 110.

## *Brian Smith scales Mt. Everest vicariously*

I had never been to Nepal the first time I saw the excellent documentary *Everest* at the IMAX movie theater in Boston. Showcasing the amazing landscapes of

Nepal's high Khumbu Valley, the rigors and dangers involved in summiting the world's highest mountain, and scenes from the Tengboche Monastery, this movie gave me a taste of what I would see for myself two years later when I hiked up to Everest Base Camp. In fact, the spectacular scenery in this movie got me interested in visiting Nepal for myself.

While the film is still great on smaller screens, the scenes of ice falls, expansive cliffs, and massive peaks are best viewed in IMAX format. The successful ascent depicted in this film took place alongside the doomed 1996 expedition described in Jon Krakauer's book *Into Thin Air*, and together, the two provide a moving tribute to all of the climbers involved.

*Everest*
www.everestfilm.com

## Music Recommendations

*Editor's Choice: Music*

**Himalaya Roots: Traditional Music of Nepal**
From Interra Records, this collection from Bharat Nepali Party features the music of various artists. Each song showcases the use of the multistringed *sarangi* (played with a bow), tabla (percussion), cymbal, and flute. These instrumental pieces offer listeners the chance to discover the meditative side of Nepali music.

**Om Mani Padme Hum**
This classic Tibetan Buddhist chant will provide the perfect accompaniment to your trip through Nepal. Numerous versions can be downloaded from iTunes, and we recommend choosing a few, for a soundtrack that will soothe you in the busy streets of Kathmandu and provide a harmonious serenade to your explorations of temples and tranquil mountain trails.

**Sindhu Malla**
For those who want a well-rounded look at Nepal, it's necessary to take time away from spiritual pursuits and explore pop culture. For a taste of the music scene, check out pop music princess Sindhu Malla. You can listen to performances of her popular "Pokhareli Kanchhi" on YouTube.

## Learning the Language

*Rex Turgano offers essentials for learning Nepali*

It had been just a little over four months, but it felt like ages since we'd left home. Both the *shreemati* and I were pretty much settled in and adjusted to Nepali culture, lifestyle, and language. We were learning new Nepali *sabdas* (words) and phrases daily, and now that we were practicing the language in context, we found that some of the resources we'd brought with us were useful, while others just sat on our bookshelf collecting dust. With suggestions from our local Nepali language teachers, we compiled this list of what we feel are the essential basics for getting a start on the Nepali language.

**Lonely Planet Nepali Phrasebook**
This handy little book is great to keep in your day pack whenever you are roaming the streets or traveling around the country. Many sections contain phrases related to going out, sightseeing, making small talk with people you have just met, and handling emergency situations. As well, there is a small dictionary/index in the back for commonly used words. I suggest using this book only as a general guide, though, for situations when you need to get a simple point/concept across. One of my teachers quickly flipped through it and found that some of the phrases and words are quite formal and slightly out of sync in relation to "everyday" Nepali.

**Ratna's Basic Nepali Dictionary**
This excellent resource is right on the money with most English-to-Nepali and Nepali-to-English word translations. There are no phrases in the book, but nonetheless, it makes a great companion to the Lonely Planet phrasebook.

**Teach Yourself Nepali Complete Course**
by Michael Hutt and Abhi Subedi

Even though this set (one book, two CDs) eventually ended up being one of the dust collectors on our bookshelf, I recommend it if you're a dedicated self-starter/learner. After my six-week language training through my volunteer program was done, I didn't have the energy to dive into learning more Nepali. But occasionally I would flip through the book and listen to the CDs, and I was always amazed that I understood everything—the lessons, the examples, and the cultural scenarios. The book is well written and a useful reference whenever I need to refresh my grammar or expand my conversation skills.

*Getting started*

Before your trip, we suggest picking up the Lonely Planet phrasebook, to introduce yourself to basic words and phrases. Once in Nepal you can easily find *Ratna's Basic Nepali Dictionary* and *Teach Yourself Nepali Complete Course*, as well as other language resources, in local bookshops.

# Epilogue

*One writer takes the time to understand Nepal*

## Brendan Work takes the time to understand Nepal

I bought a watch before I left for Nepal, to replace the one I had just lost. Little did I know, when I touched down in Kathmandu and twisted the knob to set myself half a day forward, I was beginning a time defined by time, in a way well beyond my experience.

I was coming from Swarthmore College. A Swarthmore student is rarely free of appointment, toeing tomorrow's schedule, passing in and out of the shadow of Clothier Bell Tower and the echoes of its semihourly peals. I was no exception. Indeed, my purpose in Nepal was concerned with a career based on schedules: I would be interning at *The Himalayan Times* (*THT*), a leading English-language newspaper in Kathmandu, collecting stories before 5 p.m. and copyediting them before seven.

Not only is Nepal vastly different from America, it makes even the world's other time-optional cultures seem like clock-punchers. In comparison to the way life works in Nepal, Spanish siestas may as well be overtime hours, and beach bums in the Caribbean are living in the fast lane. Happy globetrotters often cite time "slowing down" as evidence of a successful trip. But Nepal does away with slowing down and speeding up alike, because both suggest the idea of measurable velocity, and Nepal has no such thing. My own experience with this began with what passed for my job.

A workday at the *THT* office, and most other nonmedical buildings in the country, began around 11 a.m. I arrived at one in the afternoon, at no detriment to anything resembling productivity, and the first stories filtered in six hours later, after a leisurely lunch, a dozen games of solitaire, and boredom so thick it eventually became something like an out-of-body experience. I worked for two hours. When I had to leave at nine, it was not infrequent that a few stories were left outstanding and uncorrected, with improper uses of the word *the* and comical malapropisms worthy of Jay Leno's "Headlines" bit.

Receiving a story on time—the hopeful deadline being five o'clock—was just not reasonable to expect. Editing more than five stories in my allotted two hours would have been a feat. I wrangled with the writers and dropped unsubtle hints to my boss, but the office remained relaxed, and *THT* went into print every morning with sentences such as "Pradeep was awarded a death sentence."

Despite getting somewhat used to this, I continued to wonder, how is it possible that a daily newspaper could be so susceptible to the molasses pace of life in Nepal? I asked my host in Kathmandu, a family friend named Rajendra, who as a local news director has been party to Nepal's strange relationship to journalism for a long time. He also had a house with three distinctly Nepali clocks: one fifteen minutes fast, one stuck on 2:25, and the only one that worked bearing the logo of Nepal's number one condom brand. He said it was the culture.

So, I went in search of culture.

From mountain rain shadow to jungle lowland, I explored the vastness of Nepali time. Bungee jumping near the Tibetan border, I traveled a hundred feet in three seconds of free fall, but on the steep slopes of the Himalayas, I climbed the same amount in no less than an hour. I got stuck at an intersection on a motorbike and rode through it on an elephant. But dabbling in space and time, though exhilarating and enlightening and once resulting in a free T-shirt, only afforded me a paradox.

The first of two misconceptions involved in the paradox is that Nepal is stuck in time. This is abetted by the Shangri-la comparisons touted by two-week tourists and spa goers. And yes, the Tamang people north of Kathmandu still wear traditional dress and raise goats in view of eons-old peaks. And seventh-century Buddhist monasteries do still house young men in crimson robes. But custom cannot be confused with inertia. That much should be clear from Nepal's historic summer.

Just a week before my arrival in early June, Nepal bid goodbye to a monarchy older than the United States. Three days into my visit, thanks to my temporary *THT* press pass, I had the opportunity to witness the ex-king's landmark final press conference. Forty-three days later, I saw Nepal's first president take the oath of office, and as I left the country in early August, political parties were still wrestling for the all-important prime ministerial post.

Somehow, ideology had taken root in the idyll. Nepal, it turned out, is never as still as it appears to be in the postcards. Even the Himalayas are rising, about half a centimeter per year, triggering massive and often deadly landslides. But the sight of those landslides, like the smell of burning tires in Kathmandu, reminded me not to fall under any spells, because the second misconception is, of course, that Nepal is moving at all.

If it is, I decided, it is like a spinning Buddhist prayer wheel. The greatest mystery of life in Nepal is that it goes on in the face of egregious human rights abuses, beneath Biblical deluges, despite desperate fuel shortages, squeezed between China and India, without clean water, on less than $2 a day. All this, not to mention the weeks of ugly political deadlock, suggested to me that nothing was changing in this summer of change. Nepal was adapting as usual, compromising, bargaining, holding its nose as it walked around the four-foot garbage piles instead of moving them.

As I negotiated the paradox, unsure if I was half a day ahead of America, one hundred years behind it, or outside of time altogether, my own interval in Nepal was running out. Luckily for me, I found something resembling an answer in the nick of time, in a traditional haunt of answers—the Himalayas.

The story goes that some epochs ago, upon swallowing demonic poison to save the world, Shiva rinsed out his mouth at the lake of Gosainkund in the Langtang Himalayas. Pilgrims make an annual journey there to honor him under the August full moon, but I made my personal trek about a week before.

At Gosainkund, there were the usual elements of serenity: the purest air on earth, still water, white peaks in the distance. There were also what seemed like millions of rocks stacked on top of each other in the shallows of the lake. They were remarkable little monuments, because they made pleasing reflections in the water, and because they obviously stood for something, though I don't know what. But my mind was on time—what it was in Nepal and how much of the stuff I had left—and so the rock piles began to look like timepieces.

They had been assembled by the pilgrims, who carefully laid one new rock on top of the last, which might have been laid down on a previous pilgrimage, or goodness knows how long ago. But the rock piles survived the winters at Gosainkund, which freezes during the winter months, to grow a few inches taller each coming August. They recorded, with at least as much accuracy as *The Himalayan Times* on a good day, a simple fact: a pilgrim placed this rock on top of that rock.

My mind filled with other timepieces: tree rings, yearbooks, worn brass doorknobs, paw prints. But the rock piles seemed to belong specifically to Nepal. I did some thinking, and it came to make sense that in Nepal, time is neither measured nor affected by passing phases like the monsoon, or landmark events like the first president. All that matters is the contribution. A porter bearing food—that was the closest thing to a unit of time at Gosainkund. Or take the words *six-hour bus ride*. I had always figured the *six-hour* part referred to time, but in Nepal, time is defined by the word *bus*, because on the bus is the sack of potatoes, and the woman who knits the winter hats, and the freakishly skilled bus driver who can take everybody into town again. Simple contributions.

Nepal's major cultural forces, Hinduism and Buddhism, blend together effortlessly and share a belief in cyclical life and reincarnation. The country's creation stories are not measured in the achievements of one life, but by the achievements of several incarnations of life (except, of course, the Buddha, and Hindus claim he was the ninth incarnation of Vishnu). Looking at the stacks of rocks at Gosainkund, I began to see that time as contribution may be natural law: my lay understanding of Einstein's Special Theory of Relativity tells me time has as much to do with miles as it has to do with minutes. And it occurred to me that action measures time not only in Nepal, but even in places where the word *minute* means something concrete and has a (rather sacrosanct) spot in the dictionary. I thought about college. Six hours spent cramming for a text, a night out drinking beer with the guys, four years at Swarthmore, a lifetime or two—all just little rocks piled on top of each other.

Before I left Nepal, I bought Rajendra and his family a new clock. I wasn't out to make a statement. I just wanted to replace the condom clock, which to my disgust, turned out to be pretty sticky around the edges. But when I hung the new clock on the nail above the refrigerator, I was shedding an old idea and putting up a new one. I was making a small contribution to my own understanding.

# Contributor Biographies, Credits, and Index

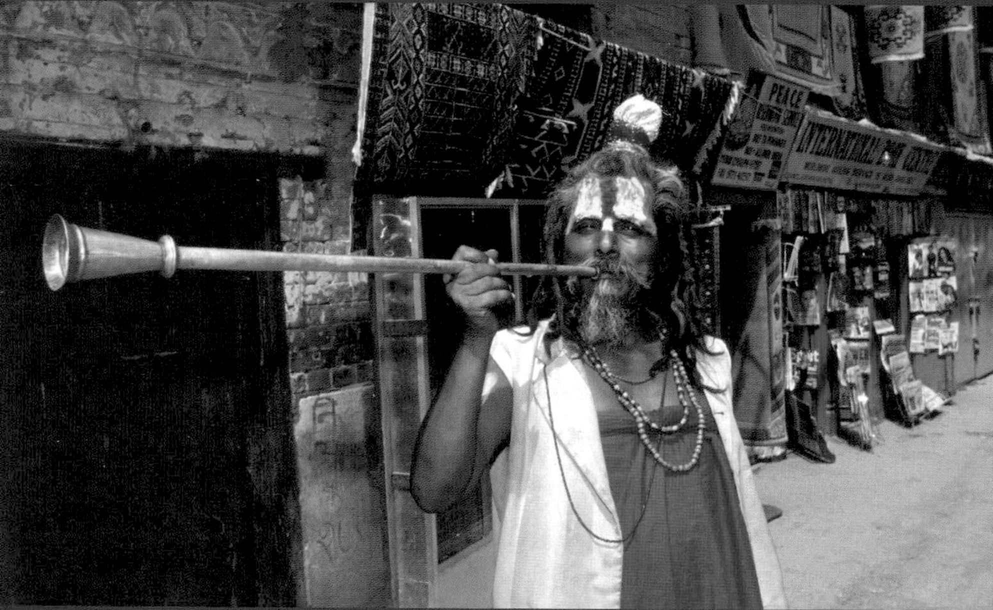

**Linzi Barber**
(Pg. 32, 126)

Linzi has traveled extensively across the globe but has a passion for Asia. Her love affair with Nepal began with an unforgettable trek to Everest Base Camp, sparking a real interest in the country. Her most recent trip included teaching English and assisting in an orphanage, which gave her an insight into the country's people and lifestyle.

**Scott Berry**
(Pg. 40, 138, 183)

Scott divides his time between Dhulikhel (Nepal) and Penang (Malaysia). His books include *A Stranger in Tibet*, *Japanese Agent in Tibet* (with Hisao Kimura), *The Rising Sun in the Land of the Snows*, and *From Goddess to Mortal* (with Rashmila Shakya). He has three granddaughters.

**Kalpana Bhusal**
(Pg. 173)

Kalpana is a senior reporter for Global Press Institute's Nepal news desk. She has been an investigative reporter covering issues of social justice and human rights since 2007.

**Joe Bindloss**
(Pg. 23, 43, 50, 78, 88, 164)

Joe has been coming to Nepal since the early 1990s to trek in Solukhumbu and explore the towns of the Kathmandu Valley. He is the author of more than fifty travel guidebooks to destinations in Asia and around the world, including Lonely Planet's *Nepal* and *Trekking in the Nepal Himalaya*.

**Charis Boke**
(Pg. 16, 35, 60, 180, 186)

Charis has spent her life looking around at the world and falling in love, as well as paying attention to injustice and imbalance in this world that she loves. It's with an eye toward both of those endeavors that she is now studying herbal medicine in her own healing practice and working on her PhD in anthropology at Cornell University.

**Cameron M. Burns**
(Pg. 128)

Cameron Burns is a writer and editor based in Colorado. He has been writing about environmental, green architecture, energy, and sustainability issues since the late 1980s as a reporter/correspondent with various newspapers and as a contributing editor for numerous magazines. His essays, articles, op-eds, features, blogs, and other material writings on sustainability have been featured in publications and on websites around the globe. He is the editor of *The Essential Amory Lovins* and coauthor of *Building Without Borders: Sustainable Construction for the Global Village*; *Writing, Etc.*; and *Contact: Mountain Climbing and Environmental Thinking*.

**Erin & Dan Cassar**
(Pg. 167)

Originally from New York City, Dan and Erin now live in Philadelphia, where Erin is a doctoral student in education and Dan is a computer programmer. They set out on their

*Sadhu blowing a horn in Kathmandu*

eight-month travel adventure in 2009. Their travels slowed down, however, with the birth of their first child in May 2011.

**Karen Coates**
(Pg. 35, 156)
www.ramblingspoon.com

Karen is an author, journalist, and media trainer who has spent many years in Asia. She was a 2010-11 Ted Scripps Fellow in Environmental Journalism at the University of Colorado, where she created the online forum Appetite-EARTH, examining the future of food. She writes the food blog *Rambling Spoon*.

**Lucy Corne**
(Pg. 48)
www.lucycorne.com

Lucy is a freelance writer with incurable wanderlust and a passion for the offbeat. Her itchy feet have taken her to over forty countries across every continent, bar Antarctica. As well as writing guidebooks for Lonely Planet, Dorling Kindersley, and Bradt, she writes travel features, which have been published in a range of newspapers and magazines.

**Kevin Curry & Zhou Zhang**
(Pg. 148, 149)

Kevin and Zhou are two young Americans who in 2009 quit their jobs, got married, and set off on a round-the-world adventure. During their ten months abroad, the "No Hurry Curry" team explored thirty-one countries in six continents. They now happily reside in Virginia waiting for the day they can do it all again!

**Emily Eagle**
(Pg. 19)

Emily works and plays as a freelance documentary media producer and multimedia artist in Seattle, Washington. With a focus on urban areas' relationships to the production of food, she hopes to be back in South Asia soon, studying vegetable markets and culinary history.

**Janelle K. Eagle**
(Pg. 74)
www.journeywithjanelle.com

Janelle is the founder of Off the Path Productions and works full time in Los Angeles as a travel blogger, independent film producer, and photographer. Her documentary and feature films/videos have been produced on three continents and for diverse clientele ranging from an orphanage in Bhaktapur, Nepal, to an NFL football star.

**Joshua Esler**
(Pg. 54)

Among Joshua's favorite experiences in Nepal was exploring the countryside by bicycle.

**Conor Grennan**
(Pg. 162)

Conor is the founder of Next Generation Nepal, a partner organization of the Umbrella Foundation, which he writes about in this book. He is also the author of the international bestseller *Little Princes: One Man's Promise to Bring Home the Lost Children of Nepal*, published in January 2011. To date it has been translated into eleven languages. Conor now lives in Connecticut with his wife and two children.

**Laura Gyre**
(Pg. 22)
http://uncertaintyblog.blogspot.com

Laura is a freelance writer and illustrator who is currently taking a break from world travel to maintain an urban homestead in Pittsburgh, Pennsylvania, with her husband and two kids. She can frequently be found online.

**David Hammerbeck**
(Pg. 102, 171)

David has spent most of the past five years in Nepal, teaching and trekking. He is co-owner of Alta Vista Treks, Pvt. Ltd., a trekking company that offers treks and trekking peak climbs in Nepal, India, and Tibet. He currently splits his time between the San Francisco Bay Area and Kathmandu, with his wife, Davika, and their son, Dev.

**Tariq al Kashef**
(Pg. 140, 163)
www.alternativeegypt.com

Tour leader, writer, expedition organizer, and all-round travel aficionado ... when not somewhere more exotic, Tariq is based in London. He is the author and editor of *Alternative Egypt*, the online Egypt travel guide for the independent traveler.

**Gerry Kataoka**
(Pg. 158)

Gerry is semiretired after a career at Kaiser, and lives in Pleasant Hill, California. He travels as much as he can, between short assignments performing Phase 1 clinical trials on investigational drugs. He also volunteers with two health-care-related relief organizations. He has traveled to every continent except Antarctica. Among his favorite destinations are Angkor Wat, Amazonia, Hanoi, Torres del Paine, Penang, Napa Valley, Hawaii, and New England. When home, he enjoys the company of his German hunting terrier, Buddy. Writing has become a passion of late.

**Alessandra Kim**
(Pg. 118)

Alessandra is an artist and lifelong traveler who has lived on three continents and traveled to more than fifty countries. Among those, Nepal remains one of her favorite places in the world.

**Srinidhi R. Lakhanigam**
(Pg. 47)

Srinidhi is a freelance travel writer with a keen interest in adventure sports, exotic festivals, culture, and heritage tourism. He has traveled extensively across the Indian Subcontinent, the United Arab Emirates, and the United States. His travel pieces provide readers with a close-up view of the culture, atmosphere, and ambience of a place. A science graduate and journalism postgraduate from India, Srinidhi has participated in varied adventure expeditions, including mountaineering in the Himalayas; underwater caving in Texas; dune bashing in Dubai; whitewater rafting in Karnataka, India; and mountain biking in Ladakh, India.

**David Lee**
(Pg. 72, 83)

David (@rtwdave) is the editor in chief and founder of GoBackpacking.com and MedellinLiving.com. He fell in love with Nepal during his first visit in 2008. David currently calls Medellin, Colombia, home. Between trips he can be found dancing the nights away in the city's salsa clubs.

**David Markus**
(Pg. 15, 52)
www.dbfoundation.org

David Markus is a PhD student in comparative literature at The University of Chicago, a contributing writer for *The Brooklyn Rail*, and a member of dBfoundation, an organization dedicated to "creating and fostering ephemeral edifices and intangible structures." While completing his master's degree at Christ Church, Oxford, David traveled to Nepal to aid in the start-up of the Kathmandu headquarters of Global Press Institute, a not-for-profit organization founded by this book's coeditor. While David spends most of his time studying art and culture from both of the world's hemispheres, the Annapurna Mountains remain the yardstick by which he measures all things beautiful and sublime.

**Caroline Martin**
(Pg. 70, 145, 180)
www.carolinemartin.org

Caroline moved to India in 2002 to complete her six-year study of Indian classical dance. A serious *Nat Geo* fixation and childhood memories of *Tintin in Tibet* have led her to adventures as a "spiritual investigative reporter" throughout India, Nepal, and Sri Lanka. She currently makes her home in New York City and Kathmandu.

**Elizabeth Mathews**
(Pg. 181)

Elizabeth is a longtime editor and sometime writer whose creative work has appeared in the journal *580 Split* and the anthology *The Moment of Truth* as well as in several obscure zines. She is currently pursuing a doctorate in English literature at University of California, Irvine.

**Patrick Moran**
(Pg. 170)

Patrick Moran is a writer and photographer from Portland, Oregon. His work has been featured in *Farther and Further, Defenestration, Blitz Weekly, Poor Mojo's Almanac(k), 52 Stitches, The Deli, Amplifier*, and many more. In his spare time he enjoys traveling to places with names that are hard to pronounce.

**Lone Mørch**
(Pg. 121)

Writer, fine art photographer, and explorer of inner and outer worlds, Lone is the author of the memoir

*Seeing Red* and the creative soul behind Lolo's Boudoir, where she helps women break free from stale self-images and embody their sensual souls. Her photography and award-winning writing has been featured in *InStyle*, the *San Francisco Chronicle*, *The Huffington Post*, and many more publications. Her memoir won the Mary Tanenbaum Literary Award from The San Francisco Foundation. Born in Denmark, Lone came of age in Nepal and now calls Sausalito, California, her sanctuary.

**Shannon O'Donnell**
(Pg. 80)
http://alittleadrift.com

Shannon left her home and life in the United States in late 2008 to travel around the world. As an active writer, photographer, and international volunteer, she travels slowly, finding unique experiences and stories along the way. She writes regularly on her website.

**Sherry Ott**
(Pg. 58, 116, 119, 152)
www.meetplango.com
www.Ottsworld.com

A refugee from corporate IT, Sherry is now a long-term traveler. She's a cofounder of *Meet, Plan, Go*, a website and national event offering career-break travel inspiration and advice. She also runs an around-the-world travel blog, *Otts World*, featuring writing about her travel and expat experiences.

**Renee Robertson**
(Pg. 112)

Renee grew up in Vancouver, Washington. She completed her BA in psychology at Rutgers University, then worked as an elementary special education specialist for six years in Washington State before meeting her husband Rick and having two daughters, Rylee and Raegan. Her husband's work has allowed the family to live abroad for more than eight years. They have lived in four different countries—Israel, Sri Lanka, United Arab Emirates, and Panama—and have had the fortunate opportunity to travel through parts of Asia, Africa, Southern Europe, the Middle East, and now Latin America. Nepal is near and dear their hearts, at the top of their list of all-time favorites!

**Clint Rogers**
(Pg. 31)

Clint Rogers traveled for ten consecutive years in highland Nepal while conducting PhD and postdoctoral research on Himalayan cultural geography. He has authored three books on highland communities living near the Nepal-Tibet border: *Where Rivers Meet* (Manaslu region), *The Lure of Everest* (Khumbu region), and *Secrets of Manang* (Annapurna region).

**Ellen Shapiro**
(Pg. 26, 28, 30, 68, 93)
www.byellen.com
www.takethekidsandgo.com

Ellen is a writer and photographer living in New York City. The author of five books including *New York City with*

*Kids* and *How to Roast a Lamb*, Ellen covers active and adventure travel destinations around the world as well as family travel, thanks to the addition of a son (and a new backpack).

**Elizabeth Sharpe**
(Pg. 25, 94, 96, 143, 154)
http://elizabethsharpe.blogspot.com

Elizabeth lives in Seattle, Washington, where she works as a writer and writing teacher. Still, her heart remains in Asia, where she lived for four years, teaching English to students in Nepal and Japan.

**Brian Smith**
(Pg. 14, 18, 89, 108, 179, 187)
http://smith-kathmandu.blogspot.com

Brian has traveled to more than thirty countries on six continents and loves nothing more than embarking on new experiences, tasting different cuisines, and meeting interesting people. He currently lives with his wife Kim in Kathmandu, serving up the best Western food in the city at Brian's Grill House.

**Jacquelin Sonderling**
(Pg. 20, 42, 63, 92, 98, 123)

Jacquelin is a Los Angeles television producer, writer, and sometimes yoga teacher who has traveled extensively through Southeast Asia. Her first eastern adventure landed her in Hong Kong. On her return, a friend took one look at her and said, "Ah, you lost your soul to the Orient. You won't be happy until you return." No truer words were spoken. Since then, Jacquelin has cycled through Vietnam, trekked twice in Nepal, and made plenty of plain old excursions through Thailand, Singapore, Korea, Japan, and Malaysia, to mention a few!

**Roberta Sotonoff**
(Pg. 132)
www.robertasotonoff.com

An award-winning travel junkie, Roberta writes to support her habit. Her passion has taken her to well over a hundred countries. Her work has been published in dozens of domestic and international newspapers, magazines, websites, and guides. She is a regular contributor to many of them.

**Robert Tompkins**
(Pg. 141)

Robert is a Canadian editor and writer. His travel stories have been published internationally through his agency Travel, Ink. He is the author/editor of-*Futurescapes*, published by Methuen. He is currently involved in the final draft of a book on linguistics, a project that he began three decades ago during his career as a high school English teacher.

**Rex Turgano**
(Pg. 20, 90, 107, 166, 172, 182, 184, 187, 188)
www.cuso-vso.org
http://thegreenpages.ca
www.reX-Files.ca

Rex is a professional librarian with an environmental background and is currently working at The University of British Columbia. He volunteered in Nepal with CUSO-VSO from 2008-2010. He is also the creator of *The*

*Green Pages*, Canada's environmental social network, and a diehard Internet enthusiast, building online communities and information resources on the side. Following his time in Nepal, Rex's adventures continue. You can follow him through his blog, *the reX-Files*.

**Laurie Weed**
(Pg. 110)
www.laurieweed.com

Laurie went off to Asia as a tourist and returned one year later as a traveler—and a writer. She now spends half of her time on the road, and the other half spinning tales from her kitchen table in Northern California.

**Kristina Wegscheider**
(Pg. 105)
www.diwyy.com

Kristina is the cofounder of *Do It While You're Young*, a website for young women interested in traveling, studying, working, and volunteering abroad. She has traveled to over fifty countries on all seven continents. When she is not traveling abroad, Kristina works as a human resources professional.

**Devon Wells**
(Pg. 45, 56, 69)

Devon Wells has written on food, movies, and travel for *The Muse*, *The Independent* (Newfoundland and Labrador), and CHMR 93.5 FM. His short story "The Viennese Teapot" won an honorable mention in the Newfoundland and Labrador Arts and Letters Awards. When he's not vagabonding through Asia, he lives in Vancouver.

**Brendan Work**
(Pg. 193)

Brendan is a reporter and translator in the Palestinian territories. He visited Nepal in 2008 while at Swarthmore College, where he received a Bachelor of Arts degree in comparative literature in 2010.

**Anju Gautam Yogi**
(Pg. 77)

Anju was born in the far western part of Nepal. She is a teacher and senior reporter for Global Press Institute. She resides in Kathmandu with her husband and her son.

## CREDITS

"David Lee forges bonds at a weekend retreat in Pokhara" reprinted in an edited and updated form from "My 3-Day Tibetan Buddhist Meditation Course," originally published at *Go Backpacking* (www.gobackpacking.com). Reprinted by permission of the author. Copyright © 2008 by David Lee.

"David Lee trades Thamel for the leisurely pace of Boudha" reprinted in an edited and updated form from "Daily Life in Boudha," originally published at *Go Backpacking* (www.gobackpacking.com). Reprinted by permission of the author. Copyright © 2008 by David Lee.

"Erin and Dan Cassar settle in at a monastery in Pharping" reprinted in an edited and updated form from "Pharping, Nepal" and "Teaching at Manjushri Monastery," originally published at *By Way of the World* (http://bywayoftheworld.blogspot.com). Reprinted by permission of the authors. Copyright © 2009 by Erin and Dan Cassar.

"Karen Coates crashes an exorcism on the Indian border" reprinted in an edited and updated form from "The Exorcist and His Wife," originally published at *Rambling Spoon* (www.ramblingspoon.com). Reprinted by permission of the author. Copyright © 2008 by Karen Coates.

"Karen Coates drinks in the flowers on the Indian border" reprinted in an edited and updated form from "Rhododendron Wine," originally published at *Rambling Spoon* (www.ramblingspoon.com). Reprinted by permission of the author. Copyright © 2008 by Karen Coates.

"Rex Turgano finds the last resort near the Tibetan border" reprinted in an edited and updated form from "The Last Resort Weekend," originally published at *the reX-Files* (www.reX-Files.ca). Reprinted by permission of the author. Copyright © 2009 by Rex Turgano.

"Shannon O'Donnell survives solitary confinement in Pokhara" reprinted in an edited and updated form from "A Little Introspection...Ten Days in Solitary Confinement," originally published at *A Little Adrift* (http://alittleadrift.com). Reprinted by permission of the author. Copyright © 2009 by Shannon O'Donnell.

"Sherry Ott faces her fears in the Annapurna Sanctuary" reprinted in an edited and updated form from "Road Work Ahead," originally published at *Otts World* (www.ottsworld.com). Reprinted by permission of the author. Copyright © 2009 by Sherry Ott.

"Sherry Ott finds her rhythm in the Annapurna Sanctuary" reprinted in an edited and updated form from "Changing Rhythms on the Annapurna Circuit," originally published at *Otts World* (www.ottsworld.com). Reprinted by permission of the author. Copyright © 2010 by Sherry Ott.

"Sherry Ott ponders positivity in the Annapurnas" reprinted in an edited and updated form from "A Mouse in My House," originally published at *Otts World* (www.ottsworld.com). Reprinted by permission of the author. Copyright © 2010 by Sherry Ott.

"Sherry Ott takes a break in the village of Manang" reprinted in an edited and updated form from "And on the 7th Day, We Rested," originally published at *Otts World* (www.ottsworld.com). Reprinted by permission of the author. Copyright © 2010 by Sherry Ott.

## INDEX

# Editor & Photographer Biographies

## Cristi Hegranes

Cristi is an award-winning journalist and a renowned international journalism trainer. The executive director and founder of Global Press Institute, she is a recipient of a Jefferson Award for Public Service and the Ida B. Wells Award for Bravery in Journalism. She is also the winner of the SPJ Journalism Innovation Prize, a New Media Web Award, a Clarion Award for Investigative Reporting, and numerous other honors. Cristi has been traveling to Nepal for more than a decade and operates a GPI news desk there. She received a Bachelor of Arts from Loyola Marymount University in Los Angeles, and holds a master's degree from New York University. Teaching news entrepreneurship at San Francisco State University and international media courses at California State University, she resides in the San Francisco Bay area with her partner, Patrick.

## Kraig Lieb

Since graduating from Penn State University in 1984, Kraig has worked, lived, and traveled extensively throughout South and Southeast Asia, and North and Central America. His experiences include Nepal, which he has been photographing regularly since 1989. Through his work with Lonely Planet, his photography has appeared in fifty-nine books and includes four covers. His images have also been featured in a variety of publications, including *The New York Times*, the *San Francisco Chronicle*, and *TIME* magazine, and have been used by organizations as diverse as Amnesty International and Kodak. He lives part-time in Northern California and part-time in Phnom Penh, Cambodia.

www.kraiglieb.com

### To Vietnam With Love
*A Travel Guide for the Connoisseur*
Edited & with contributions by Kim Fay
Photographs by Julie Fay Ashborn

### To Thailand With Love
*A Travel Guide for the Connoisseur*
Edited & with contributions by Nabanita Dutt
Photographs by Marc Schultz

### To Cambodia With Love
*A Travel Guide for the Connoisseur*
Edited & with contributions by Andy Brouwer
Photographs by Tewfic El-Sawy

### To Myanmar With Love
*A Travel Guide for the Connoisseur*
Edited & with contributions by Morgan Edwardson
Photographs by Steve Goodman

### To Shanghai With Love
*A Travel Guide for the Connoisseur*
Edited & with contributions by Crystyl Mo
Photographs by Coca Dai

### To North India With Love
*A Travel Guide for the Connoisseur*
Edited & with contributions by Nabanita Dutt
Photographs by Nana Chen

### To Japan With Love
*A Travel Guide for the Connoisseur*
Edited & with contributions by Celeste Heiter
Photographs by Robert George

### To Nepal With Love
*A Travel Guide for the Connoisseur*
Edited by Kim Fay and Cristi Hegranes
Photographs by Kraig Lieb

# Notes

# Notes

# Notes

ok 2/18

# Notes